# TOM SAYERS

*The Last Great Bare-Knuckle Champion*

# TOM SAYERS

## THE LAST GREAT
## BARE-KNUCKLE CHAMPION

Alan Wright

The Book Guild Ltd.
Sussex, England

The Book Guild Ltd
25 High Street,
Lewes, Sussex

First published 1994
© Alan Wright 1994
Set in Garamond
Typesetting by Acorn Bookwork
Salisbury, Wiltshire
Printed in Great Britain by
Biddles Ltd, Guildford and
King's Lynn

A catalogue record for this book is available from the British Library

ISBN 0 86332 929 2

# CONTENTS

# ACKNOWLEDGEMENTS

The author gratefully acknowledges the invaluable help and co-operation of the late Denis Brooks of Nottingham, Ian Stevenson and staff of Brighton Museum, Cliff Heppell, Chichester County Records Office, Swiss Cottage Library London, Chichester City Museum, the Thomas A'Becket in the Old Kent Road, *Sporting Life*, *Daily Telegraph*, *The Times*, *Famous Fights* 1901, *Memoirs of Tom Sayers* by William Wright, *Pugilistica*, *Bell's Life in London*, *All the Year Round*, *Tom Sayers–Sometime Champion*, Public Records Office London, *Illustrated Sporting News* 1865, *Sussex Advertiser*, British Museum, *Brighton Herald*, Jersey Library Service, R.Y.S. Castle Cowes I.W., *Punch* and Camden Local Studies and Archives Centre.

*To Elizabeth*

# 1

## THE NOVICE

As the train ground to a halt at North Woolwich Station on the morning of Tuesday March 19, 1848, the carriage doors flew open and a large crowd of excited fight supporters poured out upon the platform. Pushing and jostling each other in their eagerness, they swept past the ticket collectors and streamed down to the jetty to board the flotilla of small boats waiting to take them down the River Thames to an isolated field near Greenhithe in Kent.

The little convoy made an impressive sight as it sailed through the early morning mists, watched by scores of curious onlookers lining both banks of the river. An impassioned chatter of voices echoed across the water as rival factions argued the merits of the talented and formidable Abraham Couch and a novice to the prize ring, a twenty-one-year-old bricklayer named Tom Sayers, from Brighton in Sussex.

Bets were laid and odds were given on what chances young Sayers might have against the twenty-five-year-old Couch who, only two months before, had lowered the colours of the indomitable Jack Sullivan in a battle of fourteen rounds, lasting 1 hour and 38 minutes.

The sequence of events which had led to the contest between Couch and Sayers began one evening when Couch was giving a sparring ex-hibition in Somers Town, North London. After his conquest of Sullivan, he had issued an open challenge and bragged that there was no man north of London who would dare to meet him in the ring.

Presumably feeling quite justified in his boast, he had launched some scathing criticisms against several contemporary pugilists and more particularly against the promising young amateur boxer, Tom Sayers. Tom deeply resented the offensive remarks levelled against him and, in reply to Couch's vulgar abuse, promptly accepted his challenge. But the presumption of Sayers to try conclusions against a tough and experienced fighter of Couch's calibre was regarded by many as an act of unmitigated foolishness, for leading sportsmen were confident that Couch was heading for a place of stardom in the annals of the prize ring.

At the meeting to decide the venue and sign the articles binding the match, £5 from each side was deposited with the stakeholder. This figure may seem ridiculously small by today's standards, but in 1848 £5 represented more than a month's wages to a bricklayer. Unable to raise the entire stake money himself, Tom's friends and fellow bricklayers rallied to his aid and subscribed towards the outstanding balance.

So, the stage was set for the drama of Tom Sayers' debut as a pugilist and the start of one of the most remarkable careers in the history of boxing.

The little fleet of boats reached its destination on a deserted stretch of the Kent marshes shortly after midday and when the last of the stragglers had safely scrambled ashore, Tom Oliver, the ex-pugilist and designated ring-maker, led the party to a field used regularly for prize fights. By the time he had hammered home the stakes and adjusted the ropes, the two contestants had completed their preparations and stood ready to make their entry into the arena. Tom Sayers was the first to appear and, as he threw his cap into the ring in the time-honoured tradition of defiance, he was greeted with a burst of loud and enthusiastic cheering from a small contingent of navvies and fellow bricklayers. Climbing through the ropes he was joined by two leading pugilists: Jack Grant, acting as his principle second, and Dan Collins as bottle-holder. Couch entered soon after, accompanied by his two seconds; Croney (of Paddington) and a friend deputizing as bottle-holder. For a brief moment a slight frown appeared on Sayers' bronzed features at the sight of his burly 12 stone adversary; 3 inches taller and some 30 pounds heavier.

At the call of "Time!" both contestants walked to the scratch marked in the turf, and threw themselves into a fighting posture. Couch displayed all the confidence of an experienced and seasoned campaigner and lost little time in sparring for an opening. He proposed to adopt his usual tactics of dashing in at his opponent and settling the issue in double quick time. But Tom had different ideas and, as Couch launched his rush, he met him with a shattering punch on the right eye, inflicting a deep cut and drawing "First blood."

To the deafening cheers of his supporters, Sayers danced away, laughing at the consummate ease in which he had scored the first event. The two fighters came to close quarters and a sharp rally ensued with Tom pummelling away at Couch's body until both fell to the ground; Sayers falling across Couch's body and knocking the breath from his body. There came a sharp buzz of perturbation from Couch's seconds, who were clearly astonished at the rough treatment Tom had bestowed upon their fighter in so short a time. They rushed into the ring and gently carried Couch to his corner, where he was seated on the knee of his bottle-holder and supplied with a drink of water. Croney carefully sponged him down, wiped his hands and face, and removed the traces of mud and turf still adhering to his body.

Couch came to the scratch for the second round, his face still flushed from the rapid infighting of the previous round. He wore a perplexed expression on his face, ostensibly failing to comprehend why on this occasion his usual tactics had failed. Tom stood motionless, perfectly at ease, calmly watching his adversary. Couch suddenly let fly with wild swings from both hands but Tom saw them coming and danced merrily away from the punches which were short and well out of range. There followed a succession of counter hits until both fighters closed into a grappling hold. Grasping Tom in his powerful grip Couch held him tight. Unable to move a muscle, Tom became increasingly confused as he tried desperately to free himself from the vice-like clutch. A more experienced fighter would, perhaps, have known his next course of action but Tom was still a novice to the prize ring and he needed time to plan his next manoeuvre. Inch by inch and little by little, he twisted his body, altering his position until he eventually broke loose. Now it was time to reverse the roles. Locking his leg behind Couch's and, with a clever sideways movement, he threw the massive fighter to the ground.

Eager to begin, Sayers was first to jump up from the knee of his bottle-holder and hurry to the scratch for round three. The shouts of the bricklayers were deafening, and odds of 2 to 1 were now freely offered on their idol. Tom gazed intently at his antagonist and, as Couch approached, he feinted with his left and swung his favourite right. This led them into some bitter infighting, during which Tom delivered another heavy punch on Couch's right eye. Still trying to force the pace, Couch pursued Sayers around the ring, missing several easy chances to land a blow when Tom, rather unwisely, left his guard wide open. The round ended when Tom delivered another stunning right-hand punch to the jaw and sent Couch sprawling backwards on the grass.

The referee's cry of 'First knock-down blow to Sayers!' elicited spontaneous applause and prolonged cheering from Tom's ecstatic supporters. Hats were thrown high into the air, men patted each other on the back or shook hands with their nearest neighbours. Never, in all their wildest dreams, had they ever expected to witness such a scene as this.

On coming out for round four Tom literally launched himself at

Couch, landing again on the damaged right eye which by now was rapidly closing. Undaunted, Couch continued to maintain the pressure, but Tom, still almost unmarked, caught him on the nose and knocked him to the ground.

Still bleeding profusely from both nostrils and his right eye virtually closed, Couch arrived at the scratch for the fifth round clearly irritated at the punishment he had sustained in so short a time. Intent on making one last-ditch effort to finish the contest, he dashed savagely at Sayers. But Tom met him with a stinging smack on the ribs which knocked all the breath from his body. His mouth yawning open and gasping for air, he dropped to the turf in acute distress.

Tom came out for the sixth his face wreathed in smiles, well aware that the end was in sight. As poor Couch lumbered forward into the centre of the ring, still groggy from the punishment of the previous round, cries came from all parts of the arena to 'Take him away!' His seconds pleaded with him to throw up the sponge and accept defeat but, resolute to the very end, Couch tried to laugh and make light of his condition, telling them, 'I'm all right, I can carry on.'

Horribly disfigured from Sayers' severe and accurate punching, he made one last despairing effort. Tom easily avoided his lunge and delivered the *coup de grace* with a smashing hit on the nose. Couch collapsed in a heap and lay inert on the grass. His seconds lifted him gently and carried him to his corner where they worked feverishly to revive him during the 30-seconds interval between rounds. But he still remained in considerable pain and at the call of time was unable to rise to his feet.

The sheer brilliance of Tom's performance brought renewed cheering from his fellow workers who waved their arms and danced around in circles in their excitement. As the noise slowly abated, another tremendous cheer rent the air as Sayers was pronounced the victor in a time of 12 minutes and 28 seconds.

Immediately the men left the ring, a collection was undertaken on behalf of the defeated Couch. The crowd contributed generously in tribute to his indisputable courage, and the sense of fair play he displayed throughout the engagement. Tom's friends and backers were delighted with his achievement and, to express their appreciation and gratitude, presented him with the entire £10 stake money.

There were many eminent sportsmen who, having witnessed this thrilling battle, sensed that an exciting time lay ahead for the prize ring. Something extraordinary was about to happen – Tom Sayers had arrived.

# 2

## YOUNG TOM SAYERS

Tom Sayers' story begins at 11 o'clock on the evening of May 15, 1826. In a tiny bedroom of 74 Pimlico, Brighton, a shrill cry heralded the arrival into the world of Thomas Sayers, a sturdy baby with a powerful pair of lungs. Downstairs in the little brick-floored, terraced cottage where his father, William Sayers, pursued his trade as a shoemaker, there came a welcome sigh of relief, for his wife Maria was now in her forty-fourth year.

William Sayers was born in the little Sussex village of Storrington, nestling at the foot of the South Downs. Baptized in the parish church of St Mary on January 20, 1793, he lived with his two sisters and four brothers in what is now "Waterfall Cottage" in Chantry Lane, Storrington. Originally the building was known as "Fulling Mill," a cloth mill where cotton fibres were beaten by hammers operated by the mill stream (now diverted) running alongside the house. Soon after the mill ceased its production of textiles, his parents James and Elizabeth Sayers moved from their little cottage in West Chiltington into the empty premises where James set up in business as a shoemaker, tanning the hides he bought from Mr Greenfield, the local butcher.

In March 1806, tragedy struck the little family when James died at the early age of forty-two, leaving Elizabeth with seven young children to support. For the next eighteen months she struggled valiantly to provide for herself and the children. Then, on September 13, 1807, she married one Luke Butcher, from the neighbouring parish of Thakeham.

About three years later, Elizabeth, Luke and the family, now numbering eight children, moved to Brighton where Luke was employed as a sedan chair carrier. But William still yearned for the old style of village life and often returned to Storrington and the haunts of his boyhood. He was described as a good-looking young man, with a profile like an ancient Roman, when he married Maria Thomas from the neighbouring village of Sullington and took her back with him to Pimlico (now Titchbourne Street), Brighton. In those days Pimlico consisted of small terraced houses, let at half a crown a week (12½p) with one communal well as the main water supply.

The youngest of five children born to William and Maria, Thomas Sayers was baptized on December 31, 1826 by Henry Waghorn, the former tutor of the Duke of Wellington's two sons and vicar of St Nicholas Church, Brighton.

In common with the rising generation of lower-class children, young Tom grew up in a tough environment. He never attended school and, in consequence, never learned to read or write. There was little his parents could do to encourage learning, for he much preferred to spend his days on the shingly beach helping the local fishwives, or giving the fishermen a hand to push their "Hog-Boats"* out to sea. At this time in his life, no one who saw the sturdy, bare-legged, brown-faced little urchin up to his knees in water, could have possibly guessed that within the next thirty years he would become more famous than many of England's leading statesmen, politicians or literary scholars. From quite an early age, he had shown an active interest in boxing and wrestling and contemporary reports tell of him when a boy, surrounded by groups of admiring friends, showing off his prowess as a pugilist with a pair of his mother's old stockings wrapped around his fists as a substitute for gloves. Even then he had the uncanny knack of throwing, with the "cross-buttock," anyone who had the temerity to think they could better him at wrestling or grappling. In later years many a Brighton shoreman would proudly boast that he had, at times, crossed fists with the legendary Tom Sayers. At the tender age of twelve he trained a Brighton coal dealer's mule to "box." He would cross-counter with it, slipping under its belly and climbing on its back until the beast, half wild with rage, would snap round at his legs. He formed a close affinity with the coal dealer and never scrupled in dragging him home by the collar from his bacchanalian haunts.

Tom had no intention of following in his father's or grandfather's trade as a shoemaker and, when he was still only thirteen years old, he set out on foot for London to learn a trade in the building industry.

Occasionally hitching the odd lift on a wagon, he eventually arrived in the great metropolis and went to the home of his elder sister Eliza and her husband Robert King, a Camden Town builder.

*The Hog-Boat was a fishing craft peculiar to Brighton and Shoreham and no longer to be seen, except for a model in Brighton Museum. By 1886 only 3 remained out of the original 57 which were in use around 1840. The last of the fleet, the "Nil Desperandum", was burnt on Brighton beach in a 5th of November bonfire at the beginning of this century.

Robert tells how he came to his house and said he wanted to learn a trade, and asked him to give him a job. Feeling sorry for the boy and, not wanting to disappoint him after his long journey, he put him to work carrying the hod for the plasterers. However, he soon began to wonder if he had made the right decision, for young Tom gave him endless problems. Quite often, he would come down from the scaffold and set himself to work on the skilled men's jobs while their backs were turned and frequently ruined the whole thing. He recalls the occasion when Tom had been playing a few tricks while undertaking some work at a sea captain's house. One of the workmen had informed the captain of Tom's skylarking activities and the captain had lodged a complaint. Tom was called into the office where he was confronted by the irate gentleman.

'I'd like to take you to sea; I'd have some of your lazy blood out of you!' shouted the captain.

'I'd have some of your lazy blood out of you, old fellow!' replied the undaunted little Tom, 'If you dared tackle me, we'd roll overboard together.'

With that he brushed the captain aside and ran home to his sister. He was in no mood to listen to reason, and snorted, 'I'll pay the man off who reported me to the captain and, what's more, one day I'll return and make my name rattle through all London.'

With that startling prophesy, he growled through his clenched teeth, 'I'll be back in London soon; I'll learn no other trade.'

Then, without a word of goodbye to anyone, he walked back to Brighton via Portsmouth.

At the age of fourteen, young Tom began his working career as an apprentice bricklayer on the construction of Brighton's many new and elegant terraces, designed to meet the increased demands of the wealthy visitors who came down from London to sample the bracing sea air, for, since the turn of the nineteenth century when the visionary Prince Regent turned the little fishing village of Brighthelmston into the most fashionable resort on the south coast, the rapid growth of tourism had far outstripped the modest housing facilities of the town.

Despite the arduous work and the long hours, young Tom was a frequent visitor to The Druid's Head in Brighton Place, the local tavern and gymnasium where the Phelps brothers, Joe and Harry, gave boxing lessons and demonstrated their skills with the gloves. Their older brother Jack, alias Brighton Bill, had been killed a couple of years before in a desperate battle with the former featherweight champion, Owen Swift.

When he was sixteen, Tom was among the spectators at Newmarket Hill (near the present Brighton Race Course) to see a fight between a pugilist named Grady and a novice. When the main event was over, a purse was subscribed for a new challenger. A Brighton boxer named Haines offered himself as claimant and, for a while, silence descended over the crowd as they waited for someone to accept the challenge. With his pulses racing and the adrenalin coursing through his veins, young Tom piped up in a cheery voice that he was willing to take up the challenge. Although grossly overmatched in age, weight and experience, he fought a severe and hard-hitting battle.

By the end of the 17th round, Haines refused to face up to him any longer and took to hugging, relying upon his bodily weight to force the youngster to the ground. It was at this critical juncture that Colonel Paine, a local magistrate, appeared upon the scene. Making his way to the ring-side, he settled the affair by putting an end to the proceedings. With no decisive winner, the stakes were equally divided between the two contestants and Tom went home highly pleased with his performance.

Soon after this event, true to his word, Tom returned to London. One morning, when Robert King was completing a building in Holloway Road, Tom arrived on the site and set to work without asking anyone's permission.

His brother-in-law demanded to know what he was doing, but Tom would give no explanation except, 'I won't stir from here until I'm a bricklayer, so will you give me a job?'

Robert had always held a sneaking regard for the cheeky youngster and, except for his confrontation with the irate sea captain a few years before, had found him a sharp and determined lad. Given the right opportunities, he would develop into a bright and intelligent young man.

As he gazed at his cheeky and determined face, he smiled and said 'Go home to your sister, and tell her to give you a plumb-bob and trowel.'

All went well for a couple of weeks until Robert was informed that Tom was constantly fighting with one apprentice boy or another and allocating some of the prime jobs on the site to his friends from Brighton. Robert took him aside and told him he would not tolerate any flagrant misbehaviour while in his employ, but it appeared to have little effect, for Tom's only delight was in fighting.

A short time later, when Robert King was engaged on an extensive building project at the Hippodrome Race Course in Notting Hill, a poor Russian immigrant who could scarcely speak a word of English, begged him for a job as a labourer. Robert was reluctant to employ anyone who had little understanding of the language, but Tom felt a sense of sympathy for the unfortunate man and pressed his brother-in-law to give him a job of some kind, no matter how menial. Finally, after a great deal of persuasion, Robert grudgingly relented, but only on the condition that Tom accepted full responsibility for the foreigner.

During one dinner break, several navigators who were employed on the site digging trenches, began tormenting the wretched alien, who could not understand their coarse sense of humour. Tom came to the Russian's aid and told them to leave the poor fellow alone.

One big swaggering navvy replied, 'If you don't hold your tongue, I'll give you a slap round the head.'

Instantly the sixteen-year-old lad's grey eyes flashed with anger, and he promptly replied, 'Well then, you'd better try it on.'

A ring was quickly formed and the fight began. But after ten minutes of fast and furious fighting Tom had given the belligerent bully such a severe thrashing, he slunk sheepishly away to nurse his bruises. However, the navvie's mate, who had deputized as his second, was seething with anger at the manner in which Tom had punished his friend. He decided to teach the cheeky youngster a lesson he would never forget and dared Tom to take him on next. But he too was soon to regret his rashness, for in less than a quarter of an hour he was also glad to cry 'Enough,' and succumb to a mere boy.

This battle for the "underdog" gained Tom numerous friends among his fellow workers, and many remained his loyal companions in the years ahead.

On the completion of the Hippodrome contract, Tom bid farewell to Robert and Eliza and returned to Brighton to work on the construction of the massive Preston Viaduct, linking the main railway line between Brighton and Lewes in Sussex. Its architect, Rennie, had decided in favour of excavating a plateau, cutting deep into the chalk ridge, at a height of 130 feet above sea-level. For this gigantic assignment, 3,500 men and 570 horses were employed to build the present Brighton railway station and construct the impressive brick viaduct; 400 yards long and 67 feet high where it crosses the present London Road.

Among Tom's fellow workers was Bob Wade (the Dover Champion), a contemporary fighter of some considerable notoriety. Bob took an instant liking to the young bricklayer and, quick to recognize the latent talents in the impressionable youngster, took the time and trouble to instruct him on the finer points of boxing. Bob became involved in several impromptu fights during the time the construction work was in progress, and on these occasions, invariably deputized Tom as his second.

The great engineering feat was completed in just ten months and from the surrounding hills it presented a magnificent sight; its tall arches towering above the tree-covered slopes of the Preston Valley.

Having completed his apprenticeship on the great enterprise, Tom believed he could improve his financial prospects by working on the construction of the new London and North Western Railway Stations of King's Cross and St Pancras. He returned to London and took up lodgings in Agar's Town, one of the filthiest and most neglected slum areas of the metropolis. Until 1840, "Counsellor" Agar's house and grounds had retained their park-like appearance, with tall poplar and magnificent mulberry trees. The approach to the estate was by a neat little lodge and a gate leading from the King's Road, (now Pancras Road) which, at this time, maintained a rural aspect of hedgerows, skirted by trees.

In 1841, Mr. Agar sub-let the greatest part of his estate on twenty-one year leases, and immediately a shantytown sprang up of two and four-roomed cottages, erected by anyone disposed to take the ground. Many were nothing more than hovels, constructed by journeymen bricklayers and carpenters in their spare time. Consequently, with the almost total absence of drainage or sewers, the inhabitants quickly contracted diseases and fevers from the poisonous effluvia of the cesspools. The lucky few had an open ditch before their doors, but even from these the stench on a rainy morning was enough to turn the strongest stomach. The pathways, built some feet above ground level, were a complete bog of mud and filth and everywhere the roads were pitted with potholes and deep wheel ruts. The ground was naturally soft and when it rained the carts from the nearby brickyards churned it up into a secretion of cloying paste. Close to the edge of the town lay a lofty chain of cinder-heaps belonging to Mr Darke, the manufacturer of breeze-blocks used in the building industry. In general, the inhabitants exhibited a genuine apathy. Every corner of a garden contained its hut, well stocked with dirty children who played among the broken bricks and other dry materials strewn hap-hazardly in the mud. Doorways were invariably blocked with long-accumulated heaps of ashes and decaying vegetables and almost every plot contained its dog kennel, cowshed, and dung heap.

Amidst the differing styles of architecture, one dwelling resembled a dismantled windmill, another, perched upon a wall, appeared like a guard's look-out post, and the ingenious residence of Robinson Crusoe seemed to have given one builder his inspiration. One family lived in a disused railway carriage, and the house of another constituted a large yellow van on wheels, raised high above high-mud mark and having two red-painted doors with bright brass knockers, out of a tall man's reach and evidently never intended for knocking.

In Cambridge Row, a permanent crossing had been made over the mud but a signboard indicated that it was merely to facilitate the approach to the back door of the Good Samaritan public house. Another garden, bearing a board inscribed "Ladies School" contained a large pond, filled with thick green water. Next to the Talbot Arms Tea Gardens, on the corner of Cambridge Crescent, stood a small row of shops, the poorest displaying in the rag-patched windows a few apples and red herrings with the rhyming announcement "Table beer served here." Few ventured out at night, for there was not a single gas lamp to light the darkness of Agar's Town.

Tom spent little of his time in this wretched place for, in addition to his full-time work of bricklaying, he had an assortment of part-time jobs. He occasionally undertook a few chores for the ex-pugilist and well-known horse slaughterer Jack Atcheler and also for John Garratt, the proprietor of the old Copenhagen Running Grounds, near King's Cross. Here he was employed in a variety of tasks; operating the turnstiles and acting as a sort of "bouncer", ejecting trouble-makers and preventing the public from climbing over the low perimeter railings.

One evening at the running grounds he became involved in a quarrel with Con Parker, a top-class, professional prize fighter who stood six feet tall and weighed in excess of twelve stone. Words soon led to blows and the two men fought until darkness prevented any further fighting. Because a decision had not been reached that evening, they agreed to continue the conflict the next morning. At 7 o'clock the following day the pair resumed the struggle where they had left off, but Parker found he had bitten off a little more than he could chew and, although he punished Tom severely, he could not and did not beat him.

Soon after the confrontation with Con Parker, Tom learned that Robert King was engaged on an extensive construction project on Wandsworth Common. He called on his brother-in-law and asked to be reinstated; this time as a qualified bricklayer. Robert was delighted to see him again and gave him a job working on the scaffold. But inevitably, within a few days, Tom was in trouble again; this time with a big, brawny, 6 feet 3 inch Irish labourer. One morning, the disagreeable Irishman upset a whole hod full of bricks over Tom's feet. At first, he readily accepted it as an accident, and politely told "Paddy" to be more careful in future but, when it happened a second time, Tom's eyes blazed with fury and a heated argument ensued.

The burly Irishman was unrepentant and told the young bricklayer that if he didn't like it, he would give him 'a slap round the ear'. Throughout the remainder of the morning, the itinerant bully and his friends from the Emerald Isle, persistently taunted Tom until the dinner-break. By now, every-one was eager to see a satisfactory conclusion to the dispute, and the instant everyone descended from the scaffold, a fight was organized. Although Robert King listened sympathetically to the treatment Tom had so patiently endured, he was unremitting and refused permission to hold the fight on the site.

Not to be denied the prospect of a good fight, the entire work-force downed tools, and streamed off the site in the direction of Wandsworth Common. During the journey the Irishman loudly boasted to his friends that he would soon have this whippersnapper Tom Sayers ready for his coffin. On their arrival, a ring was quickly formed and the two men stripped to the waist. As they stood facing each other, the tremendous contrast between them was startling. Tom, a slim young man of eighteen, appeared diminutive beside his husky opponent who towered a full 6 inches over him.

The battle commenced, and for the first hour, Tom suffered the worst of the engagement. The ground underfoot was extremely soft, and he found great difficulty in maintaining his foothold on the slippery grass so, discarding his boots, he fought in his bare feet. Slowly he now began to gain the upper hand; his withering and accurate punching at last taking its toll. After fighting for two and three quarter hours, he caught the unhappy Irishman with a tremendous blow which laid him unconscious on the ground. While Tom did a victory jig about the ring, his opponent lay in a critical condition. He was laid on a make-shift stretcher, and carried to his lodgings where three doctors attended him all night, unsure if he would pull through. Deeply concerned over his extensive injuries, the doctors had no recourse but to report the matter to the authorities.

Within a couple of hours, all the local police stations were alerted, and patrols hurriedly sent out in a hunt for Tom. When some of his fellow workers learned that a warrant had been issued for his arrest, they took him to a stables in Tooting, and hid him in a corn bin until the hue and cry had died down. Then, at 3 o'clock in the morning, when the streets were deserted, they smuggled him back to Camden Town hidden under a cartload of hay. He remained in hiding at his sister's house for the next three days, when the search was eventually called off.

These early fights had made the name of Tom Sayers quite famous in the Wandsworth and Tooting districts, and it was not long before he received the inevitable challenge. When a Thames waterman declared he was prepared to fight Sayers for £5 a side, Tom's friends and colleagues quickly rallied to his aid and helped him raise the stakes, but when the waterman arrived for the contest he claimed he was unable to raise his portion of the stake money. Tom replied that if he could not produce the money, then he was quite prepared to give him the opportunity of fighting, if only to prove who was the better man. Evidently having second thoughts, the waterman decided to call the whole thing off; much to the disappointment of Tom and all his friends.

There is certainly no doubt that Tom was held in high esteem by his fellow bricklayers, especially after his protracted battle with Con Parker, and it was through their promise of financial backing and untiring efforts of persuasion that he was finally induced into taking up prize fighting professionally.

Peter Crawley, ex-champion of England, trained Tom Sayers early in his career.

# 3

## LOVE, MONEY, OR A BELLYFUL

By the time Tom Sayers began his fighting career, pugilism in England had fallen into disrepute. During the previous decade, the sport had attracted the attention of the criminal underworld and it became common practice for the gangs of hooligans gathered around the ringside to intimidate the referee, or interfere with the contest when their particular fighter looked like losing. Ropes would be cut, the mob would invade the ring and any pugilist who went down and appeared unlikely to return to the centre of the ring within the prescribed time could hope for a little respite when his supporters held up the proceedings. Consequently, these transgressions alienated the sympathies of the respectable and influential sportsmen who, since the inception of prize fighting, had been responsible for its very existence. Pugilism found few friends among the forces of law and order and it was sternly suppressed by the authorities. Whenever there was a possibility of a fight taking place, it became customary practice for the magistrate of the nearest town to instigate proceedings against anyone connected with the affair. However, these authoritarian measures only served to drive the sport underground and provoke further retaliation among the hierarchy of the wealthy patrons, who introduced their own security network, whereby only those who they considered trustworthy were informed of the intimate and detailed plans of a forthcoming contest. This effectively put the lower classes of society into a dilemma, for they still wanted to retain a vested interest in the sport. They congregated in the inns and taverns scattered throughout London and the provinces, where a major proportion of the leading prize fighters kept their own sporting establishments, renowned for their respectability, and which could challenge comparisons with the best kept hostelries in the land.

One hundred years before, irrepressible roars of laughter prevailed as excited crowds of wide-eyed spectators congregated around the

booths of Smithfield, Moorfields, and Southwark Fairs to watch the exhibitions of cudgelling and duelling, or to see a couple of burly contestants box and wrestle for their amusement. Here, standing outside
his booth, the inimitable Figg would loudly challenge any member of
the public to 'Step into the twenty-four-foot ring and ply your mental
maulers with the kings, princes, and hoi-polloi of the noble art of self-
defence for love, money, or a bellyful!'

These early showmen, who were prepared to meet all comers, were
the forerunners of the prize fighters who became so popular after the
Hanovarian accession in 1714. During the reign of King George I,
prize fighting had swiftly overtaken every other major sport and
throughout the kingdom, sporting houses, clubs and taverns sprang up
where the devotees of the much-vaunted "Scientific and Noble Art of
Self-defence" met with other sporting personalities, to wager on the
outcome of a "Mill" or prize fight. The prize ring actually derived its
name from these bystanders, who formed a circle and, within this ring,
two protagonists fought for a purse containing prize money. A Mill
provided an outlet for the aggressive instincts latent in many spectators
and engaged the attention of almost half the population of England.
Any pugilistic encounter between two noted contenders was considered
paramount to a national affair and, from dawn to dusk, fight enthusiasts in their tens of thousands discussed and argued the merits of
each contestant until the great event was decided. Each county had its
favourite; patronized by the nobility and gentry who moralized on its
ethical values, and admired and respected by the lower classes of
society. To every true-blooded Englishman, pugilism represented a
sport which encouraged gallantry in the individual, courage in the face
of adversity and actively inspired a feeling of self-reliance in a man's
own ability. It became the foundation stone for a new code of conduct,
in which the words "Fair play and chivalry" became synonymous with
every sportsman, and an honourable occupation in which the
exponents were expected to be totally reliable, trustworthy in the
defence of right and cause, completely dedicated to their profession
and expected to be beaten senseless rather than accept a bribe to lose
the battle. Those who did succumb to temptation were spurned and
detested by everyone and, in almost every instance, sank into oblivion
and died in abject poverty.

The wealthy aristocracy and the dedicated followers of the sport
formed their own select clubs and organizations, and developed their
own unique terminology, calling themselves The Amateurs, Corinthian's, the Blades, the Swells and many more, too numerous to
mention. Inevitably, in the succeeding years, as more clubs and institu-
tions were founded, the distinction between them became impossible to

discern. Some, like the Corinthian's, retained their identity but, to circumvent any further complications, a compromise was reached
whereby the majority integrated into what became known as "the
Fancy," – the collective noun for followers of a sport. The patrons of
the Fancy financed the ring and co-ordinated its administration until
the formation of the Pugilistic Club in 1814.

Little is known of any rules or regulations concerning the early bouts
and it remains a matter of speculation what was actually allowed. The
first indications of any rules at all was in 1719, at the time of James
Figg, the first recorded champion. Although he claimed to be a heavyweight champion, the term "Champion" at this time was used loosely
to denote a public boxer for, mentioned in The Tatler and The
Guardian – the foremost literary publications of the period – there
appears the names of two other "champions," Grettings, and Pipes,
but neither of these had any claim to the title.

Figg's portrait and fame is owed to the preservation of two great
contemporaries; William Hogarth the artist, whose celebrated picture
of Southwark Fair depicts Figg standing outside his booth and Captain
Godfrey, whose book "A Treatise on the Useful Science of Self-
defence," published in 1747, contains inherent proof of Figg's outstanding bravery. But Figg's method of fighting relied chiefly on his
great strength and ferocity, rather than his aptitude as a boxer.
Outwardly he displayed the characteristics of an honest and jovial per-
sonality but, deep down, he was a man possessed with a killer instinct.
He punished his antagonists unmercifully, particularly those who
attempted to stand up to him and fight back. Nevertheless, despite all
the criticisms, he was held in high esteem by the Fancy and regarded
as England's leading fighter.

When Figg retired as undefeated champion in 1734, he was
succeeded by George Taylor, the proprietor of "The Great Booth" in
Oxford Road (now London's Tottenham Court Road). Taylor invited
the most celebrated fighters of the age to demonstrate their skills in the
different categories of self-defence but, during his reign the boxing
booths degenerated into total anarchy, ferocity and barbarity, due principally to the drunken combatants and the various artifices employed
by the traders to swindle the gullible public. Open challenges were
freely advertised as each promoter competed with his neighbour, and
the rivalry between the booths became intolerable.

Taylor's domination ended in 1740 when he was soundly beaten by
Jack Broughton (the Waterman). With the advent of Broughton,
pugilism once again attained the rank of respectability, for according
to the best authorities Broughton appears to have been regarded as the
"Father of British Boxing." He is attributed with having invented the

boxing glove, which he developed from the padded gloves, or "mufflers" as they were more commonly known. Bare knuckles were mandatory in prize fights, but boxing gloves now became standard wear in sparring exhibitions and to prevent serious injuries during training.

On March 10, 1743 he opened "Broughton's New Amphitheatre" in London's Oxford Road. The reputation of his new establishment was beyond reproach and soon gained the distinction of boasting "Royal, Noble, and Distinguished Patronage." To curb the menace of the boxing booths, drastic action was urgently needed, so on August 10, 1743, a meeting was held between a select committee of the Fancy and the leading contemporary pugilists to formulate a code of practice. They devised a set of seven rules entitled, "Mr Broughton's Rules for the Better Regulation of the Amphi-theatre," which served as statutes for the ring for the next ninety-five years.

Broughton's methods were quite revolutionary and enormous crowds flocked to see his exhibitions of extraordinary fighting skills. He introduced the techniques of blocking, hitting and retreating, and could deflect with ease any blow aimed at any part of his anatomy. Anyone who had the temerity to enter the ring with him was soon convinced of his exceptional powers, for his stomach punch and formidable lunge under the ear generally produced a sense of trepidation in his adversaries.

After retaining his title for ten years, Broughton was beaten in 1750 by Jack Slack. A chance blow over the bridge of his nose blinded the 14 stone champion, who had developed a plethoric condition whereby, due to an abundance of red corpuscles in the blood, any heavy blow caused profuse bleeding and extensive swelling.

Jack Slack reigned as champion for the next ten years, but during that time, he acquired a dubious reputation, and there were numerous references to crookedness in defence of his title.

On June 17, 1760 Bill Stevens, alias The Nailer, became the new champion but three months later, when he met George Meggs, a collier from Bristol, he made it blatantly obvious that the fight was "fixed." Stevens was determined to lose, and with the greatest impudence, declared he would fight no longer. He later had the impertinence to claim that Meggs had paid him fifty guineas to claim the title. Following this disgraceful incident, Stevens quickly sank to the lowest depths of degredation and, although he fought several other battles, they were all against men of little consequence.

For the next twenty-two years few heads wore the conqueror's crown for any length of time. Meggs soon lost his position to Tom Milsom (the Baker) who in turn handed the title to Tom Juchau (the Pavior).

Juchau's short reign ended when Bill Darts carried off the laurels. After a reign of five years, Darts was deposed in June 1769 by Tom Lyons (the Waterman from Kingston-upon-Thames). However, having achieved his ambition to become champion, Lyons declined to continue his career in the prize ring and returned to his old trade on the Thames, leaving Darts to reclaim the title.

Two years passed before Peter Corcoran, an Irishman, laid claim to the championship. The battle proved a complete farce and Corcoran won in a single round. Darts was alleged to have been bribed with £100 to lose the battle. He departed from the ring in disgrace and died in abject poverty.

Corcoran held the title for seven years, but in his last encounter against Harry Sellers, he gave in without a semblance of a struggle. His poor Irish supporters, who had backed their "Darlin' Boy" for every farthing they possessed, were literally ruined. This shameful episode signalled the end of Corcoran's career and he too sank into poverty and oblivion. When he died, he had to be buried by public subscription.

Although Sellers retained the title for about four years, he never rated highly as a pugilist. He lost his crown to Jack (Duggan) Fearns, an Irish boatswain in just one & a half minutes, the shortest championship contest on record. Deservedly humiliated, he also faded into obscurity.

Within a short time, Fearns was succeeded by Tom Jackling (alias Johnson) an enormously powerful man weighing 14 stone. His destruction of his contemporaries was awe-inspiring and few lasted more than a few minutes. After having vanquished most of London's fighters, it became necessary to seek opponents in other directions. The search was switched to Bristol, then the hot-bed for pugilists. Here, the most promising candidate was Bill Warr. In the first round of their battle, Warr realized his position was hopeless and, after suffering all the punishment he could withstand, bolted from the ring and refused to return.

Johnson next vanquished Mike Ryan in a most controversial battle. Ryan delivered a tremendous blow to Johnson's temple. Completely stunned by the punch, Johnson was on the point of falling when his second ran into the ring to save him. Inadvertently he caught Ryan in his arms, and immediately cries of 'Foul!' resounded from the spectators clustered around the ring. Ryan's backers instantly demanded the prize money and ran protesting to the referee claiming that 'As Johnson had not fallen, it was perfectly legal for Ryan to strike him and finish the match!'

Valuable minutes were wasted during the dispute, giving the demoralized Johnson ample time to recover. When at last the battle was resumed, the temperamental Ryan was so overcome with emotion Johnson had an easy conquest. The Fancy, however, still remained in doubt on who was the better man, so a second contest was arranged. This conflict was indescribably severe and both were terribly mauled. After swapping blows like blacksmiths at an anvil, Johnson emerged victorious in 30 minutes.

His next match was against the gigantic Isaac Perrins who stood 6 feet 2 inches, weighed 17 stone and was one of the strongest men in Britain. During the conflict, Perrins received a slashing punch on the nose, slitting it open as if it had been cut with a knife. Despite his horrendous injury, he refused to submit from the heavy bombardment until the 62nd round, when he was forced away from the ring by his supporters.

Johnson's retribution came in January 1791 when he accepted a challenge from (Big Ben) Brain. The contest opened at a furious pace, each man standing toe to toe, slamming punches for round after round and each in turn being floored by the terrific blows. In the concluding rounds, his age beginning to tell, the forty-one-year-old Johnson fell repeatedly. He never fought again. He acquired the tenancy of the Grapes in Lincolns Inn Fields and settled down to life as a publican.

Brain, like Johnson, never entered the ring again. When he died in 1794 an autopsy revealed that his liver had been irreparably damaged from his many violent battles.

On Brain's death, the Jewish boxer Daniel Mendoza laid claim to the title. Bill Warr was furious at Mendoza's audacity and challenged him, but when they met at Bexley Heath on November 12, 1794 Mendoza clinched the title in twenty-three rounds.

The new science Mendoza brought to the ring was like a breath of fresh air. A cultured intellectual, he transformed the old method of standing and swapping blows to a new style of swiftness and agility.

Mendoza lost his title to John Jackson on April 15, 1795. "Gentleman Jackson" as he became more commonly known, did more to inspire pugilism than any of his predecessors. He opened a gymnasium in Old Bond Street, London, where he gave tuition in boxing to the Prince of Wales (later George IV), the aristocracy and gentry. Lord Byron, who paid tribute to him in his literary works, was a regular visitor to his establishment and a close personal friend. No one disputed Jackson's right to the title and a few years later he retired from the ring.

Jem Belcher now arrived upon the scene and appointed himself champion. This approbation caused immense confusion, for according to the Fancy, Dan Mendoza was supposed to be next in line of succession.

Born in Bristol in April 1781, Jem Belcher was the grandson of Jack Slack, the former champion. A magnificent boxer, Jem had put all the old school of celebrated heroes behind him before he reached the age of twenty. He became undisputed champion in 1800, but in July 1803, at the pinnacle of his career, he had the misfortune to lose an eye whilst playing racquets. He naturally assumed his injury marked the end of his fighting career and he believed it extremely doubtful that he would ever enter the ring again. Shortly after the accident, he introduced to the prize ring a fellow townsman named Henry Pearce. Henry, or "Hen" as he was duly dubbed, derived the nickname "The Game Chicken."

Now hailed as the new champion, Pearce entered the scene with an irresistible devil-may-care approach. On October 8, 1805 he defended his newly-acquired title against John Gully. In a bruising fight lasting 77 minutes, Gully suffered a ghastly blow to the throat. He was unable to breathe and, fearing he would choke to death, the referee awarded the victory to Pearce.

Since the accident to his eye Jem Belcher had been silently brooding over his misfortunes. Following his pupil's recent success against Gully, he allowed a hint of jealousy to creep in and foolishly issued a challenge to the Game Chicken. Despite his reluctance to encounter his old friend, as the reigning champion, Pearce could not decline to defend his title. Although Jem was still only aged twenty-six, the loss of an eye and the dissipated life he had led of late meant he stood no chance against the unsurpassed vigour of Pearce.

When Henry Pearce died of tuberculosis in 1809, Bob Gregson (The Lancashire Giant) laid claim to the title. The Fancy, however, considered him unworthy of the post and awarded the position to John Gully, but Gully declined to defend the office and announced his retirement from the ring.

The inimitable Tom Cribb, who had vanquished both Gregson and Jem Belcher, was now acclaimed eligible for the title. Immediately Jem Belcher learned of Cribb's accession, his old jealousies were aroused and he could not resist the temptation for one more battle with his old conqueror. In their fight on Epsom Race Course on February 1, 1809 Cribb emerged victorious in a contest of thirty-one rounds lasting 40 minutes. This was Belcher's last appearance in the ring. He died on July 30, 1811 aged thirty.

Tom Cribb's boxing career began when he fought the veteran pugilist George Maddox on January 7, 1805. By his conquest of the highly experienced Maddox, young Tom acquired a pugilistic fame

TOM SAYERS

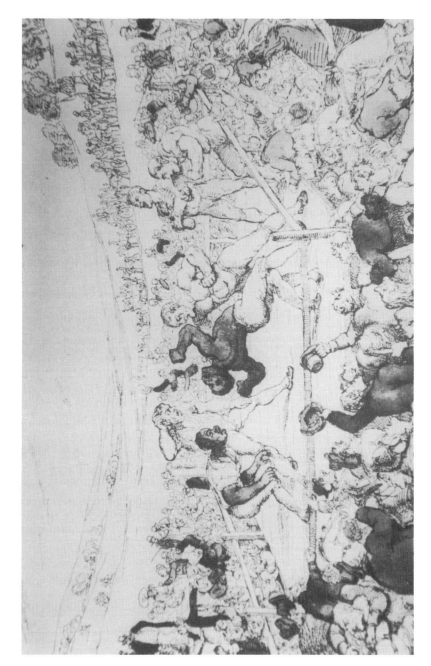

The battle between Tom Cribb and Molineux at Thistleton Gap.

hitherto unknown. Captain Barclay, the pre-eminent trainer of the period, quickly recognized his great potential and placed him under his guidance.

Cribb met many good pugilists in his career, but without doubt his most celebrated fights were with the American negro, Tom Molineaux. Their first engagement took place at Copthorn Common near East Grinstead. Seldom before had a battle of such intensity been witnessed and both men electrified the spectators with their dogged determination and courage. However strong Cribb might have been, the gallant black man was even stronger and it was only due to Cribb's predominant skill and resolution that he was able to clinch the victory.

The Fancy were captivated by Molineaux's brilliant performance, and were resolved to give him a second chance. Their second engagement took place at Thistleton Gap, in the county of Rutland. This time Cribb took a positive lead from the moment hostilities commenced and in the 9th round, as Molineaux came running in, his jaw was fractured by a tremendous blow from the champion. For his outstanding victory, Tom Cribb became the first champion of England to be presented with a belt as a badge of office. This magnificent trophy was manufactured from a lion's skin and ornamented with two large silver medallions and lions' paws.

Many pugilists laid claim to the title during the latter part of Cribb's reign but none had the courage to actually throw down the gauntlet. Among these claimants were Tom Hickman (the Gas Man), Jack Carter, and Bill Neat. In their battles for supremacy, Hickman was defeated by Neat and both Neat and Carter were conquered by Tom Spring, a protégé of Cribb. After Spring had disposed of Bill Neat in May 1823, Tom Cribb expressed his satisfaction by resigning the championship into Spring's keeping.

Tom Spring (whose real name was Winter) was soon called upon to defend his newly-acquired title and twice in 1824 defended himself against Jack Langan, the Irish champion. In their first engagement, held on Worcester Race Course, the excitement amongst the spectators reached fever pitch. Scuffles broke out as rival supporters surged forward and invaded the ring. For some time, the ring-keepers were hard pressed to keep them at bay and there were many violent clashes as these insurgents were unceremoniously ejected from the arena. At the end of the encounter, Langan was in a deplorable condition; severely cut, bruised and bleeding and barely able to stand. In their second gruelling battle at Apuldram, near Chichester in Sussex, both were in a particularly distressed condition. At the close, the gallant Irish champion made two valiant attempts to turn the scales, but he was dropped on each occasion. Finally, as Spring tapped him gently,

The climax at Spring and Langan's battle near Chichester on June 8 1824.

Langan's seconds threw up the sponge in token of defeat. So ended Spring's last epic fight. He announced his intention of retiring from the ring and again there was an interregnum until it could be decided on who should reign in his stead.

Joshua Hudson, who had defeated Jem Ward in 1823, now became the prime candidate but, within a fortnight of Spring's retirement, Hudson was beaten by Tom Cannon (the Big Gun of Windsor). Cannon now arrogated himself into the champion's seat, but as soon as he proclaimed his new position, he was immediately challenged by Jem Ward. In their conflict, Ward clinched the victory in just ten minutes. He was presented with the champion's belt which he retained undisturbed until beaten by Peter Crawley on January 2, 1827. Crawley was now proclaimed champion but, two days after the engagement, he announced that he had finished with prize fighting as a principal and Ward was welcome to resume the position he had lost. Peter Crawley had the distinction of being the shortest reigning champion in the history of the prize ring.

Jem Ward was called upon to protect his honours on two more occasions. He defeated Jack Carter on May 27, 1828 and Simon Byrne received a similar fate in July 1831. Jem retired from the ring in 1832 and announced that he would present a new belt to the first man he considered the most worthy candidate.

The first claimant was the very popular James Burke, generally better known in the fistic profession as "Deaf Burke" or "The Deaf-Un." Burke's claim to the position was disputed by the Irishman, Simon Byrne. On Thursday May 30, 1833 at St Albans in Hertfordshire, their ferocious encounter consisted of ninety-eight rounds, lasting 3 hours and 16 minutes; the longest championship fight on record. Byrne received a terrible beating, and had to be carried from the ring on a stretcher.

The following day his condition was reported as grave, and Mr Kingston, a surgeon from St Albans was summoned to his bedside. He shaved Byrne's head, bled him and applied leeches to the fearful bruising. But poor Simon never recovered from his injuries and died at 8.30 on the Sunday morning. At the inquest the following Monday, witnesses testified that in the battle both men were frequently carried to the scratch by their seconds and, at the conclusion of the contest, neither man could have made it alone to the centre of the ring.

A charge of manslaughter was recorded, naming Burke as principal in the first degree. The four seconds, Tom Spring, Jem Ward, Dick Curtis and Tom Gaynor, together with the two umpires, were charged as principals in the second degree. The coroner made out a warrant for the committal of all parties and the trial took place on Thursday July

Tom Spring's parlour.

11, at Hertford Assizes before Mr Justice Park. After hearing all the evidence, he instructed the jury to bring in a verdict of Not Guilty. Death, he said, was an occupational hazard confronting any prize fighter.'

As a result of Byrne's death, Burke remained without a fight for over three years despite his repeated offers to fight anyone in Great Britain for £100, the maximum stake he could raise. At length, in 1837, finding no one brave enough to accept his challenges, he went to the United States of America to fight the renowned Irish brawler, Sam O'Rourke. During the battle, he was forced to make a hurried escape when O'Rourke's supporters threatened to kill him with their shillelaghs and bowie knives.

While Burke was in America pugilism in Great Britain underwent immense changes. For some considerable time it had been universally recognized that Jack Broughton's set of rules were obsolete and totally inadequate to deal with the controversial issues constantly arising in prize ring battles. A complete revision was urgently needed, so in 1838 a committee of sporting gentlemen was commissioned to draft a new code of practice.

Following a succession of lengthy discussions the new statutes were formally submitted for approval at a general meeting of the Fancy. A unanimous vote of agreement was returned with the recommendation that they be known as "THE NEW RULES OF THE PRIZE RING, 1838." They specified:-

Rule 1. That the ring shall be made of turf, and shall be four-and-twenty feet square, formed of eight stakes and ropes, the latter in double lines, the uppermost being four feet from the ground. That in the centre of the ring a mark be formed, to be termed a scratch and that at two opposite corners, as may be selected, spaces be inclosed by other marks sufficiently large for the reception of the seconds and bottle-holders, to be entitled "The Corners."

2. That each man shall be attended to in the ring by a second and a bottle-holder, the former provided with a sponge and the latter with a bottle of water. That the combatants, on shaking hands, shall retire until the seconds of each have tossed for choice of position. The winner shall choose his corner according to the state of the wind or sun and conduct his man thereto, the loser taking the opposite diagonal corner.

3. That each man be provided with a handkerchief of a colour suitable to his own fancy and that the seconds proceed to entwine these handkerchiefs at the upper end of one of the centre stakes. That these handkerchiefs shall be called "The Colours" and that the winner of the battle at its conclusion shall be entitled to their possession, as the trophy of victory.

4. That the umpires shall then be chosen by the seconds to watch the progress of the battle and take exception to any breach of the rules hereinafter stated. That a referee shall be chosen by the umpires, to whom all disputes shall be referred and that the decision of this referee, whatever it may be, shall be final and strictly binding on all parties, whether as to the matter in dispute, or the issue of the battle. That the umpires shall be provided with a watch, for the purpose of calling time and that they mutually agree upon to which this duty shall devolve, the call of that umpire only to be attended to and no other person whatever to interfere in calling time. That the referee shall withhold all opinion till appealed to by the umpires and that the umpires strictly abide by his decision without dispute.

5. That, on the men being stripped, it shall be the duty of the seconds to examine their shoes and drawers and if any objection arises either as to insertion of improper spikes in the former or substances in the latter, they shall appeal to their umpires who, with the concurrence of the referee, shall direct if any and what alteration shall be made.

6. That both men being ready, each man shall be conducted to that side of the scratch next to his corner previously chosen; and the seconds on one side and the men on the other, having shaken hands, the former shall immediately return to their corners and there to remain within the prescribed marks till the round be finished, on no pretence whatever approaching their principals during the round on penalty of losing the battle.

7. That at the conclusion of the round, when one or both of the men are down, the seconds and bottle-holders shall step forward and carry or conduct their principal to his corner, there affording him the necessary assistance, and that no person whatever be permitted to interfere in this duty.

8. That at the expiration of thirty seconds (unless otherwise agreed upon) the umpire appointed shall cry "time", upon which each man shall rise from the knee of his bottle-holder and walk to his own side of the scratch unaided, the seconds and bottle-holders remaining at their corners; and that either man failing so to be at the scratch within eight seconds, shall be deemed to have lost the battle.

9. That on no consideration whatever shall any person be permitted to enter the ring during the battle, or till it shall have been concluded and that in the event of such unfair practice, or the ropes and stakes being disturbed or removed, it shall be within the power of the umpires and referee to award the victory to that man who, in their honest opinion, shall have the best of the contest.

10. That the seconds and the bottle-holders shall not interfere, advise

or direct the adversary of their principal and shall refrain from all offensive or irritating expressions, in all respects conducting themselves with order and decorum and confine themselves to the diligent and careful discharge of their duties to their principals.

11. That in picking up their men, should the seconds or bottle-holders wilfully injure the antagonist of their principals, he shall be deemed to have forfeited the battle on the decision of the umpires or referee.

12. That it shall be a fair stand-up fight and, if either man shall wilfully throw himself down without receiving a blow, he shall be deemed to have lost the battle; but that this rule shall not apply to a man who, in a close, slips down from the grasp of his opponent to avoid punishment or from obvious accident or weakness.

13. That butting with the head shall be deemed foul and the party resorting to this practice shall be deemed to have lost the battle.

14. That a blow struck when a man is thrown or down, shall be deemed foul. That a man with one knee and one hand on the ground, or with both knees on the ground, shall be deemed down and a blow given in either of those positions shall be considered foul, providing always that when in such a position, the man so down shall not himself strike or attempt to strike.

15. That a blow struck below the waistband shall be deemed foul and that, in a close, seizing an antagonist below the waist, by the thigh or otherwise, shall be deemed foul.

16. That in all attempts to inflict injury by gouging or tearing the flesh with the fingers or nails and biting shall be deemed foul.

17. That kicking, or deliberately falling on an antagonist with the knees or otherwise when down, shall be deemed foul.

18. That all bets shall be paid as the battle-money after a fight is awarded.

19. That no person on any pretence whatever shall be permitted to approach nearer the ring than ten feet, with the exception of the umpires and referee and, the persons appointed to take charge of the water or other refreshments for the combatants shall take their seats close to the corners selected by the seconds.

20. That due notice shall be given by the stake-holder of the day and place where the battle-money is to be given up and that he be exonerated from all responsibility upon obeying the direction of the umpires and referee; and that all parties be strictly bound by these rules; and that in future all articles of agreement for a contest be entered into with a strict and willing adherence to the letter and spirit of these rules and without reserve or equivocation.

21. That, in the event of magisterial interference, it shall be the duty

of the umpires and referee to name the time and place for the next meeting, if possible on the same day.

22. That should the event not be decided on the day named all bets shall be deemed void, unless again declared on by mutual agreement; but that the battle-money shall remain in the hands of the stake-holder till fairly won or lost by a fight, unless each party shall agree to withdraw his stake.

23. That all stage fights be as nearly as possible in conformity with the foregoing rules.

# 4

## THE BRUISERS

In the void left by Burke's visit to America a new breed of "Big Men" had emerged upon the pugilistic horizon. Each and every one of them was an extremely formidable customer and all more than a match for the Deaf-Un. They comprised such worthies as the 6 feet 2 inch, 14½ stone Ben Caunt, William Thompson (better known as Big Bold Bendigo) and Brassey of Bradford. During Burke's absence Ben Caunt and Bendigo had fought two incredibly controversial battles in which the cunning Bendigo had conducted a campaign of falling on every conceivable occasion. Whenever the more ponderous Caunt attempted to close, Bendigo would sink to the turf, grinning all over his face. Caunt became increasingly frustrated at these contemptible tactics and, in a fit of rage, stormed over to Bendigo's corner and struck him as he sat on the knee of his bottle-holder, telling him to fight fair. Instantly a cry of "Foul!" went up from the crowd, and Caunt was disqualified for striking a foul blow.

After this unsatisfactory conclusion a deep sense of rivalry existed between the two, until their second meeting at Selby in Yorkshire. By this time, both fighters had attracted a large following of supporters and there was an enormous muster of the troublesome roughs who were the scourge of any prize fight. The air tingled with hot contention as the two combatants hammered at each other for seventy-five rounds; the lumbering Caunt constantly thwarted by the lighter and more agile Bendigo, who again repeated his former tactics. Caunt seized him by the throat and held him high on the ropes in a stranglehold. The fight would, most probably, have ended at this point had it not been for the mob who cut the ropes and invaded the ring. When at last hostilities were resumed, Bendigo accidentally slipped on the turf and was adjudged to have fallen without a blow. Instantly fighting broke out between the rival factions and Caunt was forced to make good his escape on a borrowed horse.

Bendigo's reputation suffered nothing as a result of this defeat and, within a year, he was matched to fight Deaf Burke. Unfortunately, Burke had undergone little training and was in poor condition. Bendigo peppered his antagonist with hard and rapid punches until, in a fit of rage and despair, Burke head-butted Bendigo and lost the fight on a foul. Jem Ward now awarded Bendigo the long-promised belt but it had taken seven years for Ward to decide who should wear the coveted trophy.

On March 24, 1840 Bendigo had the misfortune to break his knee-cap whilst turning somersaults. This accident rendered him incapable of any violent exertion and unhappily forced him into early retirement. Immediately Deaf Burke heard of Bendigo's resignation, he once again laid claim to the championship. But Nick Ward, Jem's brother, proclaimed himself the new champion and, in common with all his predecessors, threw down the gauntlet to all comers.

Meanwhile, Ben Caunt who, after a bitter clash had conquered Brassey, also laid claim to the title. He accepted Ward's challenge, but from the very beginning of their battle Nick Ward adopted the policy of dropping at every opportunity. Caunt lost his temper at his deplorable actions and hit him when he was on his knees. Caunt expressed profound regret at his irresponsible conduct, and arrangements were made for a rematch. This time the verdict was reversed. At the close of the 35th round, Ward declined to continue the contest and the belt became the property of Ben Caunt.

At this time, no one appeared sufficiently venturous to dispute Caunt's right to the title so he decided to pay a visit to the United States to meet Charles Freeman (the American Giant). However, when he discovered that Freeman was 6 feet 10 inches tall and weighed 17 stone, he invited him back for a tour of England instead.

Ben Caunt returned in 1842 but remained unchallenged until 1845, when Johnny Broome offered to produce a "mystery opponent" and add a transferable belt for the winner. To everyone's amazement the mystery man was none other than the Big Bold Bendigo.

The fight was attended by a particularly large contingent of ruffians who completely dominated the arena. To prove the belt was genuine, Caunt proffered it to Bendigo for his inspection. Snatching it from his grasp, Bendigo created further uproar by donning the trophy and capering about the ring as if it were already his own property.

The fight followed the old familiar pattern with Bendigo constantly dropping to avoid punishment. Caunt's supporters screamed incessantly for the referee to intervene and cries of, "Unmanly! – Unmanly!" rent the air from his infuriated followers. In the 93rd round, some confusion arose when Caunt, believing the round had ended, sat down on the grass and was instantly disqualified for falling without a blow. Immediately the verdict was announced a vicious battle broke out between rival supporters. The huge crowd made its way to Stony Stratford, near Buckingham, where a full scale riot erupted. Shops were looted and brawling hooligans overran every public house in the town.

For several weeks a bitter controversy raged over the disgusting scenes and the unfortunate referee was unjustly accused of having been intimidated by the bullies. Caunt attempted a rematch several times, but Bendigo would not be enticed, and in 1846 both Caunt and Bendigo announced their retirement from the ring.

Bendigo's eccentricities extended far beyond the confines of the prize ring and he was constantly at the centre of some controversy or uproar. He was born on October 11, 1811 at 16 New Yard, off Upper Parliament Street, Nottingham. He claimed to be the third of triplets and the last of twenty-one children, but the Parish Register of Christenings shows only Richard and William, twin sons of Benjamin and Mary. However, the story goes that the triplets were dubbed "Shadrach, Meshach and Abednigo". Consequently William Thompson derived the nickname of "Bednigo" and, at the start of his career in the ring, actually fought under his biblical name. Later this became shortened to Bendigo and, often, Bendy. His father, a talented but improvident lacemaker, died in 1826 and young William was sent to the Parish Workhouse where he remained for nearly two years.

As a young man he made his living selling oysters on the streets of Nottingham and later gained some knowledge in the trade of iron turning, but his favourite pursuit was fishing and he was a familiar figure on the banks of the River Trent where he is credited with having saved three people from drowning. Although proficient in football, cricket, acrobatics and running, he excelled in wrestling and boxing. His contemporaries, however, found his style of boxing difficult to describe for he was the first recorded southpaw in the history of the ring. His movements were totally unpredictable; darting about the ring, sometimes circling, now retreating, sometimes with his head thrown back, or head down, boring in on his opponent.

As one sports writer pompously described his actions, "No clown in pantomime gambols ever exceeded him in the multiplicity of his corporeal evolutions."

In his early twenties Bendigo became the unofficial leader of the infamous "Nottingham Lambs", one of the unruly street gangs who terrorized the citizens of Nottingham. He was acknowledged as being a likeable fellow, always full of jokes, mimicry, comic dances and impromptu songs or poems which he made up on the spot, but when he was drunk his senses deserted him and he became a raving idiot of the most alarming proportions.

Time after time he appeared before the magistrates on charges of drunkenness and assault, but frequently escaping a prison sentence when he turned on the charm to the sitting magistrate.

Despite the leniency shown by the courts his drunken antics became almost monotonous as the headlines in the local papers wearily reported, "BENDIGO IN TROUBLE AGAIN". He was a constant source of nuisance to one Nottingham policeman who had the misfortune to bear the same name as his old rival Ben Caunt. Whenever Constable Caunt was called to the scene of a disturbance he was immediately singled out by Bendigo for "special treatment."

One magistrate once told Bendigo, 'When you are sober, you are one of the nicest men in Nottingham but when you're drunk, you 'aint! So therefore you will go to prison for two months.'

Altogether Bendigo served twenty-eight spells of imprisonment in the house of correction, but it was during his last incarceration that he heard the prison chaplain telling the story of David and Goliath. It reminded him of his fights with Ben Caunt and years later he often recalled how, 'When the preacher came to describe the fight, I listened with all my might and when it came to the wind up and David floored the giant and killed him, without thinking I was in a chapel and that it was against the rules, I bawls out "Bravo!" I'm glad the little-'un won. It was very wrong, but what made it worse was that all the prisoners and warders burst out laughing.'

After listening to the sermons and the stories from The Bible, Bendigo began to see the errors of his ways and, on his discharge from prison, refused to associate with his former cronies among the Nottingham Lambs.

As the years passed Bendigo mellowed and the turning point in his life came when he heard the revivalist minister Richard Weaver preach at a religious meeting. Weaver recognized him among the congregation and invited him to step up on the platform. The audience were understandably astounded and the miracle of Bendigo's conversion was treated with some scepticism; the general reaction being, "If he can stay out of gaol for two weeks, that'll be the miracle!"

Bendigo did stay out of gaol and did remain reasonably sober, addressing numerous assemblies in Nottingham and throughout the country.

Adopting a fighting pose, he would say, 'See them belts – see them cups, I used to fight fer those, but now I fight fer Christ.' He frowned upon any impudence from the audience with disfavour.

The photograph of William Thompson, better known in fighting circles as The Big Bold Bendigo, was taken after he turned to religion and became a lay-preacher.

There was an occasion at a meeting in Birmingham when Jack Ball
(the Fighting Gunsmith) and a handful of local bruisers turned up to
barrack him. In the midst of their sniggering and ridicule, Bendy
politely asked his audience if he could be excused for five minutes.

Descending from the rostrum, he waded into their midst with both
fists flying. Sir Arthur Conan Doyle later described the scene in his
poem, Bendigo's Sermon.

"Now, I'll tell you how it happened. He was preachin' down at Brum,
He was billed just like a circus, you should see the people come,
The chapel it was crowded and in the foremost row,
There was half a dozen bruisers who'd a grudge at Bendigo.

There was Tommy Platt of Bradford, Solly Jones of Perry Bar,
Long Connor from the Bull Ring, the same wot drew with Carr,
Jack Ball the fighting gunsmith, Joe Murphy from the mews,
And Iky Moss, the bettin' boss, the Champion of the Jews.

A very pretty handful a-sittin' in a string,
Full of beer and impudence, ripe for anything,
Sittin' in a string there, right under Bendy's nose,
If his message was for sinners, he could make a start on those.

Soon he heard them chaffin'; 'Hi, Bendy! Here's a go!
How much are you coppin' by this jump to glory show?
Stow it, Bendy! Left the ring? Mighty spry of you!
Didn't everybody know the ring was leavin' you?'

Bendy fairly sweated as he stood above and prayed,
'Look down, O Lord, and grip me with a stranglehold!' he said,
'Fix me with a stranglehold, put a stop on me!
I'm slippin', Lord, I'm slippin' and I'm clinging hard to thee!'

But the roughs they kept a chaffin' and the uproar it was such
That the preacher in the pulpit might be talking double Dutch,
Till a workin' man he shouted out, a-jumpin' to his feet,
'Give us a lead, your reverence, and heave 'em in the street.'

Then Bendy says, 'Good Lord, since first I left my sinful ways,
Thou knowest that to thee alone I've given up my days,
But now dear Lord,' – and here he laid his Bible on the shelf –
'I'll take with your permission just five minutes for myself.'

He vaulted from the pulpit like a tiger from a den,
They say it was a lovely sight to see him floor his men;
Right and left, left and right, straight and true and hard,
Till the Ebenezer Chapel looked more like a knacker's yard.

Platt was standin' on his back and lookin' at his toes,
Solly Jones of Perry Bar was feelin' for his nose,
Connor of the Bull Ring had all that he could do,
Rakin' for his ivories that lay about the pew.

Jack Ball the fightin' gunsmith was in a peaceful sleep,
Joe Murphy lay across him, all tied up in a heap,
Five of them lay twisted in a tangle on the floor,
And Iky Moss, the bettin' boss, had sprinted for the door.

Five repentant fightin' men, sitting in a row,
Listenin' to words of grace from Mister Bendigo,
Listenin' to his reverence – all as good as gold,
Pretty little baa-lambs, all gathered to the fold.

So that's the way that Bendy ran his mission in the slum,
And preached the Holy Gospel to the fightin' men of Brum,
'The Lord', said he, 'has given me His message from on high,
And if you interrupt Him, I will know the reason why.'

From the wild impetuous "buck" of his younger days, Bendigo's last years were spent quietly fishing on the banks of the river Trent or touring the country, complete with black frock-coat, hat and gloves and brandishing an umbrella and a Bible. At any prize fight he attended he could be depended upon to launch into a full-scale sermon, denouncing the Devil and all his works and the evils of the demon drink; breaking off occasionally to knock back a quartern of gin, or perhaps to lay odds on a particular race; but in the end always returning to do penance.

In 1850 Bendigo was goaded by his old and ferocious mother into coming out of retirement and accepting a challenge from Tom Paddock.

Many years later Bendigo confessed, 'She was mainly the cause of my last fight with Tom Paddock. I held the belt then and hadn't fought for some time. Well, I went to see her, she was eighty-two years old then and I found her smoking her pipe and reading a copy of *Bell's Life*.

'There you are mother,' I says. 'Yes,' she says, answering me sharp. 'Here I am. Have you seen this?' It was the paper she meant.

'No,' I says. 'I 'aint.'

She says, 'Have you seen this Tom Paddock?'

'No,' I says.

'I have,' says she. 'A needle pointer from Redditch; a fellow with no more breadth between his shoulders than between the eyes of a mouse, and he challenges you to a fight. I'll tell you this, Bendy, if you don't take up the challenge you are a coward. And I tell you more, if you won't fight him, I'll send and take up the challenge myself.'

Paddock and Bendigo fought on June 5, 1850 at Mildenhall in Suffolk. Bendigo needed all his cunning and wiles against the youthful speed of his aggressive and impetuous opponent. To escape the prolonged punishment Bendigo resorted to his usual practice of dropping on every conceivable occasion, clearly irritating the younger and less experienced fighter. In the 49th round Paddock sadly allowed his passion to rule his head. He struck Bendigo when he was on his knee and received an instant disqualification. Bendigo declared he felt extremely satisfied with his performance but this time he really did intend to retire from the ring once and for all.

With the championship title vacant once again there was not long to wait before William Perry (better known as the Tipton Slasher) laid claim to the position. He had been casting a longing eye on the proud office for quite some time and he announced that he was willing to uphold his right to all comers. He issued an open challenge, declaring he would fight any man breathing for £200 or £300 a side, or he would stake £300 to £350 and fight Tom Paddock. Paddock accepted his cartel but the contest ended without a decision. They were matched again but this too ended in a draw. The Fancy were in despair.

On December 17, 1850 they entered into their third engagement at Woking but *Bell's Life*, the sporting paper for the ring, had no terms of praise for the encounter, calling it "a mere scramble; unworthy of the name of a fight, and still less a fight for the championship."

Paddock completely lacked the resources to deal with the Tipton Slasher's unsurpassed qualities and, as Perry was retiring to his corner, Paddock ran after him and dealt him a tremendous blow behind the ear. The Tipton Slasher fell as if he had been poleaxed. Instantly, an appeal of foul was lodged and the referee had no hesitation in awarding the fight to Perry.

The Slasher now laid claim to the championship belt, but the eccentric Bendigo refused to deliver up the trophy, claiming, 'It is my own personal property, and if Perry wants it, then he will have to fight me for it.'

The Slasher accepted the challenge but Bendigo backed out, saying he would be quite content to remain merely a spectator at any future fights. Whatever became of the belt which, according to the rules should have been presented to the Tipton Slasher, was never established.

After Bendigo's retirement, the Slasher declared his readiness to defend the title for £200 a side and in May 1851 Harry Broome announced he was prepared to meet Perry for the championship. In the 15th round of their encounter, as Broome was falling to his knees, the Slasher caught him with a blow at the precise moment he reached the ground. An appeal was made to the referee, Peter Crawley, who ruled it a foul and awarded the fight to Broome.

Angry at what he considered an unjust verdict, the Slasher threatened to hit Crawley. The burly veteran's eyes blazed at the affrontary and he commenced undressing, intent on having a round with Perry. Mob violence erupted and in the ensuing chaos, hostilities were narrowly averted when the Slasher's supporters forcibly removed him from the ring.

Broome enjoyed his honours unmolested until challenged by Harry Orme in 1852. Orme carried off the prize but both men were severely mauled in a slogging match reminiscent of olden days. A second match was arranged between Broome and the Tipton Slasher, but Broome withdrew and forfeited his stake money.

Harry Orme also retired at this time and, with the title becoming vacant again, William Perry was once more dubbed "Champion of England." There were fresh discussions for a match with Tom Paddock, but the latter backed out and Perry had the course all to himself for several years until he was called upon to defend his title against the up-and-coming young middleweight contender, Tom Sayers.

Harry Orme, arch-enemy of Tom Sayers, swore he would get even with him one day.

---

# 5

## TOM SPRING'S WAITER

It was through the consistent courage and integrity of Tom Sayers that the prize ring was destined to have its last flicker of popularity. During his reign he re-created the resplendent dignity of the sport and gave it a new lease of life; long enough to recall its past glories, before allowing its existence of a hundred and fifty years to die in splendour.

Throughout the eighteen-forties the prize ring had owed its crumbling existence to the combined efforts of two men who, between them, had the subtle skill of keeping the ring loyal to the traditions of fair play. These two dedicated men, Vincent Dowling, and his son Frank, were the editors of *Bell's Life*. Its full title, *Bell's Life in London*, and *Sporting Chronicle*, was founded in 1822 and billed as containing, "News of the week. A Rich Repository of Fashion, Wit and Humour, and the Interesting Incidents of Real Life."

Circulating within a radius of 200 miles from London, it was published at 4 o'clock every Saturday afternoon from its offices at 5 Norfolk Street, Strand, and distributed that same evening for sale early Sunday morning. Priced sevenpence, its columns covered a wide variety of subjects, each headed by a woodcut. There were features on drama, the fashion world, answers to correspondents, pet's corner, the turf, and police intelligence. It also concentrated on the seamier aspects of life, giving great prominence to any sensational stories of murder, robbery, seduction and incest. Public executions were reported in unusually explicit detail, whilst the sporting section was devoted to an exclusive and comprehensive coverage on everything connected with the prize ring.

During their time in office, the two Dowlings launched a personal crusade to raise the prestige of the ring and elevate the standards of British sport. Fearlessly and relentlessly, they fought to counteract all the evil influences eating away at its foundations. Between them, their

pens commanded terrible powers of retribution against anyone who
attempted to treat them with disrespect. They were in the enviable
position to launch scathing criticisms and vent their indignation and
scorn against any malpractices of the criminal fraternity who attempted
to bring the sport into disrepute. They could exclude from their
columns any advertisements or challenges from anyone they banned
and the professional pugilist excommunicated by them could find
himself practically deprived of his livelihood.

Occasionally, bitter accusations and threats were made against them
and at one time, Frank had been compelled to fortify his office to
withstand any intruders bent on violence. He took the precaution of
positioning his desk in front of the fireplace where, at a moment's
notice, he could lay his hands on the nearby poker. But through their
determination and devotion they undoubtedly saved pugilism from
sinking into the depths of degradation and corruption currently
happening in America where, along the New York waterfront, prize
fighting had become the core of everything rotten.

In Sunday's issue of April 1, 1849 *Bell's Life* published a challenge
stating that, "Tom Sears, alias Brighton Tom, is prepared to make a
match with Collyer, of Wandsworth, for from £15 to £25 a side, and
will meet tomorrow (Monday night) at George Robinson's, The Laurel
Tree, Bayham Street, Camden Town."

Tom had taken up residence in Bayham Street and had made The
Laurel Tree his headquarters. Also at this time he had fallen madly in
love with a vivacious seventeen-year-old girl named Sarah Henderson
from the neighbouring Borough of St Pancras. Sarah had been flattered
and overwhelmed at the attention Tom had lavished upon her and,
when he asked her to marry him, she readily accepted his proposal.
However, her father Charlie Henderson, a paperhanger and decorator,
refused to give his consent to the marriage. Enraged at his decision,
she agreed to become Tom's common-law wife and, calling themselves
Mr & Mrs Sayers, they moved into lodgings at 45 Bayham Street,
sharing the house with a certain William Beale, his wife Mary and
their two children.

In August, a few months after they began living together, Sarah
became pregnant. With a wife to support and a child on the way Tom
urgently needed a match. The proposed contest with Collyer had fallen
through and, with extremely limited cash resources, he could not afford
the high cost of sparring partners, nor the astronomical fees required
by a good trainer.

One evening at The Laurel Tree he sat discussing his financial
problems with a prominent Camden Town sportsman named Mr
Viddler. After listening patiently to Tom's plaintive needs, he said he

was quite prepared to sponsor him for anything between £5 and £25 and to go ahead and make any match he chose. Overjoyed at the generosity of his new found patron, the following morning he went to the offices of *Bell's Life* and advertised a challenge.

Within a few days of its next publication, he received a reply that his challenge had been accepted by Dan Collins, his former bottle-holder in his match with Couch.

Providentially for Tom, Mr Viddler was a personal friend of Peter Crawley, the ex-champion of England and, by exerting a little benign pressure, he induced Crawley to supervise Tom's training. At a time when the prize ring was going through an unhappy and depressing phase, the burly Peter Crawley was still regarded as the embodiment of honesty and good nature. His character was above suspicion and any involvement he had with the sport was guaranteed to be beyond reproach. If any man had dared to suggest even the slightest participation of a double-cross, he would, most certainly, have found himself stretched lifeless on the ground.

As the landlord of the Queen's Head, in Smithfield, Peter Crawley was often the focal point for the enthusiastic sportsmen who would corner him in his bar-parlour and, over a jug of ale, entice him to tell his life story.

Peter's unconventional career in the ring was singularly fascinating. He was a butcher by trade, in an age when butchers were a notoriously pugnacious breed of men. Renowned for his dexterity with his fists, he was still only seventeen when he thrashed his first opponent, a huge fighting Irishman named Flanagan. The extraordinary manner in which he disposed of the man from the "peat bogs," soon attracted the attention of the Fancy and led him into his first professional match with Ben Sutcliffe. But Peter had one major drawback. He had the misfortune to suffer from a painful hernia, the result of a rupture when a boy. This handicap had sadly interfered with his prospects in the ring but nevertheless, when he was only nineteen, the Fancy thought him good enough to match against Tom Hickman (the Gas Man).

Hickman, fifteen years his senior, was in the prime of maturity and so far in his career, no one, with the exception of Bill Neat of Bristol, had ever stood up to him for long. Although Peter had not yet attained full growth and development, he fought thirteen tremendous rounds in 15 minutes. The battle ended when a spectacular punch from Hickman knocked him out of time. Despite his defeat, he was not disgraced and doubtless the prize ring would have heard more from him had it not been for his troublesome hernia.

Peter returned to his old trade as a butcher in Newington, Kent and was not seen in the prize ring for the next three years. He is next heard of at Chester races in 1822 when he thrashed a tough known as Southern's Bully. The following year he was matched with Dick Acton, a well-known contemporary pugilist who fought Jem Ward in 1821. Peter's friends thought that by beating Acton he would get the chance to fight Jem Ward, who was then laying claim to the championship.

Although Peter beat Acton in sixteen minutes, it had only taken Jem Ward fourteen. Nevertheless, his backers were well satisfied with his performance and would have matched him immediately with Ward, but his hernia incapacitated him from fighting and it was not until four years later that the two came together in the ring. During that time Jem Ward had reached the summit of his career and, after his victory over Tom Cannon, now called himself Champion of England. In response to his challenge issued in 1826 to fight any man in the world, Peter Crawley, who now considered himself fit enough to fight, took up the gauntlet. However, since his prolonged absence from the pugilistic scene, his milling pretensions were unknown. His ability with gloves was admirable, but glove performances did not afford a true criterion to his abilities with bare knuckles. Jem on the other hand, had proved his competence beyond all question in his dozen or so significant battles. The general opinion was that Crawley, alias "Young Rumpsteak", would not stand a chance against the all-accomplished "Black Diamond", the nickname Jem had derived in his occupation as a coal-whipper (black diamonds being the slang word for coal).

Enormous interest was stimulated, but sadly the great event was marred by the stubborn obstinacy and pigheadedness of Bill Gibbons, the commissary of the ring (an office in which he was succeeded by the ex-pugilist, Tom Oliver). "Gentleman Jackson", the ex-champion of England, had obtained permission from a certain Mr Wilbraham, a sporting squire living near Cambridge, to hold the contest in his park which, being private land, was beyond the jurisdiction of the magistrates.

Bill Gibbons had been offended when he was not consulted in naming the rendezvous, stressing that it was his hereditary right to select the battlefield. Consequently, on the morning of January 2, 1827, to demonstrate his contempt for the intervention, he formed the ring at Royston Heath, about thirteen miles from Cambridge and some ten miles from Squire Wilbraham's park. When the combatants and their entourage arrived at Royston Heath, they found to their dismay that at least a third of the London contingent were still a good hour's journey away, kicking their heels in Mr. Wilbraham's park and wondering at the delay. Included among these were Gentleman Jackson and many prominent patrons of the Fancy. Notwithstanding, there were still a significant number of supporters gathered around the ring when James

Paddock was disqualified for hitting Bendigo when down on his knees.

Ward and Peter Crawley stepped into the arena to do battle for the championship.

Crawley was anxious to begin, and hit out with both hands, but the Black Diamond stepped smartly back, parried the blows with beautiful precision and, as Peter pressed forward, he countered on the right eye. As Crawley dropped like a poleaxed bullock, the cheering was deafening and odds of 4 to 1 on Ward were freely offered.

Peter came out for the 2nd round, blood steadily oozing from a cut above his swollen eye. Indifferent to his injuries, he cunningly blocked all Ward's punches with consummate ease and skill. No matter how he persevered, Jem could not get past his stubborn guard. Spotting an opening, Crawley shot out a right to Jem's forehead, catching him just above the eye and almost on the temple. Ward dropped in a heap as if he had been shot and lay senseless on the turf. As the shouts of triumph from Peter's followers rent the air, the faces of Ward's supporters took on a blank look of disbelief; no man had ever before knocked out the redoubtable Black Diamond.

What did it mean? they asked each other. Was the punch a fluke? Fluke or not, the grisly fact remained that Jem was lying prone on the grass and unconscious.

His seconds worked feverishly to revive him and at the call of time, sent him up to fight. Badly shaken, he was still half-dazed when Crawley hit him on the chest and sent him down again.

Years later, Jem confided that he had absolutely no recollection of what happened in the next four rounds. He could only assume that in his state of semi-consciousness he must have fought with some inborn mechanism.

Happily for Ward, Peter Crawley was not in a fit condition to take full advantage over his demoralized opponent, for he had strained himself and was now suffering acute pain from his old rupture.

The fighting continued unabated and the hitting was horrendous. With the blood literally cascading down their faces Jem rushed in, closed, and threw Crawley with one of the most appalling cross-buttock throws ever seen in the ring. It not only shook Peter, it shook the very earth on which he fell.

There came a stupendous roar from the crowd, 'That's done him, 5 to 1 on Ward!'

Crawley came up looking dreadfully distressed. His mouth hung open, his chest heaved as if it would burst and the perspiration ran down his face and body in rivulets. 'He's done for, go and finish him!' roared the maddened crowd. But the exertion of throwing Crawley, who was nearly a stone heavier, had sapped all Jem's remaining strength. He was now so weak he dare not run the risk of closing with his opponent, who was still capable of delivering a knockout blow. The spectators were frantic with excitement; it was anybody's battle and a random blow by either side could easily decide the contest. Drawing slowly together, until they were within striking distance, a terrific rally followed before Peter fell, his features obliterated in blood.

They came out for the next round, their hands at their sides, chests and flanks heaving, the mingled sweat and blood streaming from their bruised and lacerated faces. They stood in the centre of the ring, glaring at each other, scarcely able to stand and lurching from side to side as if each would fall at any moment. There were no more offers on Ward. He was too weak to raise his arms high enough to guard his face and the sinister fist of Crawley played a tattoo on his tortured features. Although Jem did manage to land twice on Crawley's face, drawing more blood, Peter reciprocated with interest, hitting his adversary repeatedly until he was unable to lift his arms any more. Totally exhausted, they both floundered to the ropes and lowered their hands.

A quiver of expectancy rippled through the agitated crowd as the men came out for the 11th round. Ward's mouth yawned grotesquely and his heavy breathing was audible on all sides of the ring. Crawley summoned up all his reserves of strength and caught Ward with a bone-shattering punch on the mouth. Jem dropped like a stone and lay flat on his back, perfectly motionless, where he had fallen. The concerted efforts of his seconds failed to rouse him from his stupor and he was still unconscious when Crawley went over to shake his hand. The battle had lasted just 26 minutes.

Still senseless, Jem was carried from the ring and taken to the Bull Inn at Royston where he was put to bed and attended by a surgeon.

This was Peter Crawley's last fight in the prize ring.

He declined Jem's challenge for another trial, saying, 'I've licked the best man in England, and that's good enough for me.'

Crawley went on to become one of the prize ring's most celebrated trainers, and when Mr Viddler requested his services for Tom Sayers' match with Dan Collins, Peter consented without hesitation.

Collins had acquired an impressive reputation following his unsurpassed battle with Ned Donnelly of Glasgow, one of the most formidable fighters of his day. Tom Spring, the ex-champion of England, had been quick to recognize Collins' outstanding qualities and had kept a vigilant watch on his welfare. He employed him as a waiter in his taproom and encouraged him to participate in the many sparring contests held at his sporting tavern, The Castle, Holborn. The Castle was originally opened as a sporting house by Bob Gregson, the former champion, and had derived the pseudonym of "Bob's Chop House."

In later years, the prize fighting fraternity used the club for their own exclusive meetings, naming their headquarters, "The Daffy Club". When Tom Spring became landlord, it assumed the distinctive titles of "Tom Spring's Parlour", and "The Temple of the Fancy".

Collins' regular sparring sessions at The Castle had kept him in a perpetual state of fitness and he was in prime condition to meet Tom Sayers whenever a suitable venue could be arranged. "Tom Spring's

Waiter", as he had come to be dubbed, was considered a safe bet by the all-knowing ones at The Castle and, on the evening of May 27, 1850 when £2 a side was deposited to bind the agreement, Spring promised to back his protégé for the entire stake of £25.

Three days later, on May 30, Sarah Henderson gave birth to a daughter. Despite the stigma of the baby's illegitimacy, Tom was overjoyed on becoming a father and named the little girl Sarah, after her mother.

On Tuesday June 3 a meeting was held at Peter Crawley's to stake more money and draw up articles for the contest. Agreement was approved for the engagement to take place on October 22, 1850 at an appointed place to be announced later and within a radius of fifty miles from London.

Despite the great secrecy surrounding any forthcoming contest, early in September someone divulged all the arrangements to the authorities. Consequently, the magistrates knew several weeks in advance the exact date and location of the rendezvous.

Tuesday October 22 turned out to be a very warm and pleasant autumn day and the special economy tariff of ten shillings a head for first class passengers and eight shillings for second class encouraged an exceptionally large gathering for the excursion special waiting in the station. Immediately the gates were opened the train filled rapidly with the gentlemen of the Fancy, Guard's officers, sporting Corinthians, a sizeable contingent of Collins' "West End" followers and Tom Sayers' little band of enthusiasts who came principally from the North and East End of London.

Seconds before the train was due to depart the peace was suddenly shattered when hoards of yelling and shouting hooligans swarmed over the station railings. Brushing aside the bewildered ticket collectors, the unwelcome band of rabble settled themselves in the carriages, much to the indignation of the cultured and respectable passengers.

When at last the commotion had moderated, the whistle sounded for departure. The cunning fare-dodgers rubbed their palms gleefully and grinned triumphantly at the credulous individuals, foolish enough to have parted with their money on what might have been achieved with just a little ingenuity. The shrill blast of the whistle sounded once more, followed by a momentary jar and jerk as each coupling chain tightened.

'We're off now!' came the delighted cries of the dishonest rogues, but a look of dismay crossed their faces when the intrepid Station Master, Mr Weatherhead, halted the train. The ticket collectors came on board and a general inspection of tickets began. The railway officials undertaking the census promptly disposed of those passengers without means of identification by unceremoniously ejecting them from the train.

Despite the enforced delay it created great amusement to the paying clientele, who now grinned triumphantly from the carriage windows at the dejected groups of fare-dodgers, arguing amongst themselves on the platform.

As the train steamed slowly from the station, the eloquent and poetic "Milling" orator, Charley Mallet, was seen raising his fist and voice against a party of railway police who had surrounded him. Long after the train had departed, still protesting vehemently, he was forcibly expelled from the station. He returned in about an hour, cash in hand, ready to catch the next train but the remorseless officers, oblivious to his demands, still refused him entry. Angry and indignant at his mal-treatment, he launched into a tirade of abuse against the police and everyone connected with the railway. Finally, dejected and disgusted, he departed from the station threatening to report the whole sordid episode to a sitting magistrate.

An air of intense excitement and anticipation settled over the pas-sengers as the train sped through the Kent countryside, the bright morning sunshine illuminating the first golden tints of autumn in the trees. Shortly before 11 o'clock the special came to a halt a short distance from the picturesque little village of Edenbridge. Stretching themselves after their cramped journey, the travellers alighted and spread out into a field adjoining the railway line. They were soon joined by a representative of the Fancy who conducted them to a small coppice, where Tom Oliver formed the ring in the middle of a delight-ful little clearing, completely secluded from outside view. A cheer was raised as Dan Collins appeared in the arena and threw his cap into the ring. A rather curious legend was attached to this custom; if the hat blew out of the ring, then it was considered an ill-omen for that con-testant.

Collins began his preparations, but there was still no sign of Tom Sayers or his seconds. As the minutes ticked slowly away the crowd began to fidget and show signs of restlessness. Half past eleven came. Twelve came and went and there was still no sign of anyone from the Sayers camp. Anxious faces began to take on worried expressions – where was Tom?

Unknown to anyone at the ringside, he was lying down and resting in a neighbourhood house, where his attendants had ordered a late breakfast for themselves. Laughing and joking they took their time over the meal, showing scant regard for the spectators, or poor Collins, sweating it out in the little enclosure.

It was nearly twelve-thirty before the little party came into view through the trees. Instantly they were subjected to a barrage of abuse and insults from the angry and impatient crowd who, by this time, were almost on the brink of rebellion at the undue delay. The Sayers party, however, were unrepentant, and claimed that the articles of agreement stated unequivocally that they were quite entitled to delay in fighting until the stipulated time of twelve-thirty.

The next frustrating delay occurred over the choice of referee. No one would volunteer to accept the position and it began to appear as if the whole affair would have to be cancelled. To save the day Vincent Dowling, the editor of *Bell's Life*, finally consented to accept the thankless and irksome task. At last, when everything was in readiness Tom's two advocates, Alec Keene and Jack Macdonald, together with Jack Grant and Jemmy Welsh representing Collins, delivered their men to the centre of the ring. As they shook hands across the scratch, there was little to choose between either fighter; Collins just an inch taller and four pounds heavier than Sayers.

Once the crowd were convinced that the contest was about to commence they cheered up considerably, confident they were about to witness a good battle. But they could not know at this point what a tiresome and long-drawn out affair it would become.

As they took up their fighting posture the betting around the ring stood at 6 to 4 on Collins. Both were smiling as they confronted each other and Sayers was first to make a move. After some short, sporadic sparring Tom administered a right hand punch to Collins' ribs at the precise moment he was turning. The blow landed on his back with tremendous force, instantly leaving a welt and raising a crimson lump. As they faced each other again Tom delivered several short, sharp hits to the body, and Collins fell.

Round 2 began with a barrage of vigorous punching, Tom hammering home heavy punches to the cheek as Dan retorted with blows to the head. Sayers lunged out with a swinging right, but Dan stepped nimbly back and caught him with a smashing right uppercut. The terrible force behind the blow lifted Tom clean off his feet and sent him sprawling on the grass. This impressive start evoked tumultuous cheering and applause from the Bermondsey division who thought Dan was almost home and dry. There came a flurry of heavy betting around the ring and the odds went to 2 to 1 on Collins.

After some desultory sparring in round 3, there came a pause in the action. As Collins stepped away Tom leapt forward and let swing with a right. The punch was short, but quick as a flash his left shot out like a piston and landed under Collins's ear. Dan's eyes glazed over and he dropped like a stone. As he lay motionless on the turf his seconds rushed into the ring, the concern on their faces self-evident.

This unexpected success for Sayers aroused loud cheering from his little band of followers, who yelled to the opposition, 'Where's your two to one now?'

Only the expert administrations of Jemmy Welsh enabled Collins to make it to the scratch on time. It had been a close shave, and Dan never seemed to shake off the effects for the remainder of the conflict.

Tom commenced hostilities in round 5 by launching a ferocious attack, but Collins stopped his assault with punches from both hands and, after a short rally, both went down together.

Suddenly a startled cry was heard from the rear of the crowd, 'The Beaks are coming!'

An anxious murmur rippled through the ranks of the assembly and speculation mounted on whether the contest would be allowed to continue, but as neither fighter appeared unduly concerned about the threat, they came to scratch for round 6.

This was proving an excellent round, with sharp work on the eyes, hit, parry and break away, when there came a commotion amidst the crush of spectators. Everything ground to a halt as a magistrate appeared upon the scene. The crowd closed ranks to prevent him reaching the ring but, brandishing an Act of Parliament in his hand, he forced his way through the unrelenting throng until he reached the ropes and demanded a hearing. Instantly he was surrounded by a group of angry protesters and heated arguments broke out between him and some of the more aggressive supporters, who pointed out the futility of any interference by the law. Collins and Sayers saw it was pointless to continue under these conditions and stood leaning on the ropes, watching the commotion taking place outside the ring. Some of the more tolerant supporters promised to leave immediately upon the conclusion of the contest but, as much of the initial anger had moderated, the magistrate became virtually ignored and the fun re-commenced.

Both fell at the end of round 7, and Tom had just hit Collins with a vigorous right at the opening of round 8 when more confusion arose between the seconds and umpires. A halt was called to the proceedings and the men returned to their corners. Evidently believing the fight was at an end, the magistrate retired to await the decision but the crowd, anxious to see a verdict, urged the men to continue.

Sayers opened round 9 with a punch to Collins' cheekbone. Dan responded with a tooth-rattling blow to the jaw and, in a spirited welter of exchanges, Tom's fist connected on the upper and hardest part of Dan's nose. Collins now seized the opportunity to get down from the punishment, amidst the confusion caused by the magistrate's reappearance in the ring. Another hurried conference was called between the seconds and the referee and, after a short discussion, an adjournment was announced. The Justice of the Peace, evidently an extremely brave and determined man to have faced a hostile crowd of this size, refused to be intimidated and addressed the assembly in a loud clear voice saying he had received certain information on the contemplated breach of the peace and, whatever personal perils and dangers he faced, he would perform his duty.

He was instantly assured by the whole gathering that, 'Her Majesty never had a more loyal set of subjects than those present; which could be proved by their peaceful conduct at this moment.'

The magistrate then requested that some responsible person would give his word that the fight should not continue and he would then retire. Failing that and if any physical violence was used against him, then the threat of judicial action was inevitable. The majority were prepared to obey the law and considered his request justified, but amongst the more aggressive and rowdy followers of Collins were many who had invested huge sums of money in bets. Heedless of the consequences, they were convinced Collins held a decided advantage at the time of the interruption and, without a decision they could lose their stakes. Tom Paddock, then the aspiring candidate for the championship, called upon the combatants to disregard the magistrate and the law, and continue with the battle. Tempers flared and heated arguments broke out on all sides.

To avert further turmoil the officials held a council of war to discuss a practicable solution. The articles governing "Magisterial Interference", clearly stipulated that: "The referee or stakeholder should name the place of the next meeting which, if possible, should be on the same day." With the ruling clearly defined, the decision was taken to abandon the proceedings at Edenbridge and reassemble in another location later in the afternoon.

As the groups of dejected sportsmen drifted slowly away, many turned to cast a last farewell glimpse of the little clearing and to express their disappointment on what had promised to be a pleasant day's sport. When they returned to the waiting train, due to the stupidity of some and the obstinacy of others, fresh arguments broke out and more valuable time was lost. Consequently, their departure was further delayed and it was 20 minutes past 3 before they arrived at the new location on the outskirts of Red Hill, in Surrey.

In the clear and cloudless sky, the orange-coloured sun was already low on the western horizon before the men re-entered the ring. The call of "Time" came at 4.15 and both contestants walked to the scratch for the 10th round. Except for a slightly suspicious swelling at the side of his right eye, Sayers appeared scarcely marked. Collins by comparison sported a swollen nose, a puffed left ear and a large red bump on his left cheek-bone. Sayers re-opened hostilities by going on the offensive but Collins stopped him with a thundering blow on the chest, the impact sending him staggering backwards. Dan followed through with a punch to the eye and Tom fell on his face to prevent being thrown. The odds were now 6 to 4 on Collins.

Displaying an air of flamboyancy Sayers weaved and skipped about the ring in round 11, sniping and retreating until Collins slipped down.

Collins hammered Tom with his left in the 12th, drawing a profusion of blood from his lips. As he raised his hand to wipe away the blood he was instantly challenged by Jemmy Welsh for having a piece of string in his hand. The referee immediately stopped the contest and ordered him to discard it from the ring.

Between rounds 13 and 20 the fighting was extremely arduous, both men falling alternately; the scales of victory trembling first one way, and then the other.

During the next four rounds Tom exhibited some of his superb capabilities but, by the 25th, it was fast becoming obvious that a measure of the initial steam had gone from both men.

By the start of the 27th round it became noticeable that Tom had injured his right hand, for whenever he landed a blow he appeared to be in more pain than his adversary. Quick to capitalize on his new-found advantage, Collins made repeated visits to Sayers' eyes, mouth and ribs. With his right hand out of commission, Sayers now faced a major crisis. Compelled to introduce different tactics, he began making a series of double punches with his left; the first short and low in the manner of a feint, then the second a stinging, chopping blow over the eyes, nose or mouth, or as good luck might dictate. At last, tired and exhausted, they clinched and went down together. Cries came from the Sayers contingent that it was now anybody's battle and offers came of, 'Five pounds to four pounds!' But there were no takers.

In rounds 28 to 36 Collins generally made all the fighting. Catching Sayers on the hip in the 37th, he spun him over in a spectacular "Catherine wheel" throw; his feet flying through the air, his shoulders and hips striking the ground, expelling the last breath of wind from his body.

Despite his heavy fall and the injury to his right hand, Tom fought with infinite skill and discernment in rounds 38 to 43.

With darkness fast approaching, both men struggled with dogged determination to end the conflict that evening, but their hitting power was rapidly diminishing and when Collins threw Sayers in the 47th, he appeared the stronger of the pair.

There came an appeal in the 48th when it was alleged that Tom had deliberately dropped on Dan who had already fallen, but the referee declared it was an accident and overruled the objection. Unable to deliver the decisive blow, several exchanges were made with open hands in round 49 and, after a brief struggle, Collins fell beneath Sayers.

Round 50 opened with Tom receiving a particularly cruel punch on the nose which shook him to his very foundations. Caught off-guard and still dizzy from the effects of the blow, as Collins hit him again with his left the referee entered the ring and declared it a drawn battle. Amidst the groans of disappointment from the crowd, he explained that the umpires had reached a unanimous agreement that at sunset, whatever the position of the fight, a draw be pronounced. It had been a hard and determined contest, lasting a total of 1 hour and 52 minutes.

Tom found to his cost that he had relied too heavily on his right hand which, in the latter stages of the conflict had been of little service. But these were early days in his career and he never committed the same mistake twice. He was always keen to remedy his faults and to avoid them in the future.

In later years he often recalled this encounter with Collins, 'Knowing how to use the right hand is nothing; the great secret is knowing when to use it.'

On October 30, eight days after their battle, Tom attended a meeting at Peter Crawley's to double the stakes and appoint another time and place for their second engagement. But Collins was taking a benefit match that evening, and no one attended on his behalf.

Tom vigorously expressed his disgust at the arrant snub saying, 'My friends are tradesmen, and they will not be dragged about while Collins takes a benefit. They are all solidly behind me and intend to go ahead with the contest. If the opposition don't mean to go on then they had better intimate their intentions to the stakeholder. If they do decide to continue then my friends or I can be contacted at Peter Crawley's.'

This outburst had the desired effect. Within a few days Collins responded by stating that he was prepared to increase the stakes to £50 a side and fight in a month.

In the first week of November, transactions were completed for the second engagement, to take place on the same day and in the same ring, as the forthcoming contest between Young Sambo Welsh, and Jem Cross.

They met as planned on the afternoon of December 10, but the battle between Cross and Welsh was prolonged for over two and a half hours and darkness again forced a postponement.

Shortly after Christmas, Tom complained bitterly of the shabby treatment he had received from the friends and backers of Collins who were still undecided over their commitments. He issued an ultimatum, telling them they should either draw the stakes now and call the whole thing off or come to some quick decision to fight again.

'I cannot be expected to remain out of work any longer, just to suit the convenience of Collins.'

This stormy proclamation produced an instant reaction and another round of discussions was held at Peter Crawley's. This time it was agreed that their next engagement would take place on April 29, 1851 at Chapman's Marsh, Long Reach in the Thames Estuary.

With four months remaining before the contest, Tom was determined to finish the affair once and for all and, under the supervision of Peter Crawley, launched into an extensive training programme, committing himself both mentally and physically to the task ahead.

Training for the prize ring was incredibly arduous, calling for total dedication and hard work. The prescribed measures for ultimate proficiency were to rise at 5 a.m. and run at least half a mile before breakfast. Strict attention was devoted to the conditioning of the lungs and hilly districts or shingly beaches provided ideal training grounds. On returning to his quarters he would shower and, at 7 a.m., partake of a breakfast consisting of nutritious foods such as rare steak or mutton chops, a helping of stale bread and a beverage of old ale. After breakfast there would be a walk at a moderate pace of between five and six miles, returning about noon. He would then retire to bed for half an hour and on rising, embark on a four mile walk, returning at 4 p.m. for a dinner of beef or mutton with beer and bread. Occasionally, to break the monotony of his spartan existence, he would be allowed the luxury of yolks of eggs for breakfast, and a main meal of roast fowl. The whites of eggs and foods such as milk, butter, cheese and soups containing vegetables, especially turnips and carrots, were strictly prohibited. For the remainder of the day he would be encouraged to participate in the simple sports of cricket, bowls and quoits, with other light games to stimulate mental agility. After three weeks of this repetitive and boring routine, there would be an intensive period of running at least four miles, dressed in flannel clothing to induce a state of heavy sweating and, at the end of the run, he would be supplied with a pint of hot liquor containing an ounce of sugar candy, an ounce of caraway seed, half an ounce of coriander seed and an ounce of liquorice mixed in two bottles of cider. This concoction was boiled until only half of the original quantity remained. While it was still piping hot, he would consume the liquid and immediately retire to bed for half and hour, under a covering of thick blankets. After this prescribed time he would undergo a period of strenuous massage until the skin was rubbed completely dry.

Instant co-ordination of mind and body was essential and a natural partnership of brain and fist had to be practiced incessantly, combined with the ability to contract muscle power at the point of impact. Flexing the muscles brought out exterior development, but it was the muscles beneath the surface which gave each powerful thrust the full force in the concentrated attack upon the objective. Many champions possessed the essential ability to relax when they were not punching, blocking or covering, thereby giving their bodies a short respite.

Hand injuries were a constant hazard to any pugilist. Once any serious damage had been sustained, it was often likely to recur and to obviate any injury to hand or person, gloves were always worn when training or sparring. Although Tom Sayers' fists were quite small in comparison to the enormous power they conveyed, his knuckles were large and knife-edged, capable of inflicting a slashing cut when used in a chopping action. The immense power behind his right hand punch, or "Auctioneer" as it later became known, often induced a sense of terror in his opponents. A natural born fighter, he was one of that rare breed of men who are only seen occasionally throughout history. He knew instinctively how to ride a blow to lessen its impact and his sense of balance and nimble footwork were a source of admiration to everyone who saw him fight. One of his greatest specialities was his "Flit like a butterfly – sting like a bee" characterized in this century by Mohammed Ali. But his methods of fighting were not always appreciated by the old school of pugilism, who hated what they termed his "shifty" tactics. They preferred a contest where the two contestants stood toe to toe, swapping blows until one could no longer stand.

Their training completed, Sayers and Collins met again at Peter Crawley's on Monday April 28, 1851. Nobody wanted a repetition of the Edenbridge fiasco and only now was it disclosed that the contest would be fought the following day.

It was pouring with rain as the Thames steamer *Waterman No. 8* slipped its cable from Waterloo jetty on the morning of Tuesday April 29. After a short delay at Blackwall, and another at North Woolwich to pick up extra passengers, they reached their destination on Chapman's Marsh at around two o'clock in the afternoon. During the journey the betting had remained steady at 5 to 4 on Sayers, but by half past two, when the ring had been formed and both contestants stood ready, it had settled down to evens. As they entered the ring and began their preparations, the sky rapidly darkened and a sweeping shower of hail sent everyone scurrying for shelter on the bleak and deserted marshes.

At three o'clock, after the heavy rain had ceased and the majority of the spectators were soaked to the skin, the men re-entered the ring, ready to resume their preparations. Ironically, there is no detailed report extant on the fight. Only *Bell's Life* for May 4 had this to say about the conflict –

"Another proof that a great fight and a small stake often go together, was given on Tuesday last when Tom Sayers and Dan Collins met to settle the adjourned battle. It will be remembered that after two interruptions – one by magisterial authority at Edenbridge, and the other at Red Hill on the same day, their merits were considered so evenly balanced, and as each man was so anxious to avoid a draw, that fresh articles were entered into to contend for the money drawn. Sayers is a powerful, hardy-looking young fellow, and bids fair to prove a 'clipper'. We may remark that a more manly mill has not of late been seen. On this occasion, Collins was sadly over-matched in strength and stamina, while in skill, Sayers was his equal. He, however did his best and the best can do no more; while, for a ten stone man, Sayers is about as formidable and promising a one as we have seen for many a day. He, (Sayers) displayed great confidence, hardihood and courage, together with unimpaired strength and wind throughout the contest. He will prove a tough customer for whoever next has dealings with him in the fistic line."

Jack Grant was rarely seen without his battered old silk hat, and a half-chewed cigar clamped firmly in his mouth.

# 6

## THE BOROUGH MARKET PET

Nearly a year had elapsed since Tom's battle with Dan Collins and during those months his weight had increased to a little over 10 stone, making him too heavy for the lightweights and too light for the middleweights. This situation had placed him in the invidious position of trying to find an opponent in his own unique category. Despite repeated challenges in *Bell's Life* no one had responded to his offers. All his winnings and the stake money from his fight with Collins had been spent and, with a wife and young baby to support, money was in short supply. On June 11 he took a benefit match at Jem Burns' The Queen's Head in Windmill Street, Haymarket. Although the event was well supported the proceeds were not excessive.

In the autumn his backers arranged a match with Mike Madden. The first deposit was made at The Laurel Tree on November 19, but at the second meeting to draw up the articles, for some unaccountable reason Madden backed out and the match fell through. To further complicate his already overburdened budget, at about the same time as these discussions were taking place, Sarah Henderson became pregnant again.

At the beginning of 1852 Tom's financial problems came to the attention of his old employer, John Garrett, the proprietor of the Copenhagen Running Grounds at King's Cross. He sent an invitation to Tom, asking him to meet him at Copenhagen House to discuss a proposition which could have a favourable outcome to both parties. Tom listened intently when John Garratt explained that he was selling his entire estate, including the famous tea gardens, to the City of London Corporation and was on the brink of becoming an extremely wealthy man. He promised Tom full financial backing, if he would be prepared to consider him his patron. Tom grasped his hand warmly and thanked him, saying he would be delighted to accept his kind and generous offer. Ecstatic over his unexpected piece of good fortune, the next morning he went to the offices of *Bell's Life* and advertised a challenge.

In a matter of days he received an acceptance from Jack Grant, also known as 'The Pet of the Borough'. The moment the news hit the headlines that Tom Sayers was to meet the all-accomplished Jack Grant, enormous interest was stimulated amongst sportsmen from all sections of society. With the superlative skill and courage of both men, everyone anticipated a battle of attrition reminiscent of olden times. So impressive was Grant's reputation that odds of 7 to 4 against Sayers could be obtained anywhere in Southwark and the Borough.

Measuring a little under 5 feet 8 inches in height, Jack Grant was a popular figure, rarely to be seen without his old and battered white top hat tilted slightly on his head and a half-smoked cigar clenched firmly in his teeth. Currently employed as a porter at the Borough Market, the local residents believed his victory a moral certainty; he had never been beaten, and his recent success against the accomplished Alec Keene had convinced the experts that he was the best man of his weight in Britain.

At the pinnacle of his career, he was riding on a wave of success. He had defeated the inimitable James of Nottingham and, in a match of extreme severity, Haggarty from the East End of London. His notorious battle with Mike Madden in 1848 was the second longest on record, lasting five and three quarter hours. It would have been longer but after fighting 140 rounds, darkness forced a premature ending to hostilities. Although Grant did not have the best of the encounter he lost none of his prestige, for Madden was a tough nut to crack. His next contest was against the formidable Alec Keene. Long odds were offered on Grant but, after a tremendous battle lasting nearly an hour, he was proclaimed the winner.

After this brilliant performance, he was placed high in the pugilistic hemisphere, and ultimately became the chosen one of the Southwark populace. However, since his fight with Alec Keene, he had taken an extended rest from the prize ring and it was while his backers were busily searching for another competitor that he accepted the challenge from Tom Sayers.

On Monday March 24, 1852 the articles were drawn up with stakes of £100 a side. The first deposit was left in the hands of the stake-holder, Jemmy Welsh, and an agreement made for the remainder of the instalments to be paid on a weekly basis; the final settlement to be paid on June 21 at Dan Dismore's tavern, the King's Arms in Drury Lane. This would then leave the stakeholder eight days in which to select a suitable battleground.

Dan Mendoza, the Jewish boxer, devoted three years to perfecting his left hook.

Grant went into training at Northolt, under the supervision of Thomas (The Salopian) and a few days after celebrating his twenty-sixth birthday, Tom began his preparations at Sutton, where he received the expert guidance of Jackson (the American Deer) and the pre-eminent Ned Adams.

At around 8 o'clock on the morning of June 29, a large assembly of sportsmen began gathering at Shoreditch Station – now the British Railway goods depot Eastern Region – where, to the profound relief of the majority, there was a noticeable absence of the disreputable sup-porters and, more especially, the denizens of the Borough Market. Everyone was in a particularly buoyant mood and a few chuckles of amusement were raised when the stakeholder's privy counsellor, the sonorous Bishop, the gunmaker of Bond Street, related that as he was not in the habit of rising early, it had required the united efforts of his head clerk and two dogs to drag him from his bed and get him to the station on time.

Throughout the weeks leading up to the contest, the destination had remained a closely guarded secret. Only Jemmy Welsh and those present for the signing of the articles knew the full details. So, at 8.30 that morning, when the engine driver blew a blast on the whistle for departure, he was handed a large envelope, sealed with sealing wax and implicit instructions that the package was not to be opened until he reached Bishop's Stortford.

Immediately the train pulled into Bishop's Stortford station the seals were broken and the contents disclosed to the excited passengers. The train, it stated, was to proceed to a predetermined area on the outskirts of Mildenhall in Suffolk, where it would be met by an official representative of the Fancy. While the train was still at Bishop's Stortford, a decoy telegram was to be dispatched to the authorities, informing them that the fight would be staged somewhere in the region of Great Chesterford.

The police were waiting in force when the train steamed into Great Chesterford's tiny station, but when they learned of the deception and that the venue was to be outside their province, they allowed everyone to proceed on their journey, satisfied that the sanctity of Cambridge-shire was safe from defilement.

When the train reached its appointed destination at around 11.30, a trusted emissary was waiting to greet the passengers and conduct them to a secluded field, far from any road or public place.

In the lonely and deserted enclave, Tom Oliver and his assistant Tom Collins began the task of forming the two rings. The appointed ring-keepers, distinctive in their white head-bands with POLICE CONSTABLE OF THE PRIZE RING emblazoned in bold, black letters, busied themselves with their duties and ushering from the arena all those inquisitive spectators who had come to inspect the condition of the turf. Once all were safely assembled beyond the ropes of the outer ring, Dan Dismore made his appearance and, for a while, did brisk business selling the "reserved circle" tickets for any wealthy members of the party willing to pay for the privilege of a ringside seat.

Tom Oliver had thoughtfully provided a plentiful supply of straw hassocks which had been placed about ten feet from the ring. The non-paying fraternity were arranged in order a few feet from the perimeter ropes, where the ring-keepers took up their positions, separating the two sections of spectators. Thankfully, due to the almost total absence of the more questionable supporters, there was none of the usual ribald vulgarity, or "Jollying" as it was commonly known.

When all the extraneous matters had been completed and the appointment of the referee and umpires satisfactorily concluded, the two contestants proceeded to prepare themselves for the engagement. Their colours were tied to the stakes and, when time was called at ten minutes to one, the two prize fighters were conducted to the scratch to shake hands. Grant was waited upon by Harry Orme and Jemmy Welsh, with Sayers attended by Ned Adams and Bob Fuller (the Pedestrian).

The supreme condition of Sayers was a source of admiration to everyone. His good-humoured smile of confidence and the glow in his cheeks reinforced his air of invincibility. There was not an ounce of superfluous flesh upon his whole body and the sinews and tendons rippling under his tan-coloured skin emphasized the impression he was all wire and muscle. Firm and graceful in his movements, he was equally as good as he looked.

The Borough champion, muscular and brawny, looked the more powerful, but there were visible signs of a preponderance of fat around his chest and ribs; a clear indication of insufficient discipline and exercise. But Grant saw the result as a foregone conclusion.

He had openly expressed his contempt for Sayers and had told his admirers of the Borough, 'If I can't lick the Sussex yokel, then I ought to have my backside kicked.'

As they squared up to each other, Grant's stance indicated the old tactician; arms held well up and not too far from his body, head back and eyes fixed firmly on his opponent. He made it manifestly clear right from the start that he was determined to force the pace and led off with a left to Tom's forehead. Jumping neatly away from the return punch, he tried to repeat the same stratagem, but Sayers stopped him in the coolest manner and landed a thumping right to the ribs instead. Heavy counterpunching followed until Tom drew "First blood" from a cut over Grant's nose. In the next succession of counter hits Sayers received a blow to the side of his head and slipped down. The first round had clearly proved that the Borough man was not going to have the walkover he had anticipated.

Grant tried to take the initiative several times in the 2nd round but Tom thwarted his every effort. Eventually, he caught Sayers with a heavy blow under the left ear but Tom countered effectively and, in the close which followed, both went down with Sayers underneath.

Again Grant went on the offensive but Tom jumped smartly away from each attack, smiling broadly at his opponent. The Borough champion closed for the fall, but Tom refused to struggle and contented himself by peppering Grant's nose and left ear until they both rolled over on the turf.

After a deal of mutual blocking in the 4th, Tom delivered a thumping right to the Borough man's ribs; the sound echoing around the arena like a clap of hollow thunder. Counter hits followed, with Sayers on the nose and Grant on the ribs. Locking themselves into a wrestling close for the fall they were ordered to break away by the referee who declared their struggle ineffective. The round ended in the next bout of exchanges, when Tom slipped down after receiving a particularly heavy punch on his right eye.

Although they both looked flushed on coming up for the 5th, they soon went to work with a rapid exchange of counter hits; Sayers catching it heavily on the left cheek and Grant on the nose and jaw. A close and struggle for the fall ended in Grant being thrown, but not heavily.

In the 6th Grant caught Tom with a tremendous punch on the left ear. The Borough champion closed in to finish it, but Tom declined to struggle and jabbed his adversary repeatedly until he allowed him to slip down.

On coming to scratch for the 9th both men stood in the centre of the ring, their flanks heaving from their strenuous exertions in the last round. Tom's left ear was already showing the effects of Grant's repeated visitations but, nothing daunted, he delivered two stinging smacks to Grant's cheek and left ear. This brought them into a struggle and Tom eased himself to the ground.

At the close of the 15th forty minutes had elapsed, and those who had backed Grant to win in an hour began to look anxious.

The 16th and 17th were capital rounds, each man taking punishment on the nose, cheek and the side of the head. Grant dashed in and closed for the fall in the 18th, but again Tom declined to struggle and concentrated his punches to the left ear. Grant slipped down and lay on his back, blowing like a stranded whale until time was called.

In the 20th poor Jack, whose left ear had been lanced, came up with the blood pouring down his neck. Sayers caught him again on his swollen and mutilated ear, but in the exchanges which followed Tom went down under a flurry of blows.

By the 28th round Tom's left eye was beginning to show signs of closing, and they now went to work in earnest. The hitting on both sides was horrendous; Grant receiving more damage to his left ear and nose. He looked predominantly the worse for wear; his lack of condition obviously having sapped much of his strength and speed.

The Borough champion came up for the 33rd bleeding profusely from his mouth and left ear. He tried to lead off, but Sayers blocked him rather cleverly and dispensed two tremendous punches on his nose and throat. In the exchanges which led to the close, Tom received a slashing blow on the nose which removed a sliver of skin.

As they approached the scratch for the 35th round, one and a half hours had elapsed and both appeared to be suffering from fatigue. Grant stopped several well-intentioned deliveries and returned on Tom's left eye and nose, drawing more blood from both. Good exchanges led them into a grappling close and both went down.

For the next few rounds, both sparred for wind and little mischief was done. Then, in the 43rd, Grant caught Sayers with a heavy punch to the ribs and another on the nose. Tom retaliated on the throat and some massive exchanges took place on both sides, each man standing and hitting away without any attempt at stopping or gaining an advantage. Both appeared to think this was the turning point in the battle and each wished to make a decided impression upon his gallant adversary. At length, Tom slipped down exhausted, for this was unquestionably the severest round in the conflict.

On coming up for the 44th both were still suffering signs of exhaustion from their exertions in the previous round. During the 30-second interval Grant's seconds had again found it necessary to lance his ear, whilst Tom's left eye was closing under his severely swollen cheek. Both were unwilling to begin and, after some slight blows had been exchanged, Sayers slipped down.

Sayers became more active in the 46th and when, after a few exchanges they rolled over on the grass, Grant excited the admiration of the crowd by the careful manner in which he had avoided falling on his opponent with his feet or knees.

Tom attempted to make the running in the 52nd, but Grant went in to mill with both hands. He planted one punch on the nose, another to the left side of the head and a third to the nose which opened the floodgates to a torrent of blood. This round was decidedly in favour of the Borough champion and there were tremendous cheers from his supporters.

Thinking the game was now his own, Grant again rushed in but now Sayers stayed with him and, in the exchanges, dealt him a massive blow on his disfigured left ear.

Grant appeared determined to finish the matter off in the 61st round. He rushed in with a straight left and a right to Sayers' cheek and nose. Tom countered with both hands to the nose and left eye and, in the short struggle, both fell to the ground with Sayers sprawled across Grant's chest.

Evidently exhausted from their past efforts, both were slow to time for the 63rd. Although Grant was first up, he presented a truly gruesome spectacle; his face terribly swollen and flushed, his nose anything but Roman in shape and his mangled left ear steadily oozing a trickle of blood. He dashed at Sayers whose battered face still bore the ghost of a smile – although nearly on the wrong side of his mouth – but Tom stopped him cleverly and skipped away. Grant followed him up and nailed him on the right side of the head, but in the return he received another colossal blow on the left ear. At the close Grant threw Sayers and fell heavily across his body.

The Borough champion came up looking very groggy for the 64th and last round. Shaken by the repeated falls in the last few rounds, he now appeared to be suffering from internal cramp. Nevertheless he led off with a determined effort and landed on Sayers' cheek-bone. Tom retaliated on the left ear and a few sharp exchanges led into another struggle for the fall. Ultimately they came heavily to the ground. Grant hitting the earth first and Tom falling across his stomach.

Both men were immediately picked up and carried to their corners but, when time was called for the 65th round, Jemmy Welsh, on behalf of Grant, threw up the sponge in token of defeat. Grant's anxious supporters rushed over to his corner to ascertain the cause of the unexpected termination of the battle. They were informed that he was suffering intense pain from cramp and, moreover, had injured some part of his intestines and it was feared he had ruptured himself. Furthermore, he was in such excruciating pain he could no longer stand upright.

As the shouts of his excited friends reverberated around the arena, Tom was proclaimed the victor. He went over to his fallen adversary to shake him warmly by the hand and to comfort him in his distress.

Poor Jack Grant was helped from the ring and conveyed on a railway truck to a public house in the neighbourhood where, although he received every attention, he continued to be in grievous pain for some considerable time. When questioned later he admitted that shortly before the conflict, when he was in Manchester, he had suffered an accident which had left him with a weakness of the stomach muscles. Consequently, as he was not one hundred per cent fit, he was more susceptible to injury.

*Bell's Life*, who had not rated Tom's chances highly, were full of praise, and described the fight as, "A prop for the falling fortunes of the ring. – In this battle of attrition, Sayers has firmly established a reputation for courage and endurance. The manner in which he stopped the determined attacks of his antagonist, and the skilful judgement he exhibited in extracting himself from difficult situations proves that, although still a comparative novice to the ring, he is perfectly acquainted with the theory of boxing. He has proved beyond a shadow of a doubt that he is a deceptively hard hitter, having reached his pugnacious opponent so frequently, Grant's cast-iron face carries bumps and contusions, seldom seen in any of his former engagements. Grant on the other hand was not disgraced. He disputed every inch of the ground, and proved that his qualifications as a fighter were equal to those of Sayers. His stopping and wrestling were universally admired, and the care he exercised to avoid falling on his foe, gained him repeated praises from the surrounding throng."

There was great mourning and lamentations among the populace of the Borough Market at the downfall of their "Pet". Many simply refused to believe that Sayers had beaten him fairly, and had won by some devious means when he had fallen with all his weight across Grant's stomach. Among these who still earnestly believed Grant was the better man was his second and bottle-holder, Harry Orme. Normally a man of a quiet and unassuming disposition, he was quite outspoken and vociferous in his remarks, saying Sayers had taken an unfair advantage over Grant. Tom was furious at his controversial and untrue allegations and promptly challenged him to a fight, but Harry treated it all with a silent contempt. He had recently beaten Aaron Jones for the second time and, having also beaten Nat Langham the current middleweight champion, he would not be drawn into fighting for anything less than the championship.

Harry Orme never forgave Tom for his impudence in challenging him and, in his own quiet way vowed, 'One day, I will be even with Master Tom for his presumption.'

Ben Caunt.

# 7

## CLIMB TO FAME

On the evening of Wednesday July 7, 1852 Tom received his battle-money at a celebration party held at Jemmy Massey's King's Arms in Compton Street, Soho. It was a glittering and splendid occasion with innumerable toasts and showers of congratulations on his magnificent victory over Jack Grant. But amidst all the festivities Tom felt a measure of sympathy for poor Jack who, having invested all his savings on the fight, was now virtually destitute. Throwing five gold sovereigns into his hat he undertook a collection for his less fortunate opponent and, as an added favour, agreed to take a joint benefit with him at John Garratt's Copenhagen House.

Now that he was financially secure again, Tom's friends tried to persuade him to invest his capital into opening a public house; a sure and certain speculation for an up-and-coming young pugilist. They used every argument and subtlety to convince him that as the owner of his own sporting tavern, he would have a permanent base from which to conduct all his business transactions and, what was more important, should his prospects in the ring fail then he could still maintain a tolerable living as a publican. He listened patiently to all their advice and good intentions, but he was painfully aware that his fundamental lack of education prevented him from running any commercial enterprise successfully.

Eventually, becoming tired of their constant pressures, he decided to take a short break far away from everyone who wanted to control his interests and where he could have time to review his own domestic and pugilistic future. He left The Laurel Tree and all his usual haunts in Camden Town and began spending most of his leisure hours over at Ben Caunt's, The Coach and Horses in St Martin's Lane, situated close to the notorious "Rookery of St. Giles" – one of Victorian London's most infamous and vice-ridden districts. It was here that Charles

Dickens based his iniquitous Fagin and his gang of young pickpockets, and where the real felons of London came home to roost at night. Amidst the labyrinth of narrow, dingy alleyways, squalid back streets and courts were some of the most intricate and dangerous places, inhabited by the light-fingered gentry of pickpockets, cardsharps, forgers and fences, con men, thieves, embezzlers, bullies, pimps, prostitutes, vagrants and beggars. Innumerable houses were interconnected by roof, yard and cellar in such a manner that the apprehension of an inmate or refugee was almost a task of impossibility to a stranger. In the maze of passages lay an elaborate system of tunnels, low walls and holes leading into adjoining cellars, affording a ready means of escape to any fugitive from the law. Other houses were connected in a similar fashion, with communication from one back window to another by a succession of large spikes or nails, one row to hold by, and another for foot-rests. However, despite the density of the criminal element, there were also a high proportion of honest and respectable storekeepers, street vendors, costermongers and tradesmen of every description. But for the predominantly poorer and cosmopolitan inhabitants, large numbers lived in deplorable conditions among the slums, brothels and lodging-houses, where it was common for twelve to thirty people to share a room, each of whom paid about threepence a night for a bed, or a filthy mattress on the bare floor. For the majority of these, escape from their wretched poverty lay in the taverns and gin palaces, and drunken oblivion. In the taprooms of the alehouses, Black Charlie the fiddler might be seen with scores of revellers enjoying the dance, smoking over potations of gin and water, or singing the favourite songs of the period, sentimental, comic or bawdy ballads such as *The Dandy Husband, Gentle Annie, The Old Woman's Sayings, John Bull and the Taxes, The Dark Eyed Sailor*, and *The Female Cabin-boy*. Often the cheek waxed pale as a policeman opened the door and glanced around the room, but when he departed the merriment would be resumed with renewed vigour. When the pubs closed their doors at around midnight the inhabitants drifted back to their lodgings, where people of all ages and sexes, men and women, boys and girls, slept alongside each other indiscriminately. Little wonder that the conversations, and the scenes which were transacted, contaminated the morals of the young at a very early age.

Ben Caunt was delighted with Tom's visits to his famous hostelry and over the weeks they became the best of friends. Ben introduced him into his intimate circle of companions and frequently invited him into his bar parlour for one of his celebrated harmonic evenings.

But Tom hated and despised the disreputable inhabitants of the Rookery and the dubious characters who sought his company. To rid himself of their machinations, his visits to The Coach and Horses became much less frequent and they finally came to an end when Sarah Henderson gave birth to their second child, a son, on August 29. Two-year-old Sarah was thrilled at the prospect of having a baby brother to play with, whilst Tom idolized the boy, naming him Thomas.

During his weeks spent with Ben Caunt, Tom devoted a great deal of deliberation to his future and, when he returned to his loyal and trusted friends at The Laurel Tree, he informed them of his decision.

'Everything I have accomplished in the past is now behind me,' he said. 'Fighting is my ambition, and my future lies in the prize ring.'

Dedicated now in his inexorable climb to fame, he issued a formal challenge to fight anyone in Great Britain at 10 stone 8 pounds for £50 to £100 a side. His offer was readily accepted by Mr Lee, the landlord of the York Arms, acting on behalf of the very capable Jack Martin who, at the time, was in the provinces teaching the art of boxing and self-defence. Although Martin had never fought in the metropolitan ring, his proficiency as a boxer was widely known in London.

On the evening both sides met to sign the articles, the toss of a coin for choice of venue was won by Ben Caunt, acting on behalf of Tom Sayers. To the astonishment of everyone present, Caunt declared that he intended to stage the engagement on Tuesday January 25, 1853 in the neighbourhood of Hitchen in Hertfordshire, and named Stevenage Station as the destination.

Everyone doubted the wisdom of his judgement, for it was common knowledge that the police forces of Hertfordshire were much too strict and far too numerous to allow any chances of bringing the affair to a satisfactory conclusion within their county. Caunt was questioned on the advisability of his decision, but he assured everyone that his friends in the area were confident there was no cause for alarm. He concluded that if the Hertfordshire constabulary were on the alert, then the counties of Bedfordshire, Buckinghamshire and Cambridgeshire were all within a short distance, and the match could take place in any one or the other. Despite repeated protests and objections, no one could influence his stubborn conviction and everyone had to remain content with his arrangements.

The day after the articles were signed, both men went into intensive training; Sayers at the Barley Mow, Stokenchurch under the expert eye of his coach, James Key of Leamington, and Martin at The Angel, Sutton.

At the weigh-in at The Coach and Horses, on Monday January 24, 1853 both men were found to be within the maximum weight of 10 stone 7 pounds, with Martin a few ounces heavier than Sayers. Both were extremely fit and well but, from the moment everyone saw the superb condition of Sayers, odds of 5 to 4 were freely offered by his friends and backers. To forestall any leakage of information concerning the rendezvous, only now was it disclosed that the train would leave King's Cross Station for Stevenage, at 7 o'clock the following morning.

When Tom and his entourage arrived at the terminus they found the low turnout of supporters sadly disappointing. Only a few people were gathered on the platform and neither Martin nor his party were to be seen. At seven o'clock, when the train pulled out of the station, a wave of foreboding swept the almost empty carriages, and speculation mounted on what had gone wrong. Unknown to the passengers, Martin had discovered that there was no need to leave at such an early hour and had delayed his departure until the next scheduled train at 9 o'clock. In many cases the more enlightened travellers did not leave until 10 o'clock, when an express locomotive took them directly to Hitchen. By picking up another connection they arrived at Stevenage within minutes of the two prize fighters and their followers.

Despite the short notification, once again there had been a breach of security and they discovered to their dismay that the police were already at Stevenage Station awaiting their arrival. Angry with Caunt and his arrangements, the supporters of both sides loudly expressed their condemnation at his obdurate resolution in coming to Stevenage, and that a change of venue was now necessary. After a short deliberation among the organizers to plan their next objective, everyone set off, intending to make their way to Welwyn. But they were closely followed by the constabulary, who intimated that they would not allow a breach of the peace in their county and they had full authority to stay on their heels all the way back to London if necessary.

Another consultation was held, followed by much recrimination between Caunt and Martin's backers, who broadly hinted that Caunt knew there was little chance of the fight taking place long before he left London. An appeal was made to the stakeholder who decided in favour of Martin and his friends, specifying that they had been subjected to a lot of unnecessary expense by the folly of Caunt in naming a location where there was no possibility of a fight taking place. He awarded Martin and Mr Lee, his principle backer, their choice of any day that week and gave them preference in naming a new venue.

Martin declared he was anxious to fight as soon as possible, but as there appeared to be no chance of a satisfactory conclusion that day, then he was prepared to fight the following day, somewhere in the Thames estuary. Mr Lee angrily retorted that he had already offered Caunt £5 to stage the contest down the river and could not understand his insistence on coming to such a place as Stevenage, which was only a large village. He reiterated that anyone with an ounce of common sense knew there would be a massive police presence and it appeared to him that Sayers did not intend to fight.

Tom was emphatic in his assertions that he was no less disappointed than Martin and just as anxious to get the fight under way. He was perfectly willing to go down the river, or anywhere for that matter; naming the place had not been his decision. Finding both men sought an amicable settlement, the stakeholder declared the fight postponed and ordered the men to be in the ring at Long Reach between noon and two o'clock the following day.

All bets were drawn, but the great majority were instantly renewed and a number of 5 to 4s were eagerly snapped up by Martin's followers, who were of the opinion that he looked brighter about the eye and in better condition than Sayers. This was probably true, for Tom had been compelled to rise at 5 a.m., dress, shower and have his breakfast in time to catch the 7 o'clock train. Since then he had found little time for any rest, whilst Martin had enjoyed another two hours in bed.

Shortly after 5 o'clock, when the train pulled into King's Cross Station, Mr Lee hastened down to the river to hire a steamer for the following day. Handbills, advertising the excursion, were hurriedly printed and distributed during the evening to all the principle sporting taverns and public houses in London.

Despite the short notice and the thick pea-soup fog enveloping London the next morning, the Thames steamer *Waterman No. 1* was well laden with passengers when it left North Woolwich Jetty at midday. Both men and their backers were in a jocular mood and all the troubles and differences of the previous day appeared to be forgotten.

They reached their destination shortly before 2 o'clock and, by 2.30, when Tom Oliver and his son Fred had formed the inner and outer rings, Ned Adams, the appointed inspector of the ring constables, called the muster roll:

'Con Parker, Young Sambo Welsh, George Brown, Young Reed, Charley Mallet, (who this time appears to have bought his ticket), Fred Mason, Bob Castles, Spider, M'Nulty, Crockett, Harry Orme, and Alec Reed.'

Finding several absentees, he called upon the services of Mike Madden, Callaghan of Derby and the Big Bold Bendigo to fill the vacancies. Their splendid efforts in maintaining order enabled everyone to obtain an uninterrupted view of the proceedings from beginning to end.

Alec Keene and a friend deputizing as bottle-holder accompanied

Sayers into the ring, while Martin was escorted by Tom Paddock and Jerry Noon. The election of the referee and umpires was quickly fulfilled and the men prepared for the fray with all due speed. The colours were tied to the stakes and time was called at 3 o'clock.

The men approached the scratch amidst an air of breathless expectation. Sayers, taller than his adversary, looked in much better condition. His eyes had resumed their normal brightness and his finely textured skin gave the impression of extreme hardness. Martin appeared pale in comparison to Sayers' bronzed complexion but the smile on his face clearly portrayed that the word "fear" was not in his vocabulary.

As they came together for round 1, Tom opened the conflict with his left catching Martin on the nose. Martin shook his head to clear his senses, and immediately rushed in to close quarters. Some extremely heavy punches were exchanged, each simultaneously receiving a blow on the left eye and each drawing blood in some profusion from cuts above the brow. A few random shots were exchanged and both went down together. Each side now claimed "First blood", but the referee shook his head and declared it a drawn event.

As "Time!" was called for round 2 both men came to the scratch bleeding from the left eye. At this point Sayers appeared to have suffered the worst of the damage. Nothing daunted and still smiling, he led off with his left, catching Martin a stinging slap on the right cheek. The round ended with both men standing toe to toe, Martin hammering away with both hands and Sayers sniping with accurate precision until both fell together.

In the third round Martin was sent sprawling on his back from a stunning blow to the nose. Tom's supporters jumped up and down in a frenzy of excitement as "First knock-down blow to Sayers" was recorded.

On coming up for the 4th, blood was still pouring from Martin's nose. As they swapped punches, he re-opened the cut over Tom's eye and, in a wrestling struggle near the ropes, both went down.

Martin's right eye was completely closed when he came out for round ten. Sayers led off and landed again on the damaged right eye. Martin suffered the blow with his usual good humour and tried hard to raise a smile on one side of his battered face. Dashing in he succeeded in opening a cut over Tom's hitherto unscathed right eye. At length, after some sharp infighting mainly in favour of Sayers, Martin slipped down on one knee. Tom might have struck him while in this position, but he gave a loud chuckle of laughter and walked away amidst cries of "Bravo!" from both sides.

Poor Jack Martin came up for round 12, bleeding at all points yet still his cheerful and good humoured self. The heavy counterpunching which ensued left both men bleeding profusely and, as they closed into a grappling hold, Martin spun Tom head over heels with a spectacular "cartwheel" throw.

As they came out for the 13th, blood was seen pouring from a deep gash on Tom's left hand, evidently caused by hitting Martin's teeth. After some heavy pounding, principally in favour of Sayers, both went down together, each smiling benignly at his opponent.

Martin's face presented a grisly spectacle as he came to scratch for the 15th. His nose and cheek were frightfully swollen, a deep cut traversed his forehead and his lips were puffed out to twice their normal size. Again in this round he suffered tremendous punishment but, despite everything Tom threw at him, at the close he was equally as strong on his legs as Sayers.

Round 16 was rated as one of the finest exhibitions of boxing seen for many years. Martin continued to press home his attacks, drawing more blood from his adversary's left eye. At the close, Martin had the misfortune to again slip down on one knee and once more Tom walked away smiling, refusing to take advantage of the situation.

Jack Martin displayed manifest signs of weakening in the 19th round and, by the 22nd any odds could be had on Sayers, who still looked remarkably fresh. Martin made several determined attempts to turn the tables but he was stopped on each occasion. At length Tom steadied himself and waited for Martin's next rush. Shooting out his left he connected with terrific force on the right side of the jaw. Martin's knees crumpled beneath him and he collapsed unconscious, face down on the grass.

It was thought to be all over as he was carried to his corner but, to everyone's surprise, when "Time" was called, he staggered up for the 23rd and last round. As he was reeling around the ring, still obviously dazed from the last shattering blow, Tom walked calmly up to him and inflicted another deep gash on the right cheek. As he visibly winced from the searing pain, Sayers followed through with another devastating punch on the nose. Poor Martin went down in a crumpled heap and lay insensible on the ground. Tom Paddock and Jerry Noon entered the ring and, lifting him gently, carried him to his corner where they laid him on the grass. Every effort was made to revive him but it took a full five minutes before he fully recovered consciousness. A short time later, supported by his seconds, he was helped back to the steamer and made comfortable in one of the cabins.

The crowd were highly delighted with the spectacle they had just witnessed and both men received the highest praise for their performances, particularly the occasions when Sayers refrained from hitting Martin when he was down on one knee. The only sour note to mar what had been an excellent battle was the manner in which Martin had been handled by his second, Jerry Noon. Noon's usual clowning activities, designed primarily to amuse the spectators had not been appreciated and he was severely reprimanded by the leading patrons of the Fancy. They claimed he was incompetent, and incapable of holding the responsible position demanded of a qualified second. To his detriment, he had used the sponge with unwarranted force and roughness and on one occasion had actually wiped the blood from Martin while he was still fighting.

Still in animated conversation, the crowd slowly dispersed, some deciding to return to London by the steamer, while others, who perhaps did not relish a trip up the river against an ebb tide, struck out across the marshes towards Dartford. Among this throng was the eccentric Bendigo who, much to the irritation of the milling orator and poet Charley Mallet, composed and sang a long extempore poem describing the day's sport, praise of the heroes, and of course, praise of himself. His caustic wit and pantomine propensities evoked uncontrollable laughter and applause from everyone, sending them all back to London in the highest of spirits.

# 8

## THE MIDDLEWEIGHT CHAMPION

Throughout the four years they had been living together, Tom and Sarah Henderson had always expressed the wish to be properly married in a traditional wedding ceremony conducted under the established rites of the church but, because Sarah was still officially classed as a minor, they had necessarily been forced to wait until she reached the legal age of twenty-one.

In the first week of February 1853, shortly after her twenty-first birthday, Sarah and Tom went to see John Pass, the curate of St Peter's Church in the Borough of Islington, to post the Banns and set a date for their wedding. To comply with the accepted laws of the church, both couples were required to reside within the parish so, to keep up the pretence of respectability, Tom gave an accommodation address of 4 St John Street Islington, a pawnbroker's shop owned by one Robert Walker, with Sarah residing further along the street at number 21.

On Tuesday, March 8 they were married in a quiet ceremony attended by a few personal friends and close relatives. Sarah signed the wedding certificate with her usual flourish of the pen, but poor illiterate Tom simply made his customary 'X'.

A few weeks after his wedding, Tom teamed up in a unique partnership with Alec Keene, one of the prize ring's most accomplished pugilists and a highly proficient second. Alec had enjoyed a brilliant career in the ring, beating such worthy and notable exponents as Bill Cain, Young Sambo Welsh and Bill Hayes. In private life he held the rank of Captain in the 79th Highlanders and, since becoming the landlord of the propitious Three Tuns, in Moor Street, Soho, he had successfully turned the establishment into one of London's foremost sporting houses. Always closely associated in matters connected with the prize ring, he was an excellent judge of any man's fighting capabilities and he had backed Tom Sayers heavily in all his previous fights. He liked "the simple Brighton boy" as he called him and, after his last impressive victory over Jack Martin, felt quite justified in pinning his faith on the rising young star. He now put all his training facilities at Tom's disposal and frequently invited him to give exhibition bouts for the entertainment of the influential and aristocratic visitors who frequented his famous hostelry. Here, Tom was introduced to many eminent dignitaries and public figures of society: Sir Robert Peel, the founder of the Metropolitan Police, his brother Captain William Peel, Lord Drumlanrig (the father of the Marquis of Queensberry), Lord Ongly, Lord Winchelsea, the brothers Rousemont of the Stock Exchange, Sir Edward Kent and Colonel Ousley Higgins.

For over a year it had been Alec's ambition to match his "Brighton boy" against the so-called "Invincible" Nat Langham, the current middleweight champion and, in their new-found bond of affinity, found little difficulty in persuading Tom to challenge Langham for the middleweight championship at £100 a side. "Ould Nat" as he was already called, saw the challenge as an ideal opportunity to make some easy money; the only problem he envisaged was how to reduce his weight to 11 stone after his prolonged absence from the ring.

Nathaniel Langham was born at Hinckley, near Leicester, in 1820. In his first recorded ring battle in 1843 he defeated William Ellis from Sapcote, a village near his native Hinckley. His remarkable performance deeply impressed the Fancy and they advised him to go to London and seek his fortune there. In the spring of 1844, he introduced himself to Ben Caunt who soon discovered there was something extraordinary about the Leicestershire lad. A few weeks later, both were present at Long Reach for the fight between Joe Bostock of Nuneaton and Turner "The Wychwood Forester".

After their contest Tom Lowe, a successful bruiser among the longshore fraternity, threw his hat into the ring and offered to fight any man present, 'for whatever the assembled gentlemen might choose to subscribe.'

When at length a purse of £6 was contributed, young Nat Langham threw his hat into the ring in reply to Lowe's challenge. Lowe appeared to have the better of the engagement, but at the call of time for the 43rd round he rose from his corner and walked over to Nat. Shaking him warmly by the hand, he declared he would fight no more. Those around the ring who wondered at Lowe's actions, did not appreciate Langham's exceptional powers during their 50-minute battle.

Despite Nat's repeated challenges, nearly a year passed before he was matched with D. Campbell, generally known as "The Brighton Doctor". Campbell had constantly bragged of his outstanding capabilities, but within 35 minutes, Nat's "pickaxe" left (as Tom Sayers called it) had closed both the "Doctor's" eyes.

Then came his match with George Gutteridge, also known as the "Yellow-belly", a native of Bourne in Lincolnshire. On the morning of Tuesday September 22, 1846 the ring was pitched in a field adjacent to Mr Banton's, The New Inn at Bourne, before a large assembly of country gentlemen, yeomen farmers and labourers.

The battle which followed was described as one of the most orderly and well-behaved contests ever witnessed for there were no large towns nearby to send out their contingents of roughs, and they were too far from the great metropolis to be troubled by the London blackguards who, at this time, were the curse of the prize ring. Too often it was the fashion to talk of the Englishman's love of fair play, but there was precious little of it practised among the "Boys" who came out intent on seeing their man win, one way or the other.

Early in the 1st round Nat delivered two terrific facial punches, drawing "first blood" from a cut over Gutteridge's left eye. Unflinching, the Lincolnshire man pressed on regardless, oblivious to the slashing knuckles and the blood running in streams from the wounds on his face.

In the succeeding rounds Nat displayed his expertise as a strategist, dodging in as if to hit, then retreating, drawing his opponent forward and inflicting more damage to his tortured features. In Gutteridge's corner his seconds could neither stem the flow of blood, nor reduce the swollen bruises decorating his face.

Over the next dozen rounds Langham slowly took a convincing lead, but Gutteridge possessed several outstanding qualities which rendered him an extremely dangerous opponent; he had stamina and courage and he was physically much stronger than Langham. Nat resorted to every subtle strategy in his bid to conserve his ebbing strength, but Gutteridge's energy showed no signs of flagging; although his face was a ghastly sight, he could still see through both eyes and he was still strong on his legs.

By the 50th round, Langham's blows had become so feeble they no longer made any impression on his adversary and, at the close of the round, Gutteridge was still favourite in the betting at 5 to 1 on. His victory seemed merely a matter of time but suddenly, in the 51st, Langham recovered his second wind and assumed the offensive, delivering half a dozen truly tremendous hits and knocking Gutteridge off his feet. The first knock-down blow of the fight seemed to paralyse Gutteridge and, from this point onwards, the rounds were of short duration.

Gutteridge struggled on gallantly until the 93rd round when Jem

Hodgekiss, his second, seeing he was now hopelessly blinded, threw up the sponge.

Langham's only defeat came at the hands of Harry Orme in May 1851. After his overthrow, Nat went into business as a publican and became the landlord of the Ram Inn in Bridge Street, Cambridge. In the two years following his meeting with Orme the fame and reputation of Tom Sayers had risen dramatically, especially after his crushing defeat of Jack Grant. Many had prophesied that the up-and-coming young pugilist would, one day, assume the title of champion of the middleweights, but the loyal followers of Langham were amused at Sayers' audacity in wanting to meet their champion and, when the gauntlet was thrown down, they were only too willing to find the money for the stakes.

The articles were duly drawn up and signed for the contest to take place on Tuesday October 18, 1853 at Lakenheath in Suffolk, under the auspices of the Pugilistic Benevolent Association, a new body which had recently come into existence, replacing the old Fair Play Club. Eight new laws had been introduced, and slight amendments made to several of the existing rules, enlarging their scope and content.

Rule 6 now specified:- The spikes in the fighting boots shall be confined to three in number, which shall not exceed three-eighths of an inch from the sole of the boot and shall not be less than one-eighth of an inch at the broadest point; two to be placed in the broadest part of the sole, and one in the heel; and in the event of a man wearing spikes, either in the toes or elsewhere, he shall be compelled to either remove them, or provide other boots properly spiked, the penalty for refusal to be a loss of the stakes.

The old rules of 18 and 19 were deleted.

Rule 20. The referee and umpires shall take their positions in front of the centre stakes, outside the ropes.

24. Any pugilist voluntarily quitting the ring previous to the deliberate judgement of the referee being obtained, shall be deemed to have lost the fight.

25. On an objection being made by the seconds or umpires, the men shall retire to their corners and there remain until the decision of the appointed authorities shall be obtained; if pronounced "foul" the battle shall be at an end, but if "fair", "Time" shall be called by the party appointed, and the man absent from the scratch in eight seconds after shall be deemed to have lost the fight. The decision in all cases is to be given promptly and irrevocably, for which purpose the umpires and the referee should be invariably close together.

26. If a man leaves the ring, either to escape punishment or for any

other purpose, without the permission of the referee, unless he is involuntarily forced out, he shall forfeit the battle.

27. The use of hard substances, such as stones or sticks, or of resin in the hand during the battle, shall be deemed foul, and on the requisition of the seconds of either man, the accused shall open his hands for the examination of the referee.

28. Hugging on the ropes shall be deemed foul. A man held by the neck against the stakes or upon or against the ropes shall be considered down and all interference with him in that position shall be foul. If a man in any way makes use of the ropes or stakes to aid him in squeezing his adversary he shall be deemed the loser of the battle and, if a man in a close reaches the ground with his knees, his adversary shall immediately loose him or lose the battle.

29. All glove and room fights to be as nearly as possible in conformity with the foregoing rules.

At the weighing-in ceremony on Monday October 17, Langham had succeeded in reaching the stipulated weight thanks to the supervision of Jemmy Welsh and Jerry Noon, but shedding the last five pounds had only been accomplished at the cost of some degree of strength.

Unfortunately it was not the case with Tom Sayers. He had been suffering from a severe bout of influenza, followed by an outburst of boils and suppuration of the skin. His face and body were sorely affected and it sadly forced a premature ending to his training. He returned to his native Brighton for a period of convalescence, believing he would benefit from the bracing sea and air. But the moment Alec Keene learned of his condition he caught the next available train to the coast, taking with him a consultant who specialized in skin ailments. Tom responded well to his treatment and, by the morning of the contest, his doctor pronounced him fit and well enough to fight.

Tuesday October 18 dawned with the promise of a glorious day ahead. As the first rays of the early morning sun cast their subtle glow across the university city of Cambridge, many of the young sporting undergraduates decided to postpone their studies that day in favour of the great prize fight. They had received advance information confirming that when the London special stopped at Ely, instructions would be given of its eventual destination. In consequence, immediately the college gates were opened, furtive little groups of students sneaked out to join the traps and carriages awaiting at pre-arranged points along the road to Ely.

Meanwhile, many supporters had made London their overnight headquarters for, on the eve of any important contest the exclusive Limmer's Hotel always became the rallying point for the wealthy patrons of the Fancy. In the noise and bustle outside the hotel that fine

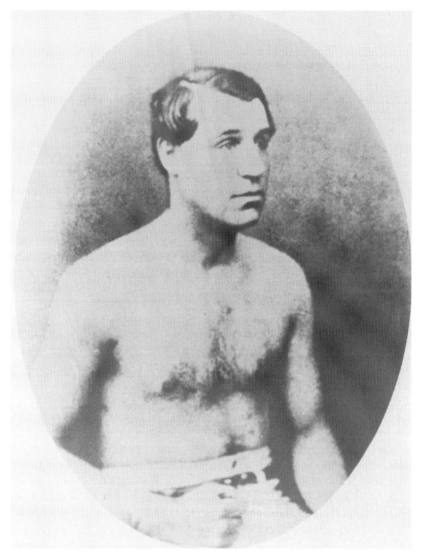

Newbolt's celebrated photograph of Tom Sayers.

autumn morning, an undercurrent of intense excitement rippled through their ranks as a large procession of gigs, phaetons and carriages of every description queued to pick up their occupants from the front door of the hotel. Since early morning the drivers of London's cabs and omnibuses had found extreme difficulty in forcing their way through the vast throng of penniless admirers waiting patiently in

Bishopsgate Street, opposite Shoreditch Station, in the hope of catching a glimpse of the two contestants.

Gathered on the platform that morning were many of the old and familiar faces of the boxing fraternity but, sad to relate, among them was Tom's old friend and former trainer, Peter Crawley. Terminally ill and much reduced by his sufferings, he still managed a cheery smile and a friendly greeting to all his old friends and admirers.

At precisely 8.30 the engine driver turned on the steam, blew a shrill blast on the whistle and, amidst the choking soot and sparks emitted from the engine's tall smokestack, the train steamed slowly out of the station, filled to capacity with over 400 jubilant supporters. On the long journey which lay ahead many travellers settled back in their seats to enjoy the brilliant sunshine and bracing air, a pleasant contrast to the dismal weather London had experienced over the past few weeks. Some passengers devoted their time to the pleasures of whist and escarte, popular games played by the Victorian gentry, whilst others, on meeting again old friends and colleagues, enjoyed a chat over bygone days, smoked their cigars or made comparisons with the ancient and modern schools of pugilism.

Shortly before 11.30 the train entered the Hockwold Fens area and pulled up about half a mile from Lakenheath Station. When everyone had alighted, they were escorted to a field about 200 yards from the railway line, where Tom Oliver and Tom Collins selected a flat piece of pasture land and pitched the ring. The ground underfoot was still soft and damp after the prolonged rainfalls of the last few weeks but the two "old Toms," with their usual foresight, had prepared a substantial supply of straw hassocks for the comfort of the paying customers.

While the officials were discharging their preliminary duties, Jem Moore, the acting ring caterer and landlord of the Old Rum Puncheon in Moorfields, produced his supply of food. Immediately the passengers saw the abundant array of fine cheeses, bread and huge joints of beef and ham spread out invitingly on trestle tables, there came a rush from all sides as hungry and thirsty individuals descended upon him to take advantage of the welcome provisions. Some travellers, who had been forced to rise in the early hours of the morning, had found little appetite at that time of day. Others, who were late in rising, had preferred to miss breakfast rather than miss the fight, but for the majority, who it seemed had considered a meal unnecessary, now found their appetites had sharpened after their long ride in the fine and bracing morning air.

At last, their pangs of hunger satisfied, all showed an eagerness to get the fight under way and a general move across the railway line brought them to the ringside where Dan Dismore undertook the sale of the inner ring tickets. Business was brisk and in less than fifteen minutes he realized the sum of twenty pounds ten shillings; more than sufficient to cover the expenses of the ring constables.

With everything now in readiness, an expectant hush settled over the crowd as they awaited the entrance of the contestants. Tom Sayers was the first to announce his arrival by throwing his beaverskin hat high into the sky. He was attended by Alec Keene and Bob Fuller, his close advisor during the latter phase of training.

Nat Langham soon followed his example, spinning his cap across the ropes and into the ring. He looked remarkably fit and healthy, a clear indication that Jemmy Welsh's discipline and training had been highly successful. Assisting him were Jemmy Welsh and Jerry Noon who, for this encounter, had been told to suspend his usual clowning activities. He evidently heeded the warning, for he adopted a quiet and attentive manner throughout the fight.

The usual tiresome procedure of choosing a referee had been settled at the time the articles were signed so, when all the remaining preliminaries were completed, the men commenced their preparations for the encounter. Time was called at eight minutes past one and, as Tom and Nat approached the scratch, each surveyed the other intently for a few minutes. The wry smile on Langham's lips portrayed little fear of what the forthcoming struggle might produce, but there were murmurs of consternation from the crowd as Tom took up the stance. His face still bore the marks of his recent outbreak of boils and he could well have spared several pounds of excess fat.

The 1st round opened with a good deal of sparring, as each endeavoured to draw his opponent into an opening. But the wily Nat was far too experienced to fall into this kind of trap and as Tom drew near he connected with two swift lefts to the nose and cheek. In the next exchange of counterpunching, Langham caught Sayers on the chin and drew "First blood" from one of the large pimples beneath his lip. Undeterred, Tom bored in, caught Nat with a terrific blow on the forehead and bowled him over on the turf.

The cry of, 'First knock-down blow to Sayers!' inspired wild cheering from the excited crowd.

Langham appeared to suffer from the after-effects of this blow for some considerable time and, to compensate against any repetition, he took the opportunity to go down on every conceivable occasion, much to the annoyance of Sayers, who hated this type of ringcraft.

In the 4th round Tom treated the spectators to a magnificent display of boxing, landing some simply bone-shattering punches with his right or, as it had now become known, his "auctioneer." But Nat was exceptionally proficient in counterpunching and one tremendous blow caught Tom between the eyes, causing the flesh to swell ominously. Sensing this was Tom's Achilles heel, Nat concentrated his punches with deadly accuracy, constantly getting past Sayers' guard and inflicting grievous blows to the eyes, nose and mouth before falling to escape any punishment. Tom bore the brunt of Langham's stinging punches until the 20th round, when he responded by delivering three crushing blows to Nat's jaw, nose and left eye, which knocked him off his feet.

At the end of the 28th round one hour had elapsed and during that time, Langham had fallen at the end of every round. But his proficiency and science was having an alarming effect as he landed punch after punch on Tom's eyes and nose.

Sayers attempted to take the initiative in the 41st round but he was met with another sharp rap on the eye and cheek for his impudence.

Tom's face was fearfully swollen as he came to scratch for round forty-seven. As he peered into the brilliant rays of the sun, his light grey eyes were now merely slits in the huge contusion running across his brow. Determined to do or die in the attempt, he caught Nat over the left eye but, in the counterpunching which subsequently followed, Langham delivered another crushing blow to his eye. A long swinging punch caught Langham on the cheek and he went down for the forty-seventh time.

As Tom led off in the 48th, Nat countered on the left eye and nose and promptly drew a fresh profusion of blood. Barely able to see through the frightful injuries to his eyes, Tom sunk wearily to the ground.

In his corner, his seconds now found it necessary to lance both eyes to prevent him from losing his sight. When he came up for the 49th, there came an audible gasp of horror from the spectators who saw he was bleeding steadily from the cuts around his eyes. Although he was still strong on his legs, he knew that if he did not finish his adversary soon he would shortly be in total darkness. Once again he dashed in but in the exchanges that ensued he received more agonizing punishment to his eyes. As he returned on Langham's mouth, Nat took the opportunity to go down yet again.

In the 55th Langham opened hostilities with a left to Tom's cheek before jumping smartly away from the return. But Sayers followed him up and some extremely heavy punches were exchanged, Nat turning on the tap from Tom's nose, while he returned the compliment with a pulverizing smash on the left eye. Langham toppled over in a state of semi-consciousness, with Tom falling across him in a not much better condition.

When Sayers came to the scratch for the next round it was obvious that his eyes would not remain open for much longer. He was finding it increasingly difficult to focus properly and he was consistently short in his deliveries. When he did catch Langham over the left eye, he received another stunning blow over the bridge of his nose. However, not to be easily shaken off, he lashed out with a left to the jaw and a series of counter hits followed, Sayers on the nose and mouth and Langham on the right eye before falling again. By now both men were completely and utterly exhausted. Any chance blow could finish Langham whilst Sayers, unless he could deliver the *coup de grace* soon, must surely go blind.

Squinting through the narrow slits of his eyes, Sayers rushed in open-handed in the 60th but Nat stepped neatly to one side and met him with two sharp lefts to the eye and nose. Unable to see anything clearly, Tom vainly tried to deliver just one connecting blow but Nat easily avoided him and administered another brutal punch on the mouth.

Suddenly the sound of a loud crack echoed across the arena as Langham delivered a stunning punch behind Tom's ear. Dazed and bewildered, he stood for a few moments as if in search of something. His seconds entered the ring and escorted him to his corner where they worked frantically to get him to the scratch on time. As he came out for the 61st and last round he looked very groggy indeed.

Anxious for his welfare, his friends called to his seconds to 'Take him away!' But with his usual dogged determination, he waved them aside and refused to submit. He was wild in his next delivery and Nat coolly waited for him and delivered a massive blow which closed his right eye completely. Once again Tom swung wildly, and once again Nat repeated the same manoeuvre as before, meeting him as he came forward with a well-directed punch which instantly closed his left eye. Seeing it was pointless to continue, Alec Keene threw up the sponge amidst loud and prolonged cheering.

After two hours and two minutes of gruelling fighting, Nat was delighted with his good fortune. Having previously been weak on his legs a sudden surge of strength coursed through his body and, after shaking Tom warmly by the hand, he vaulted over the ropes in a single bound. Tom's friends rushed over to his corner to console him after his first major defeat, but they assured him that having been beaten by such an accomplished boxer as Nat Langham was indeed no disgrace.

The spectators were in a particularly buoyant mood and, to express their appreciation for his magnificent performance, subscribed £50 in a collection for Tom.

With everything brought to a satisfactory conclusion little groups of travellers, heatedly discussing the day's events, slowly wended their way back to the waiting train. After a half hour's delay for the engineer to get steam up, the company arrived back in London shortly before eight o'clock that evening.

Within a few days of the battle, Tom's backers declared their willingness to provide the money for a rematch against Langham. But Nat was obstinate in his refusal to encounter Sayers again. He knew Tom never made the same mistake twice and he considered it would be sheer folly to risk his hard-earned laurels in another match, especially when he had hardly expected to win the first.

Despite Sayers' repeated challenges, nothing would induce him to change his mind, not even when Tom offered to stake £100, or double that amount if he was agreeable. But Nat still refused to be tempted, and announced his intention of retiring from the ring. He claimed that his friends were willing to finance him in a new business venture, much more profitable than his present establishment in Cambridge.

Having recently married a niece of Ben Caunt, he now moved to London where he became the landlord of the Cambrian Stores, in Castle Street, Leicester Square. On the lamp which decorated the entrance he had inscribed, "NAT LANGHAM, CHAMPION OF THE MIDDLEWEIGHTS." Tom was most indignant when he saw the sign, and refuted Nat's right to call himself "Champion." He declared that despite repeated challenges, Nat had stubbornly refused to fight again; therefore, according to the accepted practice of the ring, he should be the rightful title holder.

Since their battle Tom had also become a publican, having taken over the tenancy of the appropriately named Bricklayer's Arms; a small beer house in York Street (now Greenland Street), Camden Town and, as an act of defiance to Nat's claim to the title, he too sported a lamp over his doorway with his name emblazoned upon it and the legend, "CHAMPION OF THE MIDDLEWEIGHTS."

Initially Tom had been bitterly disappointed and annoyed with Nat about a rematch, but he was not a man to hold a grudge for long, especially when Nat confided that he was not in the best of health and did not feel fit enough to renew the contest. He did, however, promise to give urgent and serious consideration to his future plans and Tom would be the first to learn of his decision.

A few weeks later Tom was invited over to the Cambrian Stores, where Nat told him that he was prepared to resign the title into his keeping if he promised faithfully to defend it with honour and fulfil the obligations associated with the position. Delighted with his generous offer, Tom accepted with alacrity, guaranteeing to uphold with respect the prestigious and coveted distinction.

After relinquishing his title, Nat became one of Britain's most distinguished sporting publicans. An extremely astute business man, he had the remarkable knack of persuading the "Toffs" who patronized his house to subscribe towards the stakes and training expenses of all his protégé's. But alas, these same pugilists did not always share the same enthusiasm when they were sent to stage an exhibition for their charitable patrons. They grumbled that Nat would never allow any money to be paid directly to them. He always made a point of collecting the cash himself before paying the pugilists at a later date, minus his commission which usually amounted to twenty-five percent.

Nat had the misfortune to suffer from a speech impediment which Dan Dismore once described, 'For all the world as if he had a hot spud on his tongue.'

But despite all his faults, Nat did an inordinate amount of good work for the prize ring. He was the originator of the highly successful Rum-Pum-Pas sporting club. Every Wednesday evening its members met to wine and dine in a regulation 24-feet square ring. Quite often it became a tremendous squeeze to get the entire party into such a confined space but, the tighter the fit the merrier the company. The club's first president, Mr John Rousemont of the Stock Exchange was, by virtue of his office, custodian of the records. Nat Langham was the duly elected M.C. and the chief songster at these functions, the very talented Phil Benjamin, a man much renowned for his fine singing voice. To the applause of the audience, he would stand on a table to sing the old and established favourites such as *Tom Moody*, *Old Towler*, or *Dame Durden*.

Amongst the other regular visitors were Messrs Brown and Harris of the Stock Exchange, Lord Caledon and his brother the Hon. "Billy" Duff, Lord Edward Russell, Mr Keen (the famous mustard man), Bishop, the gunsmith of Bond Street, Harry Cooper, the bootmaker who had not missed a single prize fight in twenty-five years and other lesser known, but titled gentlemen connected with the turf and ring.

The club was famous for its principle dish, the Plum Pudding. Two of these puddings, one cold and the other hot, were supplied each week by Mrs Burnell, of the King's Arms, Hanwell. They were brought to the Cambrian Stores by her husband, punctually at 8 p.m. every Wednesday in time for dinner, the hot pudding carefully wrapped in flannel and kept warm on the journey in a hot-water plate.

After the meal, Nat frequently encouraged the revellers to make a night of it and often arranged what he termed 'A merry mill' between two young lads, well matched in weight, age and experience. As a special treat, on a fine summer's morning the whole company would travel down to a secluded spot near Epsom where, for a small purse, the youngsters would entertain the guests.

Nat made a substantial profit from running the club and, when he died in 1871, it was transferred to Alec Keene's Three Tuns, in Soho.

As the years passed away, so too did many of the old regulars, and when in 1879 it was decided to wind up the club with a farewell banquet, invitations were sent to all the known surviving members of the original Rum-Pum-Pas, asking them to meet for the last time at the King's Head, Barnes.

Surprisingly, quite a number of founder members gathered for the last reunion. Amongst those who attended were Mr Wilbraham, the sporting squire from Cambridge, Alec Keene, Jem Ward, Phil Benjamin the chief songster, Bill Burnell, who always brought the puddings, Jemmy Shaw and a few old patrons who, during the proceedings, did their best to revive some nostalgic memories of "the Good Old days" of the prize ring. They wanted to make this, the last of its gatherings, an occasion to be remembered with pleasure, rather than regret.

Jerry Noon seconded Tom Sayers in many of his early battles.

# 9

## THE EASTENDER

Having made good his title, Tom was again on the lookout for a new competitor. But much to his chagrin, nobody responded to his repeated challenges and for a while he seriously contemplated returning to his old trade of bricklaying. In his capacity as a publican he was a dismal failure and, to Sarah's intense annoyance, he gave up the tenancy of the Bricklayers Arms and returned to Bayham Street where he lived a fairly turbulent life of constant bickering and rows with his wife. Unhappy at home, and with little to occupy his time, he drifted around London, spending the odd hour or two pouring out his troubles to his old friend Alec Keene. Alec listened sympathetically to all his problems and promised he would try to find him some type of employment to take his mind off his current matrimonial entanglements.

A few days later, and quite by chance, Alec landed a contract for both himself and Tom to teach the officers of a leading London regiment stationed at a Knightsbridge barracks, "The manly art of self-defence." As qualified instructors, they would receive the princely sum of £4 a week and were to report for duty the following Monday morning.

There were many similar establishments scattered around the country where accomplished and "well-behaved" pugilists were engaged to instruct the upper classes of society in this branch of their profession. But usually, the unfortunate men they hired were literally expected to stand quietly by and allow themselves to be used as punchbags, without any attempt at returning blows, or losing their tempers.

When Alec and Tom reported at the barracks, Tom was informed that a certain stalwart, heavyweight officer, ranked as a first-rate amateur and an unquestionably formidable customer to any opponent, had been specially selected as his pupil and it was expected that he would receive preferential and specialized tuition.

Morning after morning, Tom entered the ring against this burly individual who delighted in thrashing him unmercifully, confident in the knowledge he could expect nothing in return. Eventually things became too hot even for Tom to handle and one evening, after having received an exceptionally heavy beating, he told Alec he had suffered enough punishment at the hands of this sadistic bully and if he tried it on again, he would let him have a taste of the "auctioneer."

The following morning, when Tom and Alec were at their posts awaiting the arrival of their respective pupils, an unusually large contingent of officers arrived in the gymnasium, accompanied by an equally large group of foreign officers, all expecting to see their distinguished colleague demonstrate his prowess against the current middleweight champion.

When the bout commenced, Tom began receiving much heavier punishment than usual, evidently done to impress the large gathering. True to his word, out shot his deadly auctioneer. The officer spun across the ring, dancing on his rubbery legs for a few steps until they crumpled beneath him and he pitched forward in a heap on the floor of the gymnasium. His seconds rushed into the ring and carried him to his corner where they repeatedly doused him with cold water in their efforts to revive him. One foreign officer was so delighted and impressed at the spectacle he had just witnessed, he presented Tom with a five pound note as a tribute to his courage and tenacity. But the next morning, when Tom and Alec reported for duty they were met with an icy reception and curtly informed that their services were no longer required, and they need not call again.

Out of work once more, Tom went back to giving sparring exhibitions for the entertainment of the aristocracy at Savile House. One evening, in a bout with the Jewish boxer Bendoff, everyone was most surprised to see Bendoff knock him all over the ring. When Tom's arch-rival Harry Orme learned of his defeat, the first glimmer of an idea began to formulate in his brain.

A few evenings later, Tom was visiting Alec Keene when Harry Orme and several of his friends from the East End of London came over to the Three Tuns for an evening's entertainment. Among them was a tall, slim, twenty-three-year-old pugilist named George Sims. Although Sims had fought several times in the prize ring, so far in his career he had not aspired to any real greatness. The records show that his only major victories were over Waldron, at Long Reach, on October 19, 1852 and on August 23, 1853 when he defeated Jem Parker at Rainham in Essex. But what the records did not show, was that Sims had easily beaten Bendoff on two occasions and Bendoff had trounced Tom Sayers. Harry Orme was confident Sims could beat Sayers too, but in assessing his chances he made the regrettable error of underestimating Tom's capabilities. True, Bendoff had beaten Sayers when both were wearing boxing gloves, but Tom always fought much better with his bare knuckles.

In retrospect, the events which occurred that evening were, most probably, stage-managed by Harry Orme. Tom was introduced to George Sims and each seemed to find the other quite good company. Later, as the evening wore on, they both began to give and take some light-hearted banter on the other's boxing abilities. Suddenly, in a voice loud enough for everyone to hear, Sims began making defamatory remarks about Sayers' fight with Nat Langham. Although renowned for his moderate temperament, Tom found the Eastender's insults and sarcasm intolerable and voices were raised in anger. As the argument became more heated, Sims became more aggressive and more offensive.

Everyone could see the situation was rapidly getting out of hand and they tried their best to ease the tension. But for some obscure reason, this only seemed to upset Sims even more and he offered to fight Tom there and then for £25. In one last bid to restore order, Tom politely reminded him that in his position as champion he regarded this sum as too small and he would not, under any circumstances, accept a challenge on such ridiculous terms. After this interjection, tempers cooled but an uneasy atmosphere prevailed throughout the remainder of the evening.

In the next edition of *Bell's Life*, possibly with the connivance of Harry Orme, Sims revived his former challenge of £25, (all he claimed he could raise) if Sayers would post £50. Tom thought £25 hardly worth all the bother, but as the reigning champion he could not back down without forfeiting the title. Nevertheless, grateful for a match at long last, he accepted the challenge, and the articles were ratified for February 2, 1854 at an undisclosed destination.

The Eastenders were intensely proud of Sims and his past achievements, especially in beating Waldron who was widely recognized as a tough and seasoned fighter. But to the initiated of the Fancy, the coming fight was a certainty for Sayers and it stimulated little interest.

Due to the excellent security precautions of Alec Keene and Mr Chaddock (Sims' principle backer) the whereabouts of the venue remained a total secret until the morning of the contest. In a bid to deter the lower and more troublesome classes from attending, the price of the excursion tickets was kept artificially high, so the little group of under 200 people who gathered on the platform that day consisted mainly of wealthy and aristocratic patrons of the Fancy. To guard against any action from the authorities, the small band of travellers made the short journey to North Woolwich and there transferred to the Thames *Waterman No 10* waiting at the jetty.

With such few in numbers, little time was lost in embarkation and the vessel cast off well before 10 o'clock. Because the general public had assumed the journey was to be by rail, the owners and charterers of the piratical craft which usually followed in the wake of any water-bourne excursions were blissfully unaware of the arrangements, so there was little opposition from other boats.

It was an intensely cold morning on the river and few passengers remained on deck, most preferring to huddle in the warmth of the cabins down below. After sailing for about half an hour, and when they were about two miles from Purfleet, to everyone's surprise the vessel turned about and headed for Long Reach. This unexpected move had been made to outwit a party of supporters from Cheapside who, having received veiled hints of the affair, were making for Northfleet on board a Gravesend passenger ferry under the assumption that the excursion was bound for Tilbury and the Lower Hope.

Soon after the vessel had anchored, an assortment of small cutters came alongside and began ferrying little groups of passengers ashore. Among the supporters was the old ex-champion Jem Burn, accompanied by a party of "Toffs" who had come especially to see Sayers in action after his last famous battle with Nat Langham. Jem Burn, who seldom missed a match, was heard uttering innumerable anathemas against the managers of the expedition who had deluded him into making an aquatic trip against his will. Eventually he submitted with as much grace as possible, but while being lowered into a waiting boat he launched into another tirade against an over-enthusiastic crew member who grabbed him by the head and nearly pulled off his ear.

Tom Oliver and his aides-de-camp pitched the ring near the river bank and at half past eleven, amidst as much cheering as could be raised from the throats of such a small company, the men announced their arrival by tossing their hats into the arena. Tom was accompanied by Bob Fuller and Jemmy Massey with Sims attended by Jemmy Welsh and Harry Orme. As they stripped for action, there were murmurs of appreciation for Sayers who appeared to be all rippling muscles and sinews under the skin. Scaling 10 stone 6 pounds, he looked in superb condition.

Sims, 5 feet 10½ inches in height and weighing 10½ stone, looked perfectly calm and collected, the smile on his lips portraying little fear of the difficult task he was about to undertake. But from the moment the spectators assessed the physical condition of the two men, they began laying new odds and two substantial bets were laid; one for £20 to £9, and another for £20 to £8 on Sayers. Subsequently the Sayers followers began offering three to one.

During the settlement of the preliminaries, there were loud exhortations from the ring caterer Mr Coobiddy and his Israelite assistant to, 'Come and eat!'

But as it was still fairly early in the day and hunger had not superseded discretion, the fried fish and bread did not meet with its usual patronage, especially when it became known that Dan Dismore had laid on a substantial quantity of food in the warmth and comfort of the steamer.

The umpire called time at five minutes to twelve and both men walked to the scratch to shake hands. But the moment the Eastender put up his hands, it became significantly obvious to the connoisseurs of the Fancy that he knew little of the game. The tremendous contrast between him and Sayers instantly turned the betting from sovereigns to shillings. Dan Dismore offered 4 to 1 on Sayers, but the only taker was Jem Burn who accepted the bet on the off chance that Sims might pull something out of the bag.

Sims opened the proceedings by lunging out with his left and landing on Sayers' chest. Evidently having waited to gauge his capabilities, Tom struck him on the mouth but in skipping away from the return, fell over backwards. The shivering spectators, their teeth chattering with the cold, were grateful for their warm winter overcoats and many expressed their sympathies for the two men, stripped to the waist in the freezing temperature of the Thames marshes.

Sayers came out for the 2nd round grinning all over his face. He easily dodged Sims' wildly flailing fists and hit him hard on the nose. Sims instantly closed into a grappling hold but Tom seized him around the neck with his left arm and pummelled away with right's to the ribs and left eye until they fell over together.

With no apparent plan of action, Sims led off in the 3rd with a wild swing. It caught Sayers on the mouth, but Tom countered like lightning and dealt a savage blow to the Eastender's nose. Bleeding profusely from both nostrils and resentful at such harsh treatment, Sims closed into a wrestling close. Tom hit him on the nose and left eye as before and in the ensuing struggle, both stumbled and fell.

In his corner, Sims sat disconsolately on his bottleholder's knee as Harry Orme sponged him down and staunched the bleeding. At the umpire's call of "Time" Orme sent him to the scratch, his face covered in red welts and still in a state of bewilderment from the punishment in the previous round. Again he attempted to lead off but Tom let fly with both hands, the left on the nose and his now famous auctioneer over the left eyebrow, inflicting a deep gash and instantly producing a copious flow of blood. As his head rolled back on his neck and his legs gave way beneath him Tom reached out in a bid to catch him as he fell, but the dead weight dragged him down and he rolled over on top of Sims. No one was more surprised at the startling effect of this blow than Tom, who gazed down at his prostrate foe with a look of mingled astonishment and disbelief.

Many spectators gazed horrified at his inert body, quite sure that the blow had been fatal. As Sims lay motionless on the grass, his seconds gently lifted him and carried him to his corner. They worked furiously in their efforts to staunch the river of blood pumping from the cut, until they were joined by a medical practitioner who was present as a spectator.

Sayers was wreathed in smiles as he was declared the conqueror in a skirmish lasting just five minutes, but he still appeared shocked and expressed his deep concern over his less fortunate opponent. He went across to Sims, who still lay unmoving in his corner, to see what aid he could render but a full five minutes passed before Sims showed the first signs of consciousness. He was somewhat dumbfounded when he learned of the result and begged to be thrown into the river for losing but, after a little comfort and persuasion from his friends, he agreed it would be wiser to live and fight another day.

It had been an extraordinary battle, and many who had travelled long distances on that bitterly cold morning, now grumbled that the whole affair had been hardly worth all the trouble and expense.

But for Tom, the pitifully small stake of £25 meant he could expect little profit after paying all the expenses he had incurred. Fortunately, he had to be thankful once again to the wonderful generosity of Alec Keene who, besides paying for all his training, seconds and other incidental expenditure, also presented him with the entire stakes. Consequently, the total revenue which eventually found its way into his pocket amounted to a great deal more than he had actually won.

Although Tom Sayers was now the acknowledged champion of the middleweights, he was still unable to find a competitor in his class who would respond to his repeated challenges. Of those who did show some inclination or interest none were anywhere near his weight, and for nearly two years he remained without a match. During this time he took the opportunity of touring the principle cities of England, giving boxing exhibitions and making his living in one town or another, always on the lookout for someone who might accept his challenge.

# 10

## HARRY PAULSON OF NOTTINGHAM

During the months Tom was away on tour his wife had been having a clandestine love affair with a London cab-driver named James Aldridge, a man twelve years her senior, who lived in York Street, just around the corner from Tom's house in Bayham Street. The moment he learned of Sarah's infidelities, Tom abandoned the remainder of his tour and returned to Camden Town. Immediately he confronted her about her relationship with Aldridge a blazing row developed and she stormed out of the house, telling him their marriage was finished and she intended to live with her lover. Tom's paramount concern now centred around the future welfare and wellbeing of his two young children. With no mother to care for them and uncertain about his own plans, he prudently arranged for a nursemaid to take care of little Thomas and for his daughter Sarah to attend a private boarding school.

All the money he had sent home had been frittered away, while the added expenditure and domestic upheaval had sadly depleted his own meagre savings. Compelled now to return to his former lifestyle of fighting for a living, he travelled the country for the next few months, giving boxing exhibitions and issuing repeated challenges to all and sundry in his despairing search for a match.

At length, to the astonishment of the boxing world, he offered to fight Tom Paddock at catchweight, if he could find £200 to Paddock's £100. His friends and backers were aghast when they heard of his challenge and thought it presumptuous that he should even consider himself in the same league as Paddock. The odds were totally un- acceptable and to invest any money on such a long shot would be quite ludicrous. Heedless to his pleas for sponsorship, they remained un- compromising in their resolve and he was forced to withdraw the offer.

At this stage in his career poor Tom went through a most depressing phase of discouraging setbacks. Combined with his family problems, many of his former friends and patrons deserted him and he now lost one of his advocates when Vincent Dowling, the editor of *Bell's Life*, died on October 25, 1854. Vincent was succeeded in office by his son Frank, who was in every respect a worthy chip off the old block. He knew of his father's concern for Tom's welfare and he too became a close friend and personal advisor throughout his boxing career and in private life.

By the spring of 1855 Tom had completed his tour of the provinces and he returned to London to clear up all his outstanding personal and domestic affairs. There was no hope of a reconciliation with Sarah and, with no prospects of a match within the foreseeable future, he decided to emigrate to Australia and try his chances on the other side of the world.

It was while winding up the last of his legal obligations and commitments, that the chance of a match materialized from a quite unexpected source. The first tentative approach had come from Harry Paulson of Nottingham who, like Tom, had been without a match for more than a year. Paulson's exemplary reputation was beyond reproach, but as he weighed nearly thirteen stone at fighting weight, Tom would be conceeding something in the region of two stone, a situation unprecedented at this period of time. Nevertheless, desperate for a match, he agreed to take him on for a stake of £50 a side and promptly put down his deposit of five sovereigns.

Unlike many of his contemporaries, Harry Paulson was of a singularly mild and inoffensive disposition and one of the few men who never resorted to foul language. But one glance at his powerfully square shoulders, huge barrel chest and resolute face was enough to make the worst of the rowdies think twice before picking a quarrel with him.

Harry was born in 1819 at Paxton's Court, Newark. While he was still a youngster, he moved with his parents to Nottingham where his father kept a small beershop in the Broadmarsh area of the city. He began his working career as a common labourer where the heavy manual work served to develop his muscles and harden his naturally powerful frame. At the time he became actively engaged in prize fighting, he was employed in ballast-heaving on the Trent river barges, an occupation eminently fitted to his phenomenal strength. His first reported battle was against James Cummings (alias Jemmy Walmer) in 1850. He completely outclassed Cummings, who fell without a blow at the start of the third round.

Then came his three tremendous battles with the redoubtable Tom Paddock of Redditch, near Birmingham. Although the little town of Redditch had long been famous for the manufacture of needles, it also enjoyed a notoriety of another kind. Its inhabitants, especially the lower class, had a mania for fighting. The "Pointers", as they were called, were never happy unless they were fighting between themselves or watching someone else engaged in the game of fisticuffs. They would set-to on the flimsiest of excuses and they were in their element when the canal was under construction in their neighbourhood. Quite often, the navvies employed in the digging would come over in the evening to fight the Redditch men.

On one occasion it was reported:- "About forty navigators assembled at Foxlygate-walk to engage the needlemakers in a meadow hard by, and a terrific melee ensued. Everyone had either to run or fight. From fisticuffs, they quickly proceeded to bludgeoning, for the navvies had all come armed with loaded sticks. Palings were pulled up and any weapon that came to hand was seized upon. The navvies fought with the ferocity of wild beasts and mowed down their assailants like grass. Fresh fighting men from the town continually poured into the meadow to recruit the ranks of the needlemakers until at

Fresh fighting men from the town of Redditch poured into the meadow to recruit the ranks of the needle-makers.

length, the invaders, overpowered by sheer weight of numbers, were compelled to fly for their lives; but not before they had left two of their number mortally wounded on the field of battle."

Disgusting scenes such as these did nothing to enhance the reputation of the town and it might naturally be expected that such a pugnacious community would, sooner or later, turn out some stalwart bruiser who would leave his mark in the annals of the ring. That man was destined to be Thomas Paddock, born in 1824, the son of an agricultural worker who lived in a small hamlet about a mile from Redditch. From the customs and the pastimes of the local inhabitants, it will be easily understood that young Paddock's natural desire for fighting needed little stimulation and from quite an early age he appears to have been constantly involved in the game of fisticuffs with boys of his own age. By the time he became a teenager he had acquired a formidable reputation as a fighter, having won many impromptu battles among the Redditch population and its neighbours.

His first important match took place on January 24, 1844 at Mapleborough Green near Redditch. On that eventful day Enoch Horridge of Manchester defeated James Scott, better known as Jemmy from Town, while Sam Simmonds from Birmingham lowered the colours of the veteran Thomas Murray, alias Tom the Greek. These two fights were over rather quickly and, because plenty of time yet remained, Lord Drumlanrig and a number of wealthy patrons subscribed a purse of £5 for two more contestants to round off the day's sport. Two men came forward; one, a Cheltenham man named Fred Pearce and the other, Tom Paddock.

For one and a half hours these two hammered each other until, to the delight of the spectators, Paddock floored his opponent with a terrific blow under the ear. Flushed by the thrills and excitement he had experienced that day, Tom Paddock now set his heart on becoming a pugilist. He had not failed to notice that gathered around the ring were some of the most successful fighting men of the age. All were well dressed, all had plenty of money and, to all appearances, were equal to the "Swells" who patronized the ring. If money, fame and position were all to be won from fighting, then what was to prevent him from achieving all the good things in life when nature had provided him with a strong arm, a robust constitution and an inane love of fighting for its own sake?

Jack Slagg, the landlord of the Fox and Goose, the great sporting house of Redditch, did much to foster these ideas, but he knew the youngster needed more experience and tuition before he could hope to contend successfully. Obviously the best decision would be to match him against some good local pugilist who, without overtaxing his ability, would highlight his true potential. He arranged for him to fight the veteran pugilist Elijah Parsons, at Harbourne, then a small village on the outskirts of Birmingham. In his battle with Parsons, Tom Paddock won his first noteworthy victory.

"This," said the editor of *Bell's Life*, "was certainly a promising debut for, although old Elijah was too stale to contend with such an impetuous, hard-hitting and resolute youngster as 'the Redditch needle-grinder', he certainly tested the young 'uns game, who showed he was 'all there', even if he did not possess the higher attainments of a scientific boxer."

Paddock's first big break came when he fought Bendigo in June 1850. Paddock was having the best of the encounter until he was disqualified in the 49th round for hitting Bendigo when he was down on his knees. Curiously this battle coincided with Harry Paulson's fight against Cummings and, while public interest was still aroused after their two encounters, Paddock and Paulson joined forces to stage a boxing promotion at Newark. Their proficiency deeply impressed the onlookers and within a very short space of time they entered into an agreement for the first of their three tremendous encounters.

Their first battle took place on September 23, 1851. The contest should have been fought the day before at Appleby-House, near Ashby-de-le-Zouch in Leicestershire, but before the ring could be erected a large contingent of police, who had been hiding in the woods nearby, suddenly swooped upon the startled spectators and put a stop to the proceedings.

The company then moved off to another area, somewhere near Castle Donnington, but here too they were harassed by two wagon loads of the local constabulary. In desperation, the organizers concluded that, with the increasing hostile pressure of the authorities, they had no other alternative but to postpone the contest until the following day. Because of the great need for secrecy total confusion spread through the ranks of the spectators on the exact location of the next day's venue. Rumours and speculation were rife, but in retrospect this was probably a deliberate ploy on the part of the organizers to confuse the police.

Immediately upon their return to Nottingham, the leading members of the Fancy held a secret meeting at the Dog and Bear in Bridlesmith Gate to discuss their next move. After several controversial issues and arguments were resolved, it was decided to try Lincolnshire on the morrow.

Early the next morning, those who were present for the meeting set out for Sedgebrook, near Grantham. However, there still remained a large proportion of people in Nottingham who were unaware of the new arrangements and still utterly confused by the spate of rumours circulating in the town.

*The Nottingham Journal* told the plight of these unfortunate travellers when it reported:- "Many persons of all classes started off in consequence, and on foot, for Gonerby Moor the supposed scene of action. They had, however, been misinformed for the combatants had already taken the train from Nottingham to Sedgebrook and then made their way to a point between Allington and Sedgebrook where the fight eventually took place."

This time, there were no police in waiting and everything progressed according to plan. At the call of "Time!" Paddock advanced confidently into the attack, determined to implement the same rushing tactics which had so nearly overthrown the bold Bendigo but to his amazement Paulson easily stopped his assault and, in his over-eagerness, Paddock slipped and fell full length on the turf, ignominiously terminating the 1st round.

After his highly embarrassing start, the Redditch boxer wore a look of evil rage on his face as he came to scratch for round 2. He led off hastily but was again neatly parried by Harry who planted his right under Paddock's left eye and cut a deep gash in his cheek –

'First blood to Nottingham!' came the excited cries of the Paulson supporters.

Paddock made a furious rush to avenge the blow but Harry met him square and solid with a resounding thump on the ribs which sent him tottering about the ring for a few seconds before falling.

'First knock-down' was claimed, but the referee decided Paddock had merely lost his balance. Nevertheless, Paulson clearly gained an important advantage from the punch and in the succeeding rounds, steadily improved his performance by stopping all Paddock's attacks and dealing some very hard knocks in the rallies.

At the end of the first half-hour's fighting Paddock's face and body symbolized the power of Harry's withering punches. Cool and unhurried, Paulson would wait for him, stop him and jab him heavily in the face with a left or a right. Discouraged at his harsh treatment, Paddock now resorted to dropping but it did him little good, for Paulson constantly forced the fighting, hitting him hard before he had the chance to go down.

In the 24th round, a frightful right-hand punch completely closed Paddock's left eye and in the succeeding few rounds he was frequently knocked off his feet by the Nottingham hero. Occasionally Paddock inflicted a heavy blow in retaliation, but his punches made little impression upon Paulson who kept pounding away as unconcerned as ever.

As Tom Paddock fled from the ring, Henry Paulson called for him to return.

The betting had slowly changed from 6 to 4 on Paddock to evens, and then 5 to 4 on Paulson. Paddock's naturally florid features shone like a big copper warming-pan and beads of perspiration glistened on his body in his efforts to arrest his chastisement from his stolid and imperturbable foe. To add to his misery, his hands were painfully swollen and, at the end of an hour's fighting, every blow he struck hurt him more than it did his adversary. Paddock knew his position was becoming untenable and a sullen silence had fallen over his supporters.

At the end of an hour and thirty-five minutes, and when Paddock's morale had reached its lowest ebb, a cry of 'Police!' was raised. A solitary constable by the name of Illiffe, from the Bottesford Constabulary, bravely broke through the cordon of spectators and made an attempt to seize one of the combatants.

Startled at the unexpected incursion, Paddock promptly bolted from the ring amidst cries of 'He's off, he's had his bellyful!' from the Nottingham contingent. The referee called for him to return but he sullenly shook his head and refused to re-enter the arena. Paulson ran after him in a bid to bring him back but Paddock showed him a clean pair of heels and was seen no more that day. The constable's right to intervene was instantly challenged by Paddock's supporters, particularly when the contest was taking place outside the jurisdiction of his county. But despite all their protests and objections, when Paulson returned into the ring, he claimed the victory by default.

An emergency meeting was called the next morning and, after hearing all the evidence from both sides, the referee ruled that Paulson was entitled to receive the stakes, on the grounds that when Paddock left the ring, he had failed to return when summoned to do so by the referee.

It now became crucial for Paddock to wipe out the stain of his inglorious defeat and regain his former status and reputation. His challenge for a second trial was accepted with alacrity by Paulson's backers and the date for the engagement set for December 16, 1851.

On this occasion, the Nottingham Fancy decided to keep everything to themselves. All the deposits were made secretly and no information or communiques were sent to London. Consequently, the metropolitan sportsmen took little interest in the match and tended to ignore the whole affair.

As the day of the contest drew near Tom Paddock, acutely aware that his entire future was at stake, paid the greatest attention to his training. Paulson was not an adversary to be taken lightly and he knew he would have all his work cut out if he intended to win.

Their second great battle took place near a public house named The Cross-o'-th'-Hands, at Muggington, near Belper in Derbyshire. For several weeks past, the magistrates of Nottinghamshire, Leicestershire and Derbyshire had known the contest would be fought in one or the other of these three counties and they had made no secret of their determination to prevent a breach of the peace taking place anywhere within their jurisdiction.

Early in the morning of that eventful day, hundreds of people from miles around steadily wound their way towards the Cross-o'-th'-Hands. Outwardly, everyone was in a jolly and boisterous mood but underneath this facade ran an undercurrent of impending mischief, for among this great throng were a large proportion of the worst roughs of Nottingham and Derby.

The stakes and ropes were formed by mid-morning, but a long wrangle persisted over the appointment of a referee and it was one o'clock before the men entered the ring. As Paulson stood flexing his muscles there were obvious signs of an excessive amount of flesh about his chest and back, but when he took up his stance at the scratch, feet planted firmly on the ground, square on, and hands raised high in the old fashioned attitude, he appeared capable of withstanding any onslaught.

Paddock tore in viciously, both fists flying. The tremendous impetus of his attack staggered Paulson. His knees buckled beneath him and he lay stretched out on the greensward, a trickle of blood oozing from a cut under his eye.

The referee's cry of, 'First blood and knockdown to Paddock!' evoked jubilant shouts from his followers, who yelled and cheered until their throats were hoarse.

Paulson's backers were strangely silent and looked most surprised, evidently never expecting to see such a sensational downfall so early in the conflict.

Paddock's efforts flagged a little until the 7th round when he tore in again with an irresistible force, pounding Paulson with both hands until, dazed and bewildered, Harry went down.

During the next few rounds, Paddock consistently drove his opponent back and sent him down. Suddenly there came a commotion at the back of the crowd as three Derby magistrates, Captain Hopkins and Messrs John and Jedediah Strutt appeared upon the scene, accompanied by William Wragg the Chief Constable of Belper and a small contingent of the local constabulary.

As they marched resolutely forwards to stop the proceedings, the mob closed ranks around the ring. Jedediah Strutt spurred his horse forward and tried to force a passage through the crowd, calling upon them all to disperse in the Queen's name. But the rabble amongst the vast throng refused to move and subjected him to a barrage of obscenities and prolonged jeering.

Finding his way firmly barred, he ordered Wragg and a section of policemen to clear a passage whereby he might read the Riot Act within earshot of the combatants.

Amidst shouts of, 'Keep them out! – keep them out!' the unfortunate Chief Constable stepped forward to obey the command and instantly disappeared beneath a hail of flailing fists. Jedediah Strutt and Captain Hopkins charged their horses into the thick of the fray to render assistance to their fallen comrade but they were savagely beaten back by the angry mob, who had now armed themselves with bludgeons, sticks and staves torn from the hedgerows.

When eventually the police succeeded in reaching the Chief Constable, they found him lying senseless on the ground and covered in blood. Carrying the unconscious Wragg with them, the battered and bleeding constables prudently retired to a safe distance. With the Chief Constable safely delivered from the clutches of the mob, Captain Hopkins spurred his horse and galloped off to Derby to muster additional reinforcements. The police meanwhile, calling for the assistance of some friendly farm labourers loitering nearby, carried Wragg off to

Belper where a couple of surgeons treated his injuries and restored him to consciousness.

When Paddock first saw the appearance of the magistrates, he was about to cease fighting and respect the law, but his friends yelled for him to continue as Paulson's seconds had declared they would claim the fight on a foul if he left the ring. Recalling how he had lost the last battle under similar circumstances and knowing Harry was growing weaker by the minute, he decided he had little alternative but to continue.

Terribly punished and barely able to stand, Harry prolonged his hopeless struggle until the 68th round, when Paddock dealt him a tremendous blow in the solar plexus. Paulson doubled up in agony and fell writhing to the ground.

But the most serious part of the business was yet to come. Having secured a strong force of the Derby constabulary, Captain Hopkins returned to the scene of the battle at the same moment Paddock was being proclaimed the victor. With the intrepid captain at their head, the police charged into the crowd and savagely fought their way to the ringside.

Amid the reigning confusion Paddock, his seconds and several other prominent troublemakers were rounded up and placed under arrest. Harry Paulson made good his escape in the disorder, but his bid for freedom did not last long. He was arrested at a roadblock set up on the Keddlestone Road, just outside of Derby. A keen-eyed policeman spotted him wrapped in blankets and hidden under bales of straw in a long four-wheeled drag.

Two of Jedediah Strutt's assailants were eventually apprehended near Coventry and all were duly charged, with divers other persons to the number of 1,000 and more, of having unlawfully, riotously assembled and gathered together to disturb the public peace.

When Paddock was arrested, he remarked that if he had won the toss he would have chosen any spot rather than that damned county. He added that he felt very sorry for the poor policeman who was injured and would have stopped fighting when the magistrate ordered them to disperse, but he had been told that if he did so, then he would lose the contest.

Because of the seriousness of the charges brought against them, all were committed for trial at the next assizes charged with rioting and violent resistance to the law. In court, the prosecuting counsel agreed that although neither of the combatants nor their seconds were responsible for the brutal assault on the police officers, they were, however, the principals accountable for the fight. The lawyer for the defence acknowledged that while prize fighting in itself was not a felony, it was most probable that due to the noise and bustle of the crowd the combatants, who were so busily engaged, were unlikely to have heard the reading of the Riot Act.

His testimony was totally ignored and both men were found guilty of a breach of the peace. As the judge sentenced them to serve ten months hard labour in Derby gaol they accepted the verdict with a stoic complacency, for such sentences were regarded as an occupational hazard common to all prize fighters.

Whatever effect prison may have had on Harry Paulson, it was certainly most beneficial to his rival. Paddock's fiery temper vastly improved during his incarceration and the measure of self-control he achieved was, in itself, worth the ten months imprisonment.

However, this vindication for the terrors of the law had exactly the opposite effect to that intended by the authorities. In their naivety, they believed both men would now be deterred from committing any more breaches of the peace, but on their release from prison they were even more determined to prove just who really was the better man. Harry Paulson's backers were convinced that his defeat in the second battle was entirely due to his lack of condition, and they were confident that if extra care and constant vigilance were accorded to his training, he would turn the tables in their next encounter.

In the summer of 1853, fresh articles were formally signed for a third engagement to take place in the London district, with a stake of £100 a side. The London Fancy, having been excluded from the two previous conflicts, now took a keen interest in the match and were resolved that this time they would not miss the spectacle of a really good fight between a pair of extremely competent and determined heavyweights.

On his arrival in London, Paddock went to stay with Alec Keene at the Three Tuns. Alec had pinned his faith on Paddock winning and his sound judgement was held in high esteem by the metropolitan sportsmen.

Harry Paulson, meanwhile, had made his headquarters at Ben Caunt's, The Coach and Horses in St Martin's Lane. Ben had taken a great liking to Harry, partly because he was a fellow shiresman and partly because of his quiet and unassuming disposition.

He often told his customers, 'Here gentlemen, unless I'm very much mistaken, you see before you the future champion of England.'

But many who had come to see for themselves the condition of Paulson, thought he was much too heavy for a man of his height. One critic hinted that for a man of his size and stature, he must be slow.

But Caunt laughed at his suggestion and said, 'Wait till you see him fight, and I tell ye, I mean to send him into the ring as fit as hands can make him. He'd 'a' licked Paddock last time if he'd been in anything like condition.'

Because Ben Caunt was willing to back his opinion with ready money, the customers at The Coach and Horses believed he knew much more than he was prepared to say about the merits of the Nottingham man.

Harry Paulson went into training at Brighton under the supervision of Jerry Noon while Paddock stayed at the Old Hat in Ealing, training with his future opponent, Tom Sayers.

On the morning of St Valentine's Day 1854, the usual motley crowd of curious onlookers thronged the approaches to Shoreditch Station. The first of the celebrities to arrive were Harry Paulson, Jerry Noon, Callaghan of Derby and a score of Paulson's Nottingham supporters. Although Harry was in his thirty-sixth year, he looked as fit as the proverbial fiddle, eyes bright and sparkling and a broad smile on his face to greet all his friends and admirers who had come to give him their support.

Paddock arrived shortly after the Nottingham contingent, accompanied by Mr Herbert, his principle backer, Alec Keene and Tom Sayers.

Both fighters were soon busily engaged distributing their colours with cries of, 'A guinea if I win, nothing if I lose!'

Paulson sported Bendigo's old colours, a blue bird's eye, while Paddock's flag was a chocolate coloured handkerchief with blue spots on a white border. Judging from the numerous handkerchiefs of both designs wound around the throats of the ticket-holders, sales were immensely satisfactory to both sides.

The shrill blast of the engine's whistle sounded at a quarter to nine and the special steamed out of the station, carrying 300 exhilarated sportsmen. It was a raw foggy morning in London but by the time the train came to a halt near the town of Mildenhall, the sun was shining brightly.

Tom Oliver and his two assistants formed the rings in a field adjacent to the railway line and at twelve o'clock the men were escorted into the ring. Paulson's tremendous physique electrified the Londoners, who gazed in wide-eyed admiration at his torso and the marvellous development of muscles in his arms and shoulder blades.

Most, if not all, of the metropolitan division were backing Paddock and naturally they too were interested in surveying the proportions of his opponent. But a glance from Paulson to Paddock reassured them that Paddock was also in splendid fettle. His superiority in height and reach manifested itself to such a degree that his backers no longer hesitated in laying slight odds in his favour.

From past experiences, Paulson knew his forte lay in taking an early lead and Paddock was taken completely by surprise when Harry rushed forward and delivered a thumping right on the ribs, instantly raising a bump and leaving a crimson welt. Before Paddock had a chance to recover, Harry followed through with a crushing blow to the mouth. For a second or two the Redditch boxer appeared stunned by the sheer ferocity of Paulson's unexpected onslaught. Each now peppered the other on the side of the head with short, sharp left and right hooks until they came together, clinched, and went down on the turf side by side.

In the next encounter, Paulson was first to the scratch and once again launched himself at his adversary, pounding at Paddock's face for all he was worth. Although Paddock had steeled himself for the attack he was still un-prepared for the heavy punishment he received on his nose and mouth and, when he saw Paulson about to repeat the manoeuvre, he slipped down.

Paddock was first to open fire in the 7th, shooting two quick lefts to the forehead, but Harry gave his receipt in full as he smashed his right into Paddock's mouth. The Redditch fighter stood quite still for a few seconds, dazed by the severity of the blow, blood gushing out in torrents and entirely at the mercy of his antagonist. Had Harry been a little quicker off the mark he might have turned the tide of victory, but it was never his custom to take advantage of a momentary weakness of his foe and this hesitation was long enough for Paddock to regain his scattered senses. He suffered sorely in the fierce rally which followed and he was glad when the opportunity presented itself to get down and end the round.

When Paddock came to the scratch again, his normally ruddy complexion was even more red, partly from his exertions and partly from the flowing blood his seconds were unable to staunch. Even so, he was first to attack, but the irascible Harry peppered him unmercifully and, under a hail of punches, Paddock dropped to his knees.

The succeeding rounds were generally short but busy and it was not until the 22nd round, when Harry's eye began to close, that Paddock could claim the slightest advantage.

At the call of time for the 23rd, Paddock strode rapidly across to Harry's corner and, before he could turn around from his seconds, struck him hard on the forehead. Paddock lashed out again with another vicious left and Harry slipped down in the scramble. There were hoots and shouts of disapproval from the Nottingham division, who were quite justified in protesting against Paddock's unethical conduct.

Not to be caught napping a second time, Harry was up promptly and ready at the scratch for the call of "Time!"

During the next dozen rounds Paddock steadily played on Harry's right eye, which his seconds kept open by judicious lancing.

At the close of the 50th, except for Paulson's right eye, neither had taken a decisive lead and it was still anyone's battle.

For the next five rounds, Paddock strained every muscle and fibre to deliver the one commanding blow which would put an end to his relentless adversary. He concentrated all his attacks on Paulson's right eye which, in all probability, would be closed long before his strength failed.

Then, in round 56, he delivered a simply shattering blow to Harry's right eye and knocked the brave Nottingham fighter off his feet. Everyone believed the battle must be over, but Harry came up to the call of time looking little the worse for wear. Nevertheless, the mischief was done. The eye was beginning to close.

Although he was fast losing precision from his failing eyesight, Paulson refused to yield and in the 89th round attacked with such astonishing vigour that he knocked Paddock down.

The roar of frenzied delight from the Nottingham supporters seemed to cleave the air with a sound like hollow thunder. 'Harry wins! – Harry wins! – Nottingham forever! – the Redditch beggar's beat!'

Paddock's backers looked crestfallen; were they going to lose their money after all? Those at the back of the crowd, eager to see what was happening in front, surged forward like some gigantic tidal wave. In their frantic excitement they crowded right up to the ring, the ropes and stakes straining under their weight of numbers.

At the umpire's call of "Time!" everyone craned their necks forward in their desire to see the condition of the two combatants. Both were terribly distressed, although Paddock looked in slightly better form than his foe. Paulson, well-primed with brandy was resolved to make one last determined bid for victory. Steadying himself for a moment he dashed forward as fast as his shaky legs would allow, boring down on Paddock, and swinging wildly with both hands. The Redditch fighter hardly knew what to make of Harry's sudden resurrection and, fearing he may yet have a dangerous punch left in him, retreated so quickly he crossed his knees and went down on his nether end. The squelch as he landed was audible all round the ring, and shouts of derisive laughter greeted his ludicrous collapse.

Paddock sat where he had fallen, gazing around with a comical expression of astonishment and bewilderment on his face. Deprived of his knock-out blow, Harry stood over his aggressor his legs planted wide apart and looking as if he could have dearly loved to hit him where he sat.

Indeed, he probably would, had not Jerry Noon yelled, 'Harry, Harry, for God's sake mind what you're about!'

Chief Constable Wragg, and Jedediah Strutt the magistrate, are attacked by the mob
at Paulson v Paddock's second battle.

A feeble, foolish smile crossed his battered features. Lowering his
arms, he turned around, gave a lurch and fell full length beside his antagonist. He was carried back to his corner amidst the deafening
shouts of his supporters, who still believed he would pull the fight out
of the fire. But Jerry Noon knew better. This had been the last flicker
of the candle; Harry's strength had gone and he had shot his bolt.

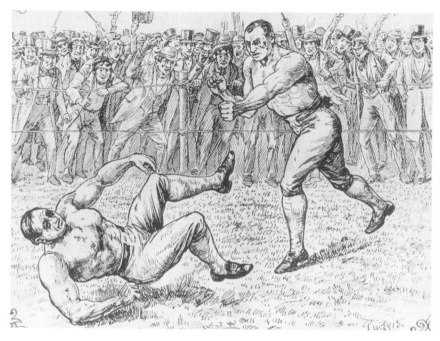

Tom Paddock floors Harry Paulson.

However, Harry Paulson stood up for another dozen rounds, despite the urgent remonstrances of his seconds who told him his position was hopeless. At the close of the 102nd round, Jerry Noon threw up the sponge on humanitarian grounds and refused to allow Harry to continue fighting.

Paulson's backers strongly condemned Noon for his actions, declaring he had no right to give in for his principal when the latter was willing and anxious to continue the battle. They insisted Harry was still a potential danger to Paddock and might have beaten him at any moment. But the Fancy disagreed with their assertions and commended Jerry for his conduct.

'Everyone,' they said, 'could see Paddock had his opponent at his mercy, and could have done with him as he pleased.'

So ended their last gallant battle. The rubber had been played out; Paddock had scored two games to his adversary's one, proving beyond all doubt that he was the better man.

Almost two years had passed since this last eventful conflict and when Tom Sayers' backers learned that he intended to fight Harry Paulson, they hesitated once more. They were well aware of Paulson's tremendous fighting capabilities and considered it a wild and rash decision on Tom's part to match himself against someone so much heavier, without seeking their consent or approval. Most showed their reluctance to back him while others pulled out completely, thinking the whole idea preposterous. But despite all their objections and threats of desertion, Tom was even more determined to proceed with his plans, emphatic in his belief that he could win.

In his quest for sponsorship, he was horrified to find just how few of his so-called friends had remained loyal. The burning question now facing him was who, among his tiny band of faithful sympathizers could he turn to for help and advice? His old friend Alec Keene had been recalled to his regiment and was now serving in the Crimea, but fortunately he was still blessed with having his one constant companion, the ex-pugilist and horse slaughterer Jack Atcheler who, years before had employed him in his pet-food industry. Jack Atcheler, known throughout London as Knacker Jack, but whose real name was Henry Mansfield, promised Tom full financial backing for sparring partners and training expenses. He never forgot this charitable act and when Jack died, to record his gratitude for his innumerable acts of generosity and kindness, Tom dedicated his memoirs to, "His most esteemed friend and early patron, Jack Atcheler, – By his most grateful servant, Tom Sayers, Champion of England."

With virtually no one else remaining, Tom decided to seek the advice of Nat Langham. "Ould" Nat pondered over Tom's dilemma, and thought he might be in the position to solve all his troubles if he exerted his unique ability in influencing the sporting nobility to contribute towards the stakes. He called upon Sir Edward Kent, one of the staunchest of the Corinthian sportsmen, and told him how Sayers had been deserted by his backers. Sir Edward listened sympathetically to Nat's story and, for a few moments, sat silently contemplating how he could help.

Gazing intently at Nat, he remarked, 'I think it's a great pity that such a plucky effort on the part of Sayers should be thwarted, especially when he intends to take on such a large and accomplished adversary as Harry Paulson. Therefore, I will give the matter my most urgent consideration and will inform you of my decision shortly.'

Sir Edward Kent then sent invitations to all his wealthy sporting colleagues, requesting them to attend a special counsel meeting at Limmer's Hotel to discuss the proposed fight between Sayers and Paulson.

Within days, Nat was summoned to Limmer's where Sir Edward waited to inform him of the committee's decision. While Nat was at the conference, Tom spent his time at the Cambrian Stores anxiously awaiting his return.

At last, Nat burst through the door, brandishing in his hand a cheque for £50 and saying, 'The good sport that Sir Edward is, he wouldn't allow the fight to fall through for that amount.'

At the meeting to ratify the articles it was decreed that the engagement would take place on January 28, 1856 at Appledore in Kent. A strict security clampdown was immediately imposed; nothing was mentioned in any fixture lists and only a privileged few among the Fancy were informed of the arrangements.

During the weeks that followed, numerous applications were received from dedicated supporters requesting information on the venue, but the destination remained a closely guarded secret until the train left London Bridge Station on the morning of the fight. The only scrap of information released throughout the rigorous security blackout was that the contest would be held within a seventy mile radius of London.

Tom returned to London on Monday January 27th, the day before the engagement and went to stay with Nat Langham. News of his arrival, and that he was serving drinks behind the bar of the Cambrian Stores, quickly spread to the other sporting houses and within an hour he was besieged by a large number of his "upper-crust" supporters, all eager to catch a glimpse of him and judge his condition. But to their consternation, they found him a little too fleshy and almost half a stone above his usual weight. Tom was now forced to disclose that he had only received three weeks training for, prior to that, he had been locked up in a Suffolk jail for the part he played in seconding Bill Hayes in his fight with Jemmy Massey.

While Tom had been languishing in prison, Harry Paulson had undergone a strict and intensive training programme under the guidance of Jem Burn and Bendigo. Harry was now in excellent health and in splendid shape, with every muscle in his powerful frame beautifully developed. Bendigo, who knew of Tom's imprisonment and of his lack of training, was confident he stood little chance of success against a superbly fit Paulson and he had backed his fellow townsman for a considerable fortune. Jem Burn was equally certain Sayers could ill afford to give away so much weight, and he too had induced many of his sporting colleagues to back Paulson with everything they possessed. Consequently there was an enormous amount of money riding on the fight, both in London and the provinces.

A few days before the contest, Harry Paulson and Bendigo arrived in London and took up lodgings at Jem Burn's The Rising Sun in Air Street, Piccadilly. At The Rising Sun on Monday January 27th, preparations had been under way since early morning for a big eve-of-battle party in honour of Harry Paulson. The festivities continued throughout the day and when Harry made his appearance later that evening, he was instantly greeted by a host of cheering friends and supporters who subjected him to innumerable toasts and good wishes for the morrow. He thanked them warmly for their hospitality and friendship but, thinking ahead to the big day before him, retired to bed early and left everyone to enjoy the rest of the celebrations. The eccentric Bendigo kept the whole company in perpetual laughter until midnight, when someone reminded him that he too had work to do that same morning.

Whereupon he immediately wished everyone, 'a very good morning' and, along with Jem Burn, retired to bed for a few hours' rest.

By five o'clock in the morning, when the first of London's sportsmen were astir, they discovered that during the night a very severe frost had set in and the temperature had fallen to minus 5 degrees centigrade. The thin film of ice covering the cobblestones now created havoc for many travellers, who found it extremely difficult to hire a cab. The shortage of transport had been caused by the drivers of the vehicles waiting impatiently at their stables while the farriers roughened the horses shoes to alleviate slipping on the icy roads. In consequence many travellers missed the train which left London at 8 o'clock sharp.

In all probability, Tom would also have been left behind, had it not been for the opportune arrival at his house of a private coach belonging to an old friend. He cut it so fine that when he arrived at the station he found the gates were about to close. Brushing aside the ticket collector, he sprinted down the platform and jumped aboard the train as it was pulling out of the station. Only now, when they were safely on their way, was it revealed that their destination was Appledore Station, a mile from the small village situated midway between Rye in Sussex, and Ashford in Kent.

The journey of some sixty-four miles was completed by eleven o'clock, and within half an hour the ring stood ready and waiting. For the convenience of those who could afford the price of an inner circle seat, Tom Callas had come provided with an abundance of basketwork stools, but with so many people left behind in London, most were superfluous to spectators' needs.

With such a relatively small attendance, there remained a remarkably passive air as Harry Paulson entered the arena, accompanied by his two seconds, Bendigo and Bob Fuller. Close behind the trio came Tom Sayers, assisted by Nat Langham and Jemmy Massey. In the penetrating cold of the Romney Marsh, and surrounded by shivering spectators, the two contestants stripped to the waist and shook hands across the scratch.

On the umpire's call of "Time!" Paulson threw himself into the old-fashioned attitude adopted by Tom Cribb, both hands held high and both feet planted firmly on the ground. In contrast to Paulson, Tom assumed his usual stance, resting lightly on his left foot, right arm laid across his chest and the left well extended. He sparred a little until Harry charged in with a left and right to his head. A sharp rally brought them to close quarters and as Tom delivered a weighty punch on Harry's nose, both went down together with Paulson underneath.

'First blood to Sayers' was registered in the 4th round, when he caught Harry on the right eye and ear and produced a faint smear of blood.

On coming up for the 10th, Tom displayed the visible signs of Harry's repeated visits to his nose and with a profusion of deep red knuckle marks on his ribs. He feinted for an opening before letting go with a left, but Harry parried the punch and returned once more on the sore ribs. Tom cross-countered with exceptional speed, and sent Harry to grass with a sharp left hook to the temple.

'First knock-down to Sayers!' came the cries of the elated spectators as Harry was helped back to his corner.

Bendigo and Bob Fuller worked frantically to revive him during the thirty second interval, sponging him down and pouring ice-cold water over his head and body. But when he came to the scratch for round 11, his eyes were glazed and he was still dazed from the last tremendous blow. Tom danced nimbly around him, penetrated his guard and delivered a cracking punch over the right eye before Harry had a chance to return the compliment. When they finally came to a close, Tom knocked him down with a terrific right to the jaw. He received a rousing chorus of cheers from his own supporters, but only some black looks from the Nottingham contingent.

Paulson sent Sayers down in the 16th with a stupendous blow to the mouth, and when he came up for round 17, blood was still pouring from his stricken nose and lips. Although a lot of energetic infighting ensued, little material damage was done and Tom took the opportunity to slip down on the muddy turf.

By the 20th, Tom's left eye was showing signs of closing and, in the next round, Paulson concentrated all his efforts into closing it completely.

The already soggy ground had become a veritable quagmire by the end of the 38th and both slipped to their knees opposite each other, the spikes in their boots ineffectual in the soft mud.

A dreadful right from Paulson closed Tom's left eye in the 41st, and in the next half dozen rounds he slipped down repeatedly to avoid the heavy punishment. But his constant resort to the detested dropping method induced incessant sighs, groans, and cries of foul from the

Nottingham supporters. At one point, when he was exceptionally weak, he slipped down rather questionably.

By the 50th round, and evidently suffering from the terrible blows to his ribs, Tom could only raise his left arm with a strenuous effort. Paulson went in again, delivered another rib-bending punch and Sayers went down again.

In round 52 Harry Paulson received loud cheers and applause for a very sporting gesture. Having brought Tom down, he slipped in the mud and overbalanced. With the utmost care, he avoided dropping on Sayers by placing a knee on either side of his body. This was not the only occasion he had exercised caution during the fight and he well deserved the highest accolades for his careful actions.

After some rapid exchanges in the 73rd, the tide suddenly turned in Tom's favour when he landed with both fists on Harry's mouth and left cheek. Paulson retaliated on the nose, but in the close for the fall Tom hit him again on the mouth and sent him sprawling in the mire. A new vitality now surged through Tom and it became noticeable by the 75th round that Paulson's head was beginning to swell ominously. Remembering the lessons he had learned at the hands of Nat Langham, Tom now concentrated his attacks solely on Harry's eyes. One had already closed and the Nottingham fans were looking serious. Paulson was gradually going blind, while Sayers appeared no weaker than an hour ago, added to which he still had one undamaged eye.

When they came up for the 83rd both were looking decidedly battle-worn and weary. Harry's left eye was fast following his right and it was becoming increasingly obvious that if Sayers could only keep his distance the result would be a foregone conclusion.

Another ding-dong slogging match astonished everyone in the 85th round. Sayers eventually went down, with Paulson on his knees beside him.

At the call of time for the 93rd round, nearly two and a half hours had elapsed. Tom walked slowly to the scratch, his fatigue obvious. Still forcing the fighting, Harry landed again on Tom's sore ribs and once more he went down.

After some slight exchanges in the 99th, Paulson landed a crushing right and knocked Sayers flat. The Paulsonians waited anxiously for the call of time, debating on whether or not he would stand but, to their profound surprise, he came up as strong as ever for the 100th. He skipped lightly around his antagonist, delivered two quick jabs to the nose and left eye and danced away without a blow from Paulson. Tom followed up his advantage with a punch to the throat, but while getting away from the return, slipped and fell in the mud.

Repeated cries of 'Foul!' echoed from the Nottingham ranks in rounds 102 and 103. In the latter, Sayers saw Paulson lumbering towards him, but as he stepped back his legs slowly slipped in the mud. Unable to maintain a defensive attitude, or extricate himself from his ridiculous position, he slid slowly down in the sludge as a shriek of 'Foul' was raised by the Nottingham fans.

The referee, Ned Smith, declared he had been unable to see the incident due to Paulson's supporters crowding forward. After holding a consultation with the umpires, he pronounced the objection overruled on the grounds that his collapse was unpremeditated and purely accidental. However, it was some considerable time before the uproar subsided and order was restored. The prolonged delay provided a welcome respite for Tom, but it had the opposite effect on Paulson, whose remaining eye had almost closed during the course of the dispute.

At the start of the 106th round, Paulson dashed in for one last-ditch effort. Heavy blows were exchanged with Sayers landing again on the left eye, and Harry once more on the ribs. Squinting through the slit of his swollen eye, the Nottingham fighter gave Tom a resounding crack on the left ear, the force of which toppled him over.

Sayers came up slowly for the 107th, weak on his legs and blood oozing from his ear. Another rally followed and another blow from Harry sent him down again.

Round 108. Paulson's brutalized face presented a sinister spectacle, fearfully swollen and scarcely a glimmer to be seen from his bloated left eye. Again Harry bored in, forced Sayers backwards and delivered another crushing body blow on his sore ribs. Forcibly sucking in a supply of air, Tom retaliated with a smashing left to the jaw and knocked Paulson completely off his feet. His seconds rushed into the ring, picked him up and, with an arm around each of their shoulders, half-dragged him back to his corner.

The last blow had marked the beginning of the end for Harry, and at the call of time he meandered slowly to the scratch, still dazed and in a semi-trance. He attempted a swinging right but it missed its mark completely and, as he lumbered forward, Tom delivered the *coup-de-grace* with a stupendous right to the jaw, bowling him over. Harry was carried to his corner where he was tenderly treated by his seconds, but when time was called for the 110th round he was unable to rise to his feet. Still semi-conscious from the last shattering punch, it took several minutes for him to recover sufficiently to realize that it was all over. He expressed his bitter disappointment at the unsatisfactory and unexpected termination of the battle, but with the terrible injuries he had sustained to his eyes it is extremely doubtful he could have lasted much longer.

Tom complained of the brutal treatment he had received about his body and the repeated visits to the side of his head, but the fact of having emerged the winner went a long way towards relieving his physical suffering. He climbed rather stiffly through the ropes and walked unaided to The Railway Hotel, the little public house adjoining the field of battle. Close on his heels came an enthusiastic and loudly cheering party of friends and supporters, triumphant in his success.

Harry Paulson, horribly disfigured, both eyes completely closed and still weak on his legs, was carried by his loyal followers to the same public house where, after taking a short rest and some light refreshment, he soon recovered and became his old jovial self once again.

In his long and arduous battle Tom had proved himself capable of holding his own against a twelve stone man, a thing never before attempted in the annals of the prize ring. But perhaps of more importance than the prestige and profit of his victory over Paulson was the unique alliance which now developed between himself and John Gideon, one of Paulson's principle backers. This singular friendship was destined to have far-reaching consequences, for not only did it gain him a lifelong friend and philosopher, it also forged the links in the chain which subsequently secured the eminent position he held as champion of England.

John Gideon, businessman, sportsman, and entrepreneur, was born on June 10, 1821. His interest in the prize ring originated at the age of nineteen, when he witnessed his first fight at Grays in Essex. In 1854 he joined the exclusive Victoria Club, then situated in Victoria Street, Ludgate Hill and, at the instigation of Lord Drumlanrig, was made a member of Tattersall's on the Saturday before Blink Bonny won the Derby in 1857. But of all his commercial enterprises and designations, his proudest claim of all was his partnership with Tom Sayers and his rise to fame.

"My first real days of friendship with Sayers began in a curious way," he once wrote. "He was matched to fight Harry Paulson of Nottingham. Paulson had previously beaten Tom Paddock and others. Bendigo thought this a certainty for Paulson and backed him for all he could raise, seconded him, and lost his money. I also thought it a real good thing for Paulson, who was favourite at 7 to 4 on with very few takers. These odds I laid and lost. I also knew from good authority that Sayers was not well and was unfit to meet Paulson in a twenty-four foot ring, and he never entered one in worse condition, having had but three weeks training, which were too merrily passed at the quarters of Tom Oliver, at Prestbury near Cheltenham, who was then training horses for Mr Cartwright. Also I knew that on the Sunday night before the fight, 'Tom was dead pals with the distiller', and on the Monday night he was serving behind the bar at Nat Langham's, where he hailed from. His reason for not going to bed was that he was waiting for his fighting boots to arrive, and wait he did, for they were not delivered until a quarter to twelve. He had then to turn in, and turn out at half past five, have his cold bath and his breakfast and catch the train at London Bridge for Appledore, Kent. Knowing these things, I excused myself for losing as it did me, or rather my purse, no harm in the future, for I stopped Tom after the fight from going to Australia and matched him against Aaron Jones, so that we were inseparable friends until the day of his death.''

Gideon went on to say: "It may be remembered that at 'Ould Nat's' there was held a weekly winter gathering of the Rum-Pum-Pas, and among its members was a Mr Henry Cuthbertson, who was then studying for the medical profession and working at Charing Cross Hospital. On the night before Tom went into the ring to meet Paulson, the young surgeon impressed Sayers with the never-used, valuable notion of keeping his eyes shut from the instant a round was finished until time was called to begin the next. The idea tickled Tom's fancy and he tried it the following day and, having won, never forgot it in all his pugilistic engagements afterwards. I have always found that prize fighters when in action will not be attended to with their eyes closed. They wish to look about them to see what is going on. That's all pride and flashness, as they labour under the delusion that their backers and friends at the ringside will think they are getting beaten if they don't wink and 'office' them at every opportunity.

"In all my knowledge and experience in prize ring matters, I never saw the equal of 'The Bonny Boy from Pimlico, Brighton' and it would have been difficult to have found a cleaner and more honest bill of health than that shown in the fighting life of the game, Tom Sayers."

The conquest of Harry Paulson was unquestionably the turning point in Tom's career. Now, firmly established as a man with whom no man under twelve stone must meddle, from this period onward his name is involved with every question of the belt and the championship.

# 11

## A NEW BELT

In 1855 a number of leading patrons of the ring put forward a proposition to raise, by subscription, enough money to purchase a belt of greater intrinsic value than anything presented before, including the missing belt which had "gone astray" during the many and frequent squabbles between Ben Caunt, Bendigo and the Tipton Slasher.

Immediately it was reported that a fund had been launched, money began pouring in and the target of £100 was reached within a matter of weeks. A committee was then inaugurated to supervise the financial management of the trust and formulate the terms and regulations governing the acquisition of the trophy. Their first assignment was to place an order with Mr Hancock, the silversmith of New Bond Street, to design and manufacture a new belt worked in frosted silver.

There then followed a series of discussions which subsequently culminated in the following measures:

1. That the belt should not be handed over to any person claiming the championship until he had proved his right to it by a fight.

2. That any pugilist having held it against all comers for three years without a defeat, should become its absolute possessor.

3. That the holder should be bound to meet every challenger, of every weight, who should challenge him for the sum of £200 a side.

4. That at the final deposit for every match within the three years, the belt should be delivered up to the committee until after the battle.

5. That on the belt being given up to the winner of any championship fight, he should deposit such security as should be deemed necessary in the hands of the committee, to ensure the above regulations being carried out.

No sooner did it become known that the belt was ready for contention than there came a general stirring up of the big men of boxing.

The Tipton Slasher, the current reigning champion roused himself; Harry Broome shook himself together; Tom Paddock was torn between hope and fear of disappointment and Aaron Jones who, although having recently fought and lost two tremendous battles with Tom Paddock, sat up and took notice, issuing a defiant sort of grunt. The only man who declined to show any interest at all was Harry Orme, who was quite content to rest upon his well-earned reputation.

Initially no one appeared sufficiently venturous to tackle the Tipton Slasher. Then suddenly, not one, but each and every one of the heavyweight aspirants to the belt sent him a challenge. The first to reach him was from Aaron Jones and immediately arrangements went ahead for the ratification of the articles.

The challenges from Broome and Paddock arrived soon afterwards, but the Slasher informed them that they must wait until the issue between Jones and himself had been resolved. Broome and Paddock were too impatient to await the result of this event and they made a match between themselves to decide which of them should take on the mighty Tipton Slasher. However, while they were in training, news reached them that Aaron Jones had met with an accident and was compelled to forfeit to the Slasher, so there now appeared to be a clear course for the winner of their contest. In their battle, in spite of all the will and courage Broome displayed, his age was against him and his strength failed at the crucial moment.

The way was now open for Paddock to meet his old adversary, but when £80 of the deposits had been staked Paddock's renowned foul temper got the better of him and, in a fit of pique, he insulted his friends and backers. To demonstrate their contempt for his deplorable actions, they instantly withdrew their support and cash. Unable to raise the entire stakes by himself, Paddock was now compelled to forfeit the match. This came not only as a bitter disappointment to himself, but also added to the frustration of the Tipton Slasher whose efforts to gain the coveted belt had foundered once again.

William Perry, the Tipton Slasher, arrived in London to receive his forfeit from Tom Paddock and to attend a "champion's dinner" held in his honour at the Cole Hole Tavern in the Strand. During the course of the evening, there came a surprise announcement that Aaron Jones had recovered from his accident and a match was now pending between him and Tom Sayers. Because the acquisition of the belt could only be obtained by a fight, Perry had no other recourse but to await the result of the contest between Jones and Sayers and then challenge the winner.

There had been overwhelming surprise at the presumption of Sayers to meet Harry Paulson, but this time there were many who thought him far too over-ambitious in taking on the redoubtable Aaron Jones. However, there were those who had seen him dispose of the mighty Paulson and thought it a strong possibility he could also succeed against Jones. But, whatever the chances, they had to be carefully studied and analysed before setting any odds. Paulson was seven years Sayers senior; Jones was five years his junior. There was also a great disparity in their heights and weights. Jones was three inches taller than Sayers and twenty-three pounds heavier with the reputation of being a punishing hitter, a scientific boxer and, what was more, one who aspired to the championship.

A Shropshire lad by birth, Aaron had just turned eighteen when he attracted the attention of some sporting military officers at Shrewsbury. Confident he had a promising future in the ring, they sent him to Jem Burn to acquire some professional coaching.

In due course, his military patrons received such glowing reports of his progress that they requested Burn to find him an opponent. His debut was against Harry Orme on December 18, 1849. Although Aaron was a complete novice to the ring, it took the more experienced Orme 2 hours and 45 minutes of tough and arduous fighting to emerge victorious.

After conquering the veteran Bob Wade in 1850, Aaron remained without a match until 1852 when, with the avowed intention of redeeming his lost laurels, he came back for a second bout with Harry Orme. The police, however, were extremely officious on this occasion and they were constantly harried wherever they went. They fought a few rounds at Bourn Bridge near Cambridge and a few more at Newmarket, Orme getting the advantage at the former location and Jones at the latter. The referee then named a third venue but, before the ring could be erected, Jones declined to renew the contest and the stakes were awarded to Orme. No satisfactory explanation was ever given for Aaron's refusal. There were conflicting reports circulating at the time that he was scared to continue the engagement, but it was more probably due to a recurring congenital ailment than cowardice. His courage and tenacity were beyond reproach as he proved two years later when he challenged Tom Paddock.

Seldom before had a battle of such intensity been witnessed. Aaron suffered appalling punishment in a contest of 121 rounds, lasting 2 hours and 20 minutes. Although he was defeated, his backers were enraptured by his performance and had no hesitation in backing him for a second match with Paddock. This encounter, which took place at Mildenhall on June 26, 1855 was once again a battle of bravery and determination by both men. Jones was having the best of the conflict when he had the misfortune to break his collar bone. He was unable to strike an effective blow and Paddock pounded him unmercifully until he capitulated in the 61st round.

Jones was then matched with the Tipton Slasher but, due to his unfortunate accident, the contest did not materialize. In the interim, he arranged to meet Tom Sayers on January 9, 1857.

At this period there was a concerted persecution against the prize ring by the provincial magistrates and it was proving a very risky business indeed to attempt a match anywhere in England. The eastern counties had always been a favourite venue for the Fancy but, with the constant vigilance of the police in every region, it had become extremely dangerous for large parties of sportsmen to congregate at any railway station.

For several days before the event, John Gideon had supervised the distribution of handbills to all London's sporting houses, advertising that a special excursion would be leaving King's Cross Station at nine o'clock sharp on Tuesday the 9th of January.

Forewarned that the contest would be fought the following Tuesday, the police in the Home Counties now put all their forces on full alert. Realizing his mistake in disclosing the date of the engagement, Gideon did not dare risk a confrontation with the authorities. Mindful of the consequences, he now faced the dilemma of changing all the preparations to forestall any action by the police.

Early on the Tuesday morning, hundreds of people arrived at the station only to discover that they were the unwitting victims of a plot to deceive the police. It was perfectly true that there was an outgoing train at 9 o'clock, but it was never intended to take any passengers to the fight. There were turbulent and angry scenes when the crowd realized they had been used as decoys by the organizers, and throughout the remainder of the morning groups of disgruntled fight fans slowly dispersed from the station threatening all kinds of retribution to the people responsible for their deception.

The new starting point was Fenchurch Street Station where, at eight o'clock that morning, fewer than 130 people were gathered on the platform; the majority of these having been informed of the destination at a benefit match they had attended the previous evening. Therefore, the elite little company consisted mainly of patricians of the boxing world and a small band of pugilists engaged as ring constables.

The little party arrived at Tilbury at nine o'clock and boarded the steamer *Jupiter* chartered from Messrs Churchward of Lombard Street. Many travellers grumbled at the abnormally inflated price of a guinea for a return ticket but, due to the limited attendance, the organizers had reluctantly been forced to increase the fare, merely to break even.

There was a stiff north-easterly gale blowing when the steamer set

Handbills were hurriedly printed and circulated to every sporting pub in London.

sail for Canvey Island, then an isolated spot on the Essex marshes. As an added precaution, to throw the police or their informers off the scent, the Captain of the vessel was instructed to proceed directly to the mouth of the Thames and then double back to their intended destination.

Despite the biting wind and a deepening depression, everyone enjoyed the journey to the Nore Light, but when they reached the open water in this area the excessively choppy seas soon created an adverse effect on many passengers who, unaccustomed to aquatic excursions, began to feel sea-sick. To a great extent it proved fortuitous that the number of passengers was relatively small, for there were many and frequent calls to the stewards for swabs and buckets.

After tossing about on the waves for nearly an hour, to everyone's immeasurable relief, "About ship" was ordered and the vessel re-entered the estuary. Since their departure from Tilbury, the weather had rapidly deteriorated and the leaden-coloured sky, combined with the icy wind blowing off the river, brought with it flurries of driving sleet and snow, chilling everyone to the bone. The steamer slowly inched its way through the dark and murky waters until it came to rest close against a mudbank. Amidst the swirling snow and biting wind, the passengers disembarked into the black, ankle-deep mud of the river bed and began their journey across the mudflats. Many luckless individuals had the misfortune to slip and fall as they trudged grimly through the blizzard and the foul-smelling, treacherous slimy mud.

On reaching the shore, Tom Oliver and his two assistants, Callas and Pug, spent some considerable time in their search for a suitable piece of flat land, for the ground was essentially uneven and furrowed due to the recent heavy rains and the freezing depths of winter. Eventually a promising area was found quite near the shoreline and they hurriedly formed the rings.

Sayers and Jones had completed their preparations in the comparative warmth of the steamer and they hurried into the enclosure, wrapped in blankets as protection against the piercing cold. Both were loudly cheered, and both looked equally confident as they tied their colours to the stakes: a light grey and white for Sayers and a neat white and blue check for Jones.

Shedding their protective garments, they stood stripped to the waist, teeth chattering and shivering violently in the bitter easterly wind blowing off the sea. Tom was escorted to the scratch by Jemmy Massey and George Crocket, and Jones by Alec Keene and Mike Madden.

"Time!" was called at 1 o'clock and, as hands were clasped Tom watched his heaving opponent with an element of caution. Jones was also under no misapprehension that this would be an easy conquest.

Several minutes of weaving and feinting ensued until Jones lashed out with a quick left and right. As the blows passed harmlessly over Tom's shoulders, he tapped Aaron on the face but without any real force. Then Aaron stepped in, planted a left on Tom's right eye, delivered another blow with equal severity on the same spot and a mighty punch on the nose. Evidently shaken by this ferocious onslaught, Tom attempted to smile, but his face merely twisted into what was described as 'a sort of ghastly contortion.' Shortly after this assault, Jones inflicted a deep cut over Sayers' eye.

As he staggered back a few paces, the air was rent with exultant cries from Aaron's supporters of 'First blood to Jones!'

Undeterred, Tom came back with renewed determination until Aaron again reached the cut above his eye and drew more blood. Sayers returned the compliment with a straight punch to Aaron's nose and removed a fragment of skin. A brief period of energetic infighting followed until they locked into a wrestling close and both fell. The first round had lasted half an hour.

The fighting became much faster and much more aggressive in the next five rounds with Jones clearly in command. Hitting with deadly accuracy, he buffeted Tom unmercifully about the ring. Suddenly, due without doubt to the penetrating cold, Tom's face became distorted in pain as he was seized with violent cramp in his stomach and legs. Seeing his obvious distress, his seconds feared they may have to throw up the sponge, but he refused to quit and in the next half-dozen rounds silently suffered all the tremendous punishment Jones could administer. His forehead and mouth became swollen and lacerated and his left eye almost closed.

In the 22nd round, Aaron bestowed a resonant smack on Tom's forehead and knocked him off his feet.

A burst of exuberant cheering echoed from the Jones contingent, and cries of 'First knock-down to Jones!'

This pulverizing blow unsettled Sayers and allowed Aaron to inflict more terrible execution in the next few rounds. Battered, weak and tired, and bleeding profusely from his left eye and ear, Tom faced up to the unrepressed ferocity with his same stubborn resolution until Aaron floored him a second time with a vigorous punch on the nose.

In round 48, and after nearly two and a half hours, Tom suddenly snapped out of his lethargy and it became anyone's battle again. Jones continued to press home his attacks with his usual ruthlessness, but now Tom stood his ground in the encounters and closed Aaron's left eye.

Sayers had vastly improved by the 52nd round and was now exhibiting some of his accomplished skills, his clever foot-work repeatedly saving him from further punishment. He delivered several stunning punches to Aaron's face, and it now became the turn of Jones to show signs of weakening. Realizing he must soon finish the fight or lose it, Aaron closed Tom's left eye with two stinging punches.

During round 55, it began to look as if the end was in sight for Sayers. Out to finish it, Jones bored in but Tom met him with a straight punch on the cheekbone and Aaron collapsed in a heap. Everyone thought it was all over for Jones, but the skilful administrations of Alec Keene and Mike Madden enabled him to come to scratch at the call of "Time." As Aaron stood swaying in the centre of the ring, still obviously numbed, Tom dispensed another terrific blow to the same cheek and he dropped again. As he lay semi-conscious on the ground, his seconds climbed into the ring and carried him to his corner. They roughly shook him and slapped his face but he only showed the first signs of recovery when the smelling salts were waved beneath his nose.

Tom responded first to the call of time and dashed over to administer the *coup de grace* but, foolishly going into the attack with his guard down, he ran full-tilt into a swinging left from Aaron. The massive punch landed full on his nose and sent him reeling about the ring.

So the ding-dong battle continued until the 62nd round when both men, totally exhausted, stood quite still in the centre of the ring peering at each other through the slits of their swollen eyes, neither capable of striking an effective blow. Seeing the impasse, their seconds entered the ring, covered them with rugs and led them back to their corners.

At length the referee and umpires, believing they had been allowed adequate time to recover, called for them to return and finish the fight. Both went to the scratch as ordered, but as Sayers advanced Jones retired into his corner. Tom started to walk after him, but in obedience to the commands of his seconds, he did not follow for there was a reasonable chance that a random blow from Jones could finish him too.

With darkness fast approaching and the blizzard intensifying, the referee called once more for Jones to go to the scratch but again, the moment he saw Tom coming towards him, he walked back to his corner. The referee could see that Jones was reluctant to continue the struggle and that Tom was not sufficiently strong to subjugate Aaron, so he ordered them to shake hands and declared the match a draw.

It had been a particularly aggressive encounter lasting three hours. Tom's left eye was completely closed and Aaron's right eye was fast following his left but, because Jones had also sustained an injury to his right hand, the referee decided that a second meeting later in the week was entirely out of the question and another date would have to be agreed.

Everyone now hurried to regain the warmth and comfort of the steamer before the inky blackness of the January night descended upon the river. There were many amusing incidents and minor accidents on their return journey across the mudflats, but luckily, nothing of a serious nature to mar the pleasures of the day's sport.

After the fight *Bell's Life* was inundated with complaints from the irate travellers who had wasted their time and money by going to King's Cross Station. One party of unfortunate individuals stranded at King's Cross received some veiled hints of the actual destination. Determined to witness the fight at any cost they hurried down to the river and, at great expense, hired a boat to take them to Canvey Island. They arrived in the area late in the afternoon, in the teeth of a howling snowstorm. But in the hurry to put them ashore before darkness fell, they were landed on the wrong island. Before they discovered the mistake the boat had put to sea again and was well out of earshot. Marooned miles from the nearest civilization, cold, hungry and thirsty, they had to weather the night sleeping under a haystack, huddled together for warmth.

Many who attended the match that dreadful day, grumbled that they could never understand why so many prize fights took place on winter mornings such as these; surely the summer would be more agreeable to both the men and the spectators instead of the biting winds, rain and frost so common on a January morning.

Jones too, had a number of complaints and recriminations to make on the way the event was handled. He lodged a strong protest that had it not been for John Gideon, he would have won, despite the handicap of having sustained an injury to his right hand in the ninth round. The weather, he claimed, had also been against him, it having been the worst day for a fight in living memory. For three hours he and Sayers had faced each other through showers of frozen sleet and flakes of snow. Having lost the toss for choice of corners, he had been left in the unenviable position of facing the strong headwind blowing off the river. He admitted that the weather had also affected Sayers who, at one time, was seized with acute stomach cramp.

'Seeing him standing there, suffering intense pain and watching his teeth chattering with the cold, I thought is was all over but the shouting. But then I heard Jemmy Welsh calling for the brandy. John Gideon, who held the bottle, refused to allow Tom to drink it neat for fear it may go to his head and make him dizzy, insisting it should be administered in a cup of tea. The tea was prepared by Johnnie who had brought a kettle, some wood, turpentine and a tin fire-stand. Having made the drink, he diluted it with the brandy before crawling into Sayers' corner and making quite sure he drank it between rounds.'

Aaron then went on to relate how his backers had remonstrated with Gideon, vainly begging and imploring him for a hot drink and some brandy for Jones, but he refused to part with a drop, telling them, 'If Jones' seconds had failed to make similar provisions for their man, were they naive enough to expect the other side to help them in their own negligence?'

Moreover, to protect his investment, Gideon had hired the services of Harry Savage, the ring caterer Coobiddy, Tommy Tyler, Splawger Spriggins, Jerry Noon and Bendoff. This septet, all armed with hand coshes, were quite prepared to prevent by force anyone who attempted to touch the drink.

'When Tom had drunk as much tea as he required, Johnnie Gideon, for fear I should have any, ran to the sea wall and threw the kettle, teapot and fire-stand into the Thames. I shall never forgive Gideon for his unkindness to me that day. Naturally, Sayers gained renewed life and strength from the hot beverages, enabling him to prolong the fight until darkness fell.'

On hearing these allegations, Frank Dowling, the referee, admitted he had not witnessed the incident, saying, 'Due to the inclement weather that day, for most of the time I could not even see across to the other side of the ring and, as darkness was rapidly approaching, this had been the principle reason which forced an end to the hostilities and proclaim the contest a draw.'

At the next meeting to decide the venue, Tom and his backers offered to add another £100 to the stakes if Jones would agree to a rematch within six or eight weeks. Aaron's backers declined to increase the existing stakes and remained inflexible in their attitude. They insisted that due to the extensive injuries he had sustained to his right hand, he should be permitted at least another two months in which to recuperate. Aaron interjected and proposed that if he could abstain from fighting for these two months, he would then reconsider Tom's offer to double the stakes. But the Sayers' party were uncompromising and rejected all the proposals, claiming they were totally unacceptable to them and that the final decision should be left to Frank Dowling. After giving the matter his due consideration, Frank Dowling directed that they split the difference and fight in a month. The date for the engagement was then set for Tuesday February 10, with stakes of £200 a side.

Quick to capitalize on all the publicity, Tom announced that before he commenced training, he would take his benefit match at the Chandos Street Rooms on Monday January 19.

The day after the benefit and with a tidy sum in his pocket, he returned along with Jemmy Massey to his favourite training quarters in Newmarket.

Because Jones had promised to attend the match of Bill Cleghorn, one of his training companions, he delayed his departure until Wednesday January 21, when he left London for a secret rendezvous, somewhere in the neighbourhood of Brighton. He was now under the supervision of Charley Jenkinson, the trainer who had coached Sayers in his last fight with Aaron. Since then, due to some underlying friction between himself and Sayers, he had switched his allegiance to Jones. This move was heralded as a great coup for Aaron, for Charley would now be in the position to furnish some invaluable tips on how to circumvent Tom's success.

Soon after Jones and Sayers had departed from London, a backer of Jones put forward a proposition that if Sayers was agreeable, he was prepared to add a further £100 to the stakes, to be regarded as a bet. This offer was eagerly snapped up by Tom's backers and as soon as the general public became aware of the news, Sayers immediately became the favourite in the betting.

As the day of the engagement drew near, so the interest intensified. In the absence of racing and steeplechasing that winter, the followers of

Tom delivers his notorious "auctioneer" in his second battle with Aaron Jones.

As the winter blizzard swept across the marshes, John Gideon kept Tom supplied
with cups of hot tea, laced with brandy.

the turf now turned their attentions to the ring and the betting among
the racing fraternity ran very high.

   Tom and Aaron returned from their training the day before the
contest. Jones went to stay with Jem Burn at The Rising Sun and Tom
went directly to Dan Dismore's to settle a bet on his fighting weight.
After drawing the beam at 10 stone 9¾ pounds, he joined Nat
Langham at the Cambrian Stores. Later that evening Tom and Aaron

attended the joint benefit of Bob Travers and Bill Cleghorn. Immediately they entered the auditorium, they received a rapturous welcome and a standing ovation from the enthusiastic audience.

During their weeks in training many unsuccessful attempts had been made to find a secluded but easily accessible location for their next engagement. But time had run out and once again it became necessary for another journey down the Thames. As usual on these occasions, an early start was imperative and at the London terminus that morning there was an exceptionally large turnout of sportsmen of all classes. Many of the older campaigners claimed it was a wondrous sight to behold, reviving for them nostalgic memories of olden times and proving that for over a century, the sport of boxing remained predominant in the hearts of all red-blooded Englishmen.

On their arrival at Tilbury, they found a steamer berthed at the pier ready to take them to their destination. This time, however, to everyone's profound joy, they discovered the fare had been reduced to ten shillings a head for a return ticket. The vessel set sail against the flood tide a few minutes before 10 o'clock but, as usual on any water-bourne excursions, following in their wake were a couple of pirate craft loaded to the gunwales with noisy supporters.

The steamer returned to the same location off Canvey Island and dropped anchor close to the shore. Gangplanks were run out and disembarkation began. Everyone waded through the shallow water and mud to the same field close by the river bank. Regrettably at this point, unknown to anyone among the company, the owner of the land was a Justice of the Peace who chanced to be out coursing on his estate that morning.

When he saw the hundreds of people struggling through the mud and water and assembling on his property, he galloped across to enquire what was happening. Questioning the organizers, he was astounded to learn that they intended staging a prize fight in his field and even more surprised to hear of the previous contest held there on that bitterly cold day in January.

Fortunately for everyone concerned, he possessed a lively sense of humour and saw the lighter side of the situation. He was extremely amiable about the whole affair and listened sympathetically to their persuasive arguments, but he pointed out that as one of Her Majesty's magistrates he could not, and would not, permit an infringement of the Queen's Peace, particularly when it was their intention to hold it on his estate. He courteously informed them that if they all moved on, and out of his jurisdiction as quickly as possible, they would have his assurance that no further action would be taken and no one would bother them further.

It had all been intensely annoying, but everyone accepted his instructions in good humour as once again they all trudged back through the treacherous mud and water to re-embark aboard the steamer.

Another short journey brought them to a promising piece of open park-land, close to where the Tipton Slasher fought Charles Freeman the American Giant back in 1842, and disembarkation began again under the same tortuous conditions. This time everything went according to plan, and by half past one the ring had been pitched and the preliminaries completed. The ring-keepers called for everyone to clear the ring, and both men announced their arrival by throwing their beaverskin hats high into the sky.

Tom was escorted by Jemmy Massey and Bill Hayes, with Jemmy Welsh deputizing as bottle-holder and advisor in his corner, whilst Aaron received the assistance of Jack Hicks and Alec Keene, with Jack Macdonald presiding over the resoratives. The inner-ring company, whose investments to the Pugilistic Benevolent Associated amounted to £18, took their seats and a hush settled over the crowd of an estimated 1,000 spectators.

This time each knew the capabilities of his opponent, and when time was called at two o'clock Tom made it crystal clear he intended to pursue different tactics to those he had adopted in their previous meeting. He dodged about for a few seconds and with great rapidity shot out a left and a right. Jones successfully blocked both punches but fell in getting away. Aaron's friends and backers could not conceal their surprise that he had allowed Sayers to take the lead despite the change in tactics, but at this early stage in the conflict they were not unduly worried and were confident his performance would improve in the second round.

Full of confidence, Tom came up, a beaming smile illuminating his face. He feinted with his left and then tried his favourite double. The first hit was stopped but the second caught Aaron on the chin. Twice in quick succession Tom repeated the punches and each time escaped without a return blow. The phenomenal speed of these punches took Aaron completely off guard and for a moment or two he stood gazing around in utter bewilderment. They went to close quarters and some intense and rapid infighting ensued, mainly in favour of Sayers, who landed a left on Aaron's nose and drew "First blood". Jones then delivered a slight hit on Tom's head and both fell.

Quick to the call of time, Tom went straight in with his left. Jones countered heavily and both acquired a blow on the forehead. Heavy exchanges followed with Tom renewing the flow of blood from Aaron's nose. After a few dodges, Tom again advanced, delivered a thumping blow to Aaron's solar plexus and followed it through with a stinging smack between the eyes before dancing away, chuckling with laughter.

During the next period of wild fighting, Tom inflicted a cut on Aaron's left eye and split his nostril open. Sayers was now hitting as he pleased, his magnificent footwork the admiration of friend and foe alike. Dumbfounded by the sheer speed and ferocity of his onslaughts, Aaron's face wore a worried frown as again Tom stole in, slipped under his guard, banged his fist on the smitten eye and drew more blood. In the heavy rally which ended the round, Jones sustained a sharp left as he slipped down. Aaron's backers were bitterly disappointed with his performance; his punches lacked any real decisive power, and he appeared to have lost all sense of judgement.

At the umpire's cry of "Time!" Tom was on his feet in an instant and walked smartly to the scratch for round 4. Smiling broadly at Jones, who bore a contusion over his left eye, a sorely swollen nose and his morale at a low ebb, Tom planted his double yet again; the left on Aaron's right eye, and the famous auctioneer on the left side of the jaw, laying Jones horizontal on the turf.

'First knock-down to Sayers!' evoked a roar of frenzied cheering from his delighted supporters who threw their hats high into the air, shook hands with their nearest neighbour, and slapped each other on the back in their excitement.

As Aaron sat up on the grass, eyes glazed and wondering what had hit him, his seconds entered the ring and carried him to his corner. Although they worked furiously during the 30-second interval, he remained semi-conscious for most of the time and only fully regained his senses at the call of time. The atmosphere was electric. Odds of 2 and 3 to 1 were freely offered on Sayers but found few takers for most people were confident he would finish the contest in the next round. In his hurry to complete his handiwork and quash Aaron he went straight in with a left and a right, but lacking precision, all he could muster was a meek slap on the face which would not have hurt a child. To the utter frustration of his supporters, at the very moment he needed the power to deliver the last crushing blow, all his calculated coolness and sense of judgement deserted him and at the close for the throw, both went down together.

Jones' backers gave a long sigh of relief; Sayers, it seemed, had outworn his strength and had given Aaron the breathing space he so badly needed. John Gideon was worried that Tom was fighting too fast, and by not pacing himself would quickly tire. He cautioned him in his corner and warned him of the consequences, but Tom simply shrugged his shoulders and told him not to worry; he knew what he was doing and what suited him best.

Revived by the short respite Aaron took the initiative in the next
five rounds, and Tom's face was flushed a deep crimson when he came
to scratch for round 10. Jones rattled into a clinch and some rapid infighting developed, followed by a long struggle for the fall. During the
scuffle Tom brought one foot into contact with Aaron's legs as he fell
on him.

A cry of 'Foul!' was echoed by Jones' seconds, but the referee disallowed the objection as purely accidental.

The conflict continued but with rounds of short duration. In the
20th, Aaron floored Tom with a tremendous right to the jaw. This
triumph raised a storm of cheering from his host of followers who
were confident he now held the whiphand and was back on the road to
victory. Amidst all the clamour, the Sayers' backers were verging on a
state of near hysteria. They had warned Tom he was playing a
dangerous game, and he was now suffering the consequences. He
listened attentively as they voiced their protests, but still persisted in
his argument that he knew what suited him best.

Elated by his knock-down, Jones rushed in to finish the fight but,
summoning up some hidden resources of power, Tom met him with a
straight right to the left cheek and Aaron dropped to the grass. His
collapse was instantly greeted with a chorus of cheering and a waving
of top hats from the Sayers' supporters who, only a couple of minutes
before, had thought him a beaten man.

Jones came to the scratch with a look of grim determination on his
face. He launched himself at Sayers, and in the subsequent scramble
bull-dozed Tom to the ground – the match was alive again.

At the end of the 37th round, and after 65 minutes of tough and
aggressive fighting, Aaron's eyes were showing signs of closing. His
punches too were lacking their former power and having little effect
on Tom, whose most formidable enemy at this moment was his own
fatigue.

The steady concentration of Tom's withering attacks to Aaron's eyes,
nose and body between rounds 62 and 82 gave renewed optimism to
his backers, and as they came up for the 83rd round Tom saw that the
time had arrived to put an end to Aaron's misery. He went in, planted
a left and a right on the right eye (the left had long since closed) and
Jones fell.

Aaron made one last despairing bid in the 85th and last round.
Tom blocked the punch and, as Jones twisted slightly, he caught him
with a terrific hook on the right eye. It was the finishing touch;
Aaron's head rolled forward on his neck like that of a rag doll and,
with his one remaining eye closed for good, he lay like a log where he
had fallen.

Realizing it was pointless to continue, Alec Keene threw up the sponge and Tom Sayers was hailed the victor in a gallant battle lasting exactly two hours. Amidst the prolonged cheering, Tom went across to shake hands with his brave antagonist before leaving the ring and returning to the steamer. He was followed a little later by Aaron, who had remained behind for medical treatment to his stricken eyes. Although severely mauled, he did not feel the pain so acutely as he did his injured pride and the bitter resentment of having been beaten by one so much smaller and lighter than himself.

Soon after Tom had dressed, he went round among the passengers making a collection for Jones and, by the time they returned to London, he had raised the sum of eight pounds.

In the opinion of many this had been Tom's most skilful and creditable feat; nevertheless it had taken him a total of 5 hours and 147 rounds to beat Aaron, and that was twice as long as any other man had ever stood up to him before. Without a doubt the two hardest nuts Tom ever had to crack were Harry Paulson and Aaron Jones, but of the two, the latter was incomparably the finer fighter.

William Perry, better known as the Tipton Slasher, lost his title of Champion of England to Tom Sayers.

# 12

## THE NEW CHAMPION

Delighted with his brilliant performance against Aaron Jones, and as a fitting tribute to his courage and daring, Tom's friends and backers honoured him with a celebration victory dinner at Nat Langham's Cambrian Stores on Thursday February 19, 1857. Among the invited guests were Baron Nicholson, John Gideon, Mr Lupton, "Farmer" Bennett the well-known contemporary bookmaker, Tom's two seconds Bill Hayes and Jemmy Massey and his bottle-holder Jemmy Welsh. As further tokens of their admiration, Tom was awarded the entire stakes from the contest and presented with a magnificent silver cup donated by Captain Webster of the 79th Highlanders.

The facing side of the cup bore the inscription: 'Presented to Tom Sayers by his sincere friend Captain Webster, as a mark of appreciation of his gallant and manly conduct in his victorious fight with Aaron Jones, February 10th 1857.'

On the obverse side was a circle of laurel with a lion inside the wreath, and underneath the words: "Courage! fight it out; a crown or a glorious tomb." – SHAKESPEARE.

In recognition of his ostentatious trophy, Captain Webster was duly elected chairman for the dinner, and his cherished cup was filled with champagne and passed around the company who individually drank a toast to Tom's continued good health and happiness. During the evening's festivities, there were innumerable toasts and after-dinner speeches, interspersed with traditional songs and entertainment from the guests.

When the tables had been cleared, the pipes lit and the drinks served, the conversation turned, quite naturally, to the topic of prize fighting. Jemmy Massey sat expounding the merits of William Perry, the Tipton Slasher, adamant in his opinion that there was no one among the heavyweights capable of beating him. Tom Paddock, he claimed, was the only one in his class, and even he stood little chance of success. John Gideon joined in the discussion saying the Slasher was too old, long past his prime, and had really no right to hold the title of champion. With his usual astuteness, he glanced across at Tom to gauge his reaction, and suggested that the guest of honour should be given a crack at the title as he was only too anxious to take on either Tom Paddock or the Slasher.

Tom pricked up his ears at the remark, and immediately joined in the conversation saying, 'Well, if anyone would care to back me, I would be quite willing to take on the Slasher for the championship.'

Jemmy Massey jumped to his feet, and banging his fist on the table shouted, 'Then I'll back the Tipton against you for £200 a side, and here's a fiver to bind the match.'

Tom turned to Gideon and said, 'Take him Mr Gideon, take him; down with a fiver to cover his. It's a bargain. I won't back out.'

Five pounds from each side was deposited with Nat Langham, and it was proposed that the friends and backers of both men should meet at Jemmy Massey's the following Wednesday evening to draw up the articles. Most of Tom's friends were amused at the notion and looked upon the whole affair as a bit of after-dinner bravado, hardly believing he was serious, least of all Jemmy Massey, who failed to communicate with the Slasher.

When Tom and John Gideon arrived at Massey's on the appointed evening, they were astonished to find that nobody else had turned up and nothing had been done. Tom was furious. He told Massey that if the match did not proceed immediately, he would have no other alternative but to draw the first instalment, and then publish a formal challenge to the Slasher in *Bell's Life*. Having seriously underestimated Tom's intentions, the following morning Massey sent an urgent communique to Perry, requesting him to come at once to London.

Events then moved rapidly. At Nat Langham's the following Monday (March 3) the articles were drawn up and signed for £200 a side and the Champion's belt, and the provision that the contest be held on June 16, 1857, within a radius of 100 miles from London. Twenty pounds were then deposited with Frank Dowling to bind the match and negotiations completed for the payment of the weekly instalments.

Now the match for the championship was on, the excitement in sporting circles mounted rapidly and the relative chances of the two contestants were heatedly debated. The vast majority thought it unbelievable that a man, admittedly the acknowledged champion of the middleweights, was boldly throwing down the gauntlet to the equally acknowledged heavyweight champion of England.

'Was it possible?' they speculated, 'for even the most scientific of little men, to even consider his chances in trying to beat such a huge mass of muscularity as The Slasher, an old and seasoned warrior, a tremendous hitter and undoubtedly the best heavyweight in the land?'

Even Perry had scoffed at the idea and had openly confessed that he had absolutely no intention of capering about the ring like Sayers; he would stand until the "Little 'un" came within range of his mighty fists.

'I cud take 'im like a boiled turnip, and squeeze the life out 'o 'im,' he said, laughing.

Tall and muscular from the waist upwards, the Tipton Slasher possessed an almost Herculean body. His only deficiency was in his legs, which were somewhat in the shape of the letter "K", generally attributed to having contracted rickets when a boy. He stood half an inch above six feet, and weighed in the region of 14½ stone. Sayers would be conceding something approaching four stone, and four inches in height.

According to Perry's own account he was born in Tipton, near Birmingham, in 1819. If he is correct in this statement, then he must have begun his pugilistic career at the early age of sixteen. He would then have weighed less than 10 stone 10 pounds, as the records show that on November 3, 1835 he beat Barney Dogherty of Chelsea, who was in that class. The following year he defeated Ben Spilsbury in nineteen rounds at Oldbury and a year later, on November 22, 1837, he obtained his third victory against Jem Scunner (the Gornel champion). When Ben Caunt returned from America with the 6 feet 10½ inch, 17 stone Charles Freeman, Perry was matched twice with the American Giant.

In their first encounter at Sawbridgeworth in Hertfordshire, darkness forced a premature end to hostilities. In their second battle a week later on Cliffe Marshes, near Gravesend, Freeman was proclaimed the victor in the 38th round when the Slasher fell without a blow. On December 19, 1843, Perry met Tass Parker for the first time, but the police intervened and the fight was postponed until February the following year. In this engagement, after fighting 133 rounds in 2 hours and 32 minutes, Parker fell without receiving a blow. The pair met again on August 4, 1846, when the Slasher won conclusively in twenty-three rounds lasting 27 minutes.

For the next few years, except for a futile attempt to make a match with Ben Caunt, little was heard of the Slasher until September 1849, when he was found forfeiting to an up-and-coming young pugilist named Con Parker. Perry made his first appearance as a bona-fide claimant for the championship when he met Tom Paddock on December 17, 1850. After fighting twenty-seven rounds in 42 minutes, Perry clinched the title through a foul blow from Paddock.

As the new Champion of England, Tom Sayers is pictured with the championship belt, and the handsome silver cup donated by Captain Webster, for his victory over Aaron Jones on February 10th, 1857.

With a mighty heave of his shoulders, he threw his opponent clean out of the ring.

The following year, Johnny Broome undertook to find a man who would fight him for £200 a side and the championship title. To everyone's surprise, the Slasher was challenged by Johnny Broome's brother Harry. In their contest at Mildenhall, the referee Peter Crawley awarded the verdict against the Slasher on the grounds that he had struck Broome when he was on his knees. The Slasher contested the verdict, and he and Crawley nearly came to blows. Eventually a fresh match was agreed upon, but Broome retired from the ring and the Slasher regained the title; plus a forfeit of twenty-five pounds.

In private life, William Perry was the landlord of the appropriately named Champion Inn in Spoon Lane, Tipton, Birmingham. A popular hero among the local community and widely known throughout the Birmingham area, he led a wild and boisterous life, was frequently drunk and usually on the look-out for trouble. Besides his public house, he also ran a very lucrative business selling refreshments at the Midland race meetings.

Almost as eccentric as his contemporary, the big, bold Bendigo, there were many amusing anecdotes told of his exploits. David Christie Murray, the celebrated Victorian novelist, recorded some of his recollections of the Slasher (his boyhood idol) in an autobiography published in the eighteen-sixties.

"On one occasion," Murray writes, "I played truant from school and followed the Slasher to a small race meeting held at a place called 'The Roughs' on the side of the Birmingham Road, in Handsworth. The Slasher was surrounded by his usual rag-tag-and-bobtail admirers and was in one of his most swaggering moods, aggravated no doubt by alcohol. As he roamed over the course he saw a machine for trying your strength, an apparatus where you pay a penny and hit your hardest and a dial records the force of the blow. The target was a figure of a circus clown, with a buffer around his midriff, at which you were invited to strike.

'The Slasher tossed a penny to the proprietor and prepared to strike, when the latter cried out, 'Don't strike, not you Mr. Perry! not you!'

" 'Gerrout,' he said, as he spat on his hand, clenched his fist and smote.

"Crash went the whole machine into ruins; the wooden uprights splintered and the iron supports doubled into uselessness. The destroyer rolled on rejoicing; but the crowd made a subscription and the owner of the machine stowed away his property, well pleased."

Murray also tells of the notorious Morris Roberts who had a boxing booth at these races.

"Standing on the platform outside, he was calling, 'Walk up gentlemen, walk up, and see the noble art of self-defence as practised by Englishmen. Not like the cowardly Frenchman or Italian, as uses sticks, knives and pistils, and other fire-arms, but the weapons provided by nature. I've got a nigger inside as won't say 'No' to any man. Also George Gough, as has fought fifteen bare-knuckle fights within the last two years, and won 'em all. One man down, and the next come on. If there's any sportsmen 'ere as cares to 'ave a turn, there's half a crown and a glass of sperrits for the man who stands before George Gough five minutes, no matter where he comes from.'

"Up went the wicked Slasher's old silk hat upon the stage.

"Morris Roberts, who was bawling, 'Twopence does it – first rate sample of the noble art for twopence!' froze at the sight of Perry.

"Come, come, Mr Perry,' he exclaimed when he had recovered himself a little. 'You can't expect George to stand up against the champion of England. That doesn't stand to reason, that doesn't; now does it Mr Perry?'

"The Slasher smiled, 'All right, hand down that half a crown and that there glass o' sperrits.'

'You don't mean it Mr Perry?'

'Don't I?' cried the Slasher.

A sudden inspiration illuminated Mr Morris' mind.

'All right, come up Mr Perry; sixpence does it, sixpence does it.'

"No sooner was it known that the champion was resolved on

business than the booth was besieged. It turned out that Mr Gough had been impertinent to the Slasher, and the offended dignitary punched him, it was thought, a little too unmercifully. At the close of the first round, the man of the booth said, truthfully no doubt, that he had had enough of it and the entertainment came to a premature end.''

Stories such as these serve to illustrate the Slasher's capricious nature and his undisciplined behaviour during his reign as England's champion. Both Tom and Gideon knew he drank too much and of the indulgent life he led. They were convinced that, nearing forty, he was too old and incapable of prolonged exertion against a younger and more agile man. Tom knew he stood no chance of success if he attempted to stand and swap punches with Perry; his objective was to wear down his older and heavier opponent until he was too exhausted to continue fighting.

Both men scorned the idea of defeat and each invested every penny they possessed. The Slasher even sold his public house to raise the extra capital with which to back himself so defeat could mean his total and absolute ruin. Tom was still in comparatively good condition after his recent battle with Jones but the Slasher was in poor shape. So, after disposing of all his business interests, he left Tipton and settled down to a steady training programme at Boxmoor in Hertfordshire.

With three months remaining before the contest, Tom thought it time to take a short vacation in which to relax and give some urgent consideration to his family commitments. For a long time he had nourished a sense of guilt that his two young children had been denied all the tender love and affection they so badly needed, and how little he contributed towards their moral and religious upbringing. Since his separation from Sarah, his whole life had consisted of touring the country to earn a living, or training for his next engagement.

In restitution for his negligence, he went to see the minister of St Pancras Old Church, and on Friday March 20 young Sarah, now aged six, and Thomas four, were baptized in a double Christening ceremony. With one of his prime objectives successfully accomplished, he spent every available moment with the youngsters until, with great reluctance, he had to bid them farewell and resume training.

From the time the match had been made, the excitement had mounted rapidly and the highly controversial fight became the major topic of conversation throughout the realm. The immediate public reaction was that by his victory over Aaron Jones, Tom Sayers had risen a little above his station and this overwhelming sense of confidence he possessed could now lead him into serious trouble. In many quarters it was widely predicted that the match could only end in a forfeit. But the Sayers party maintained their own opinions, unshaken in their belief that the Slasher, by not having fought for several years, would be stale and much too cumbersome to compete against the exceptional speed and hitting power of Sayers.

While the controversies raged, the magistrates, fully aware of the date and details of the impending contest, issued a warrant for Tom's arrest. Fortunately a certain well-wisher within the judiciary warned him about the directive, and he slipped away a few hours before the arresting officers called at his lodgings. For the next few weeks he avoided apprehension by adopting various ingenious disguises and carefully covering his tracks as he moved about from county to county.

During the time he was on the run from the law, exhaustive efforts had been made to find a suitable location within the allotted time specified in the articles but, with less than a week remaining before the event, nothing conclusive had yet been settled. With the authorities on full alert, it was much too dangerous to attempt a journey by rail and it began to appear that another sea-bourne excursion was inevitable. Plans were then implemented to hire two vessels; one to carry the men and their companions, and the other to convey a select company of wealthy Corinthian sportsmen. But to the consternation of the organizers, by the morning of Friday June 12, they were still unable to charter a boat.

Then, to everyone's profound relief, later that day there came an offer of a vessel, but only at a high price and on the condition that it carried no more than 250 passengers. Grateful for their last-minute reprieve, they hurriedly called a meeting at Owen Swift's Horseshoe situated on the corner of Titchbourne Street and Coventry Street, to negotiate the arrangements and itinerary. There it was decided that the vessel should put to sea immediately, and sail directly to Southend where it would await the arrival of the company on Tuesday morning. In the interests of security, it would then set sail to a secret destination only to be revealed after the vessel had put to sea. It was also agreed to limit the number of passengers to 200; only a restricted number of tickets would be issued to the general public, a certain portion allocated to the combatants and the remainder entrusted to bona-fide patrons of the ring. Surprisingly, considering the significance of the match, little more than half of these were actually sold.

At ten minutes to eight on Tuesday June 16, the small company of supporters left Fenchurch Street Station bound for Southend. During the journey word quickly spread through the carriages that Mr Clarke of the Adelphi had chartered a boat in opposition to the official craft and was running his own excursion at a specially reduced tariff. The vessel, they were told, would be waiting at Tilbury for any passengers who wished to take advantage of the cut-price offer.

At first, many were annoyed to hear this disturbing news as any un-authorized excursion usually ran the risk of attracting the undesirables but, upon further consideration, many agreed it could be a blessing in disguise as they had already objected to the high fares being charged, even if it was for the better boat.

The Slasher travelled down to Southend on the evening before the fight, but Tom, still on the run from the authorities, made his own way to the town so heavily disguised even his best friends failed to recognize him. This move proved extremely fortunate, for all down the line from London to Southend police officers had been stationed with orders to arrest him on sight.

When everyone arrived at the coast, they found to their dismay a south-easterly gale blowing, a heavy swell running and the steamer still lying at anchor offshore, unable to berth at the pier. It now became a particularly hazardous undertaking to board the vessel, for the small craft ferrying the passengers out to the steamer were grossly overloaded in the very high seas. It took Tom Oliver more than half an hour to clamber aboard with the stakes and ropes and even longer for the remainder of the passengers. Only people who already held tickets, or those willing to pay a couple of sovereigns before boarding, were allowed on the vessel. Many who had made the perilous journey out to the steamer, now found they could not afford the fare and were forced to return to the shore. Amidst all this confusion a large proportion of the dreaded mischief-makers had managed to infiltrate the vessel without paying. Due to the gullibility of several officials, they were allowed to remain on board until it was discovered that no more boats were available to ferry them back to the shore. The organizers were now posed with the question of whether they should be allowed to stay, or swim for it back through the choppy seas. Nobody could accept the responsibility for anyone drowning so, however unwelcome they may be, all were allowed to remain.

When the last of the stragglers were safely aboard, the steamer cast off and headed out to sea. Down in the cabins, Messrs Pinkstone, Coobiddy and Barney Aaron had provided a lavish banquet of cold chicken, ribs of beef and salad, and a nip of brandy at sixpence a small glass.

The vessel ploughed its way through the choppy seas until it rounded the Nore Light. The voyage now became a nightmare, espe-cially for the bad sailors. Clutching at their top hats, they were seen leaning over the rails, offering their contributions to the waves. A measure of sympathy was also extended to those unfortunate passen-gers packed together in the forecastle of the steamer. They were con-stantly drenched with salt spray every time the vessel dipped its bows into one of the deep troughs. Sailing in their wake came the other cut-price vessel, *The Widgeon*. The unhappy passengers on this steamer fared even worse than their counterparts in the official craft, for theirs was a much smaller boat and they were tossed about unmercifully on the huge waves.

Wet and thoroughly miserable, they arrived off the Kent coast at half past one. The skipper dropped anchor in the deep water channel and everyone now disembarked with just as much danger as they'd had on boarding, for the swarms of small boats which came alongside to ferry the passengers ashore were once again grossly overloaded. Perhaps the greatest miracle of the day was that there were no serious mishaps.

Soon after Tom Oliver had formed the rings and the crowd began taking their places, a man on horseback galloped up and demanded to know what they were doing on his master's land. Not seeking any trouble at this late stage of the proceedings the organizers squared the servant with a sovereign to keep him quiet until after the contest.

The preliminaries having been completed, the men were about to toss for choice of corners when another scare took place. This time there was to be no question of bribery, for running towards them came a squad of uniformed police officers. The Kent constabulary had become suspicious of the unusual activity on the river and had sent a party of constables to investigate the disturbance.

As the alarm was raised, the two combatants and their seconds made a bolt for the shore, closely pursued by the crowd who stampeded back to the two steamers. For a time there was utter chaos as many, in their anxiety to escape the clutches of the police, clambered aboard the wrong vessels. However, despite the panic, everyone re-embarked on one boat or the other and, waving a cheery goodbye to the constables on the shore, steamed away towards the opposite bank of the estuary.

The two boats sailed on for a few miles until they reached a lonely and secluded stretch of shoreline on the Isle of Grain. While the second disembarkation was taking place, Tom Oliver and his assistants pitched the ring in a small depression in the ground, much resembling a miniature amphitheatre. His prudent choice in selecting the site allowed everyone an uninterrupted view of the whole proceedings.

The sale of inner-ring tickets proved most lucrative, realizing £47. 2s. 0d., the largest sum ever raised on behalf of the Pugilistic Bene-volent Association. At four-thirty, Tom and the Slasher made their ap-pearance in the arena, Tom attended by Nat Langham and Bill Hayes, and the Slasher by Tass Parker and Jack Macdonald. With the odds stationary at 6 to 5 on the Tipton, several last-minute bets were laid by those who had been holding back for longer odds. The colours were tied to the stakes; a blue handkerchief with large white spots for Sayers, and a blue birds-eye for Perry.

At twelve minutes to five, Tom and the Tipton were escorted to the scratch by their seconds.

The stark contrast between the two men was quite extraordinary. The Tipton, with his immense frame and muscular arms and legs, looked quite capable of taking on perhaps 3 or 4 men such as Sayers. His only deficiency was his stance, which appeared rather ungainly due to his crooked leg. Full of swaggering confidence, he clearly assumed he had an easy task before him. But however optimistic the Slasher may have felt, Tom made it perfectly obvious that he too, felt the same. As he took up his stance, his broad shoulders, small loins, and powerful arms and legs, vividly emphasized his potent energy and athletic development. Tapping the ground lightly with his left foot, he peered at his hulking opponent and laughed. Everyone knew the Tipton's intentions were to play a waiting game, but the arrogance of Sayers was too much for Perry and instantly his plan of action was thrown to the winds. He now abandoned his preconceived ideas and went on the offensive.

With more vigour than good judgement, he lumbered forward like a huge bear, swinging wildly with both fists. But the wily Tom could see the punches coming a mile off and he stepped smartly aside to let the blows whistle through the air. Again the Slasher advanced and, as Sayers stepped back a pace, he slipped and fell to the ground. As he quickly scrambled to his feet the Slasher lurched forward, registered a slight hit on Tom's skull, and he fell once more.

Tom was in a frolicsome mood and, as he taunted Perry in his corner, his seconds reminded him to stick to his plan and treat the derision with contempt.

Perry came out for the 2nd round with even greater confidence, beaming with his broad, toothless grin. Lunging forward, his right fist connected with terrible force on Sayers' ribs. Tom countered with his usual lightning turn of speed and delivered an equally devastating punch on the Slasher's mouth, splitting his lip. An impulsive burst of cheering heralded the first event and there came jubilant cries from the supporters in Tom's corner of "First blood to Sayers!"

The Tipton stood dumbfounded, staring around with a blank look of disbelief on his face.

'The owdashus little monkey!' he yelled. 'Wait till I catch 'ee!' Then, swinging his great arms like the sails of a windmill, he charged.

Quick as ever on his feet, Tom danced lightly away before any blows came anywhere within range. Springing in, he hammered the Tipton with a tremendous smash on the bridge of the nose before skipping away, an impudent smile illuminating his face. Smarting with pain, and hungry for revenge, a deep frown crossed the Slasher's furrowed brow. Swinging his right arm in a gigantic circle, the uppercut, should it have landed, would have almost taken Tom's head off his shoulders.

Sayers came into the attack again and, with a mighty chopping punch, crashed his hard fist into the Slasher's already bleeding nose. Exercising his refinement of footwork, Tom now began to make the veteran boxer look foolish, first dancing around him like an Apache brave, uttering wild-indian war-whoops, and then running from him as if in fear of his life. Bobbing under Perry's arm, banging him on the head as he passed, he reappeared from behind and hit him on the nose. Torn to distraction, the old giant lost his sense of reason and sadly became guilty of the very folly he vowed to avoid: he stupidly played into Tom's hands and began chasing him about the ring.

His incredible actions were beyond the fulfilment of Tom's wildest dreams, for this was his one and only chance of winning. His only requisite now was to undermine the Slasher's physical powers until he was incapable of striking an effective blow and then go in and finish him off. Rushing around like a mad bull, the Tipton battled with thin air as Tom skipped nimbly away from every impetuous attack.

Suddenly Sayers feinted and dispensed a slashing punch on the Slasher's right cheek, inflicting a deep gash and instantly producing a stream of blood. A second crushing punch followed on the same spot and enlarged the cut even further. Once again the infuriated Slasher chased him around the ring, swinging punches wildly but with very little precision. Finding his attacks were leading him nowhere, he lowered his arms and retired into his corner for a wipe of the sponge from Jack Macdonald. His seconds implored him to remember his plans, but the sight of the "little monkey" and his relentless taunts re-kindled his wrought up anger and more futile efforts followed as he tried repeatedly to hit his elusive opponent.

The Slasher's supporters were disgusted with Sayers' actions and called for him to stand still and be hit, but Tom merely smiled at them and wisely declined; his instructions were to keep his antagonist on his feet and fight at a distance. Again and again the Slasher missed com-pletely or was stopped. Tom wore a wry grin on his face as he stood quite still, watching the Slasher intently. Launching himself at Sayers, his arms flailing wildly, he narrowly missed his slippery foe and smashed his fist into one of the stakes. Tom raised his arms in aston-ishment and burst out laughing as the Tipton vigorously shook his injured hand. Visibly slowing down now, the old veteran tried to spar for a time to regain fresh wind, but this only prompted more frisky dancing from Sayers, and more exhaustive efforts by Perry. Suddenly

Tom sprang forward and caught the Tipton with a severe jab on the nose, drawing a fresh stream of blood. With a savage scowl on his face the Tipton stood for a moment contemplating his next move. Then, rushing in, he hit Tom on the side of the head and knocked him to the ground.

A spontaneous burst of applause and cheering rent the air; 'Time, fifty-two minutes!' yelled the umpire above all the clamour.

As Tom was assisted back to his corner, the Slasher turned to the crowd and flexed his muscles as if to imply he was still as fit as ever.

Although he was grinning broadly as he came to scratch, the Slasher was still breathing heavily from his exertions in the previous round. Nevertheless, he still adhered to his usual practice of forcing the fighting as he dashed again at Tom, driving him into his corner. Evidently thinking he had him secure, The Tipton wound himself up to finish it, but when he let fly with his left and right he found Tom had slipped beneath his arm and was away, laughing in the middle of the ring. Clearly irritated that his opponent would not stand to be hit, he lumbered after him like a gigantic elephant. Tom blocked another left and a right before turning away, laughing and shaking his head.

Confounded by Sayers' sublime agility, and finding he could do nothing with him, Perry retired into his corner where he stood leaning on the ropes. Tom stood in the centre of the ring, a beaming smile on his face, beckoning to the Tipton to come to the scratch. Having taken a short respite, he came out and attempted a feint and a punch but Tom, quick as a flash, hammered him heavily on the right cheek. The Slasher tried again, and this time, as he landed on the ribs, Tom fell. One hour and four minutes had elapsed.

So the combat proceeded, much after the same style for the next few rounds. Had Perry stood his ground and not chased the more nimble Sayers around the ring he might have won, but contrary to the advice of his seconds and the orders of his backers, he stubbornly refused to stand still. As the excitement and uproar intensified, the Tipton's followers threatened to break into the ring and for a time the ring keepers were hard pressed to keep them at bay and restore order.

At the close of the 8th round, and when it was too late, the Slasher realized the errors of his ways. He came up very slowly for the 9th, having fought himself to a virtual standstill. Severely mauled, and his morale in shreds, he had never before fought a man whose brilliant footwork had been so completely dazzling and bewildering. Sayers was now taking greater liberties than ever, and he delivered three tremendous facial punches in quick succession, one of which further enlarged the ghastly wound on Perry's cheek.

Morose and dejected, he walked wearily back to his seconds for more attention, with Tom following in close pursuit. Angry at the intrusion into his corner, he tore in again. Swinging his right with all the force he could muster, Tom jumped smartly back as the vicious blow whistled past, missing him by inches. With a quizzical frown of uncertainty on his brow, the Slasher paused, and returned again to his corner for a drink of water. With nothing else to occupy his time, Tom followed his example. At length, feeling refreshed, they went back to work with a vengeance, Sayers continuing to concentrate his attacks on Perry's damaged nose and cheek.

The Tipton was noticeably becoming weaker by the minute, but he carried on resolutely until Tom rammed a straight left to his mouth, a right to the nose and followed it up with another sharp rap on the mouth. The impact staggered Perry and, still stumbling forward from the momentum of the last punch, he tripped and fell. This practically settled the fight; the last three blows in particular had been tremendously hard.

His resistance crumbling, the game old fighter was very slow to the call of time. Stunned, dazed, and unsteady on his legs, he crawled painfully to the scratch for the 10th and last round. He attempted to lead off, but it was, however, only an attempt. Tom easily avoided the punch, and planted another bone-shattering smash on the nose. Two more futile attempts by Perry were stopped, and as he lashed out a third time, Tom jabbed his left on the mangled cheek and his auction-eer on the mouth, ripping his upper lip like paper. The Slasher lay prone on the grass.

His seconds carried him to his corner, and it was only with considerable difficulty that they brought him round in time to go to the scratch. His appearance was grotesque; his face was fearfully bruised and swollen and his gaping, cavernous mouth, with its hideous cut presented a truly pitiful sight. A hollow sough escaped his lips as he exhaled in a state of fatigue and despair. Without the ghost of a chance, he was entirely at the mercy of Sayers. Owen Swift, the Slasher's principle backer, seeing his lamentable condition, stepped into the ring and declared he should fight no more. The old veteran was unwilling to give in without just one more try, but Owen insisted they shake hands, and the Tipton accept defeat. It had been a dismal ending to the Tipton's long career.

As they clasped hands and gazed compassionately at each other, the sponge was thrown into the air from Perry's corner. The fight had lasted 1 hour and 42 minutes. Amidst the prolonged cheers of his supporters, Tom Sayers was proclaimed the winner of the contest and the new Champion of England.

It was extremely fortunate that the fight ended when it did, for scarcely had the men left the ring when the same detachment of policemen who had interfered before, arrived upon the scene, too late to put the result in jeopardy.

Everyone hurried to rejoin the two vessels in the estuary but, when they reached the shore, they discovered to their dismay that the skipper of *The Widgeon* had steamed away almost upon the conclusion of the contest and had abandoned the majority of his customers to their fate. The great crowd of supporters left stranded on the shore now made a headlong dash to board the larger steamer. The already chaotic situation was further aggravated by the residual passengers of *The Widgeon* pushing aside the people from the official craft in their hurry to scramble aboard before any demands could be made to check their credentials.

Eventually, when all the passengers had safely re-embarked, a consultation was held between the managers to plan their next course of action. Rather than give everyone another turn around the dreaded Nore Light, they decided that the vessel should head on up the Medway and make for Strood, near Rochester.

During the return Journey, Tom took up a collection among the passengers for his fallen but game opponent. Most contributed generously, and raised the quite considerable sum of £22.5s.0d.

The steamer berthed at Strood shortly before 8 o'clock, in good time for the travellers to catch the next connecting train to London which arrived in the capital at 11 o'clock that evening.

Alec Keene, landlord of the Three Tuns, in Moorhead Street, Soho, an early patron of Tom Sayers.

# 13

## THE BLINK BONNY RIOT

The Slasher's defeat heralded a revolution in prize fighting, for never again could it be dictated that weight alone should be the definitive factor in a championship contest.

By his victory over Perry, Tom Sayers became the marvel of the age and, as a mark of approbation on his outstanding conquest, a celebration dinner was given in his honour at the Cambrian Stores on Monday June 22, 1857. Dressed for the occasion in a high starched collar and cravat, Tom looked immaculate in a richly ornamented three-quarter-length smoking jacket with astrakhan cuffs and trimmings, fastened down the front with neat wooden toggles.

During the course of the evening, the inaugural presentation of the brand new belt was made by Lord Drumlanrig and, to the applause of the assembly, Tom proudly buckled the magnificent trophy around his waist before giving a short speech of thanks to all his friends and supporters.

To record the event for posterity, he posed for a photograph, holding Captain Webster's silver cup in his right hand, and his left resting on the new belt. Although the general topic of conversation centred around Tom and his achievements, a marked degree of sympathy was extended towards the old Slasher, now completely ruined and finished professionally. He had lost everything of value: his proud title of Champion of England (the position he had held for about seven years), his public house, and every penny he possessed.

To alleviate Perry's current financial difficulties, Tom launched a fund-raising scheme in London, and within a few weeks, collected the quite considerable sum of one hundred pounds. There were countless occasions when many pugilists had reason to thank Tom Sayers for helping them out in their time of need, for he was indeed one of the most generous of men to any of his less fortunate colleagues, always ready to make a donation on their behalf and rarely refusing to give his services at any fund-raising benefit or exhibition.

In addition to the money raised in London, a further subscription to aid the Slasher was opened in the Midlands, and from the contributions donated in this area enough money was collected for him to open a modest beer-house in his native town. Regrettably the enterprise soon failed when he quickly returned to his old lifestyle of self-indulgence and drink.

He was never known to refuse a glass of anything alcoholic; 'For the good of the house' as he would say.

In his reminiscences of Perry's declining years, David Christie Murray wrote; 'He was dying when I saw him again, his once vast chest and shoulders were shrunk and bowed, so that one wondered where the giant frame had fallen to. He was despised and left alone, and he sat on the side of his bed with an aspect altogether dejected and heartless. In his better days, he liked what he used to call "a stripe o' white satin", which was poetic for a glass of Old Tom gin. I carried a bottle of that liquor with me as a peace-offering and a quarter of a pound of Birdseye tobacco. He did not know me, and there was no speculation in his look, but after a drink he brightened. When I had entered, he was sat twirling an empty clay pipe with a weary and listless thumb and finger, and the tobacco was welcome.

"They mought ha' let me aloon," he said, when his wit grew clear. "I held the belt for seven 'ear. Tum's a good 'un. I've sin 'em all, and nivver sin a better. But he owed to ha' let me be. There was no credit in hammerin' a man at my time o' life. All the same tho', I thowt I should ha' trounced him. So I should if I could ha' got at him, but he fled hither and he fled thither, and was walkin' about me like a cooper walkin' round a cask. An' I was fule enough to lose my temper, an' the crowd began to laugh and gibe at me, an' I took to racin' after him, an' my wind went, and wheer was I then? He knocked me down fair-an'-square he did it. The only time it ivver chanced to me. I put everything I had on that fight, an' here I bin."

Could anything have been more pathetic? Perry died on January 18, 1881 at his home near Wolverhampton. He was talking to some friends when he was seized with a fit of apoplexy, and never recovered.

After Tom's decisive victories over Aaron Jones and the Tipton Slasher, there remained only one other aspirant with which to link his name with the championship, and it was not long before Tom Paddock issued the inevitable challenge. Before the match could be ratified, however, Paddock was admitted to hospital suffering from rheumatic fever. With his usual thoughtfulness, Tom paid him a visit in hospital and left him with a five pound note, together with the promise to raise a subscription to help ease the financial burden on his wife and family. With Paddock incapacitated, and no one to dispute his right to the title, Tom seized the opportunity to make a tour of the northern counties, to exhibit his trophies and demonstrate his fighting skills.

During his travels through Yorkshire Tom and his old friend, the ex-champion Jem Ward, were in the vicinity of Doncaster on the Friday of the Doncaster Race Week. As keen betting men, and with plenty of spare time on their hands, they could not resist the temptation of spending a day at the races. Entered in the Parkhill Stakes that eventful day was the outstanding racehorse of the year, Blink Bonny, owned and trained by William I'Anson, and ridden by Jack Charlton. The three-year-old filly had won the two major classics in the racing calendar: The Derby and The Oaks. Two days before, on Wednesday September 16, she was favourite in the St Leger, running against her old adversary Imperuse, who had finished in fourth place and 16 lengths behind her in The Oaks. However, in the St Leger the positions were completely reversed; Blink Bonny finishing a disappointing fourth behind Imperuse.

On this memorable Friday, Blink Bonny ran over the same course and distance as the St Leger, but this time she won in a canter and, what was more astonishing, in a much faster time than Imperuse just two days before. The first hint of trouble came when the time was hoisted and angry voices were raised in the crowd. A group of protesters began shouting that Blink Bonny had been deliberately pulled in the St Leger and they had not had a fair run for their money.

When Charlton rode into the unsaddling enclosure, he was met with a chorus of mingled hoots and hisses from a gang of malcontents encircling the paddock. Scenting impending danger, he hurriedly dismounted and quickly stripping the saddle from the horse, attempted to thread his way through the threatening crowd fast closing in around him. The meagre police presence was totally inadequate to defend him from the ever increasing fury of the rabble and the situation suddenly turned desperate when several of the ring-leaders began kicking him and William I'Anson. Several of the more tolerant spectators tried to offer them some protection, but the pent-up feeling of wrath now gave way to a chorus of yelling, which rapidly swelled into a thunderous crescendo of screaming as the mob went completely berserk, frenziedly attacking any innocent by-standers who had the misfortune to be in the vicinity of the paddock. A group of hooligans detached themselves from the main body, and made a dash for the unfortunate mare, evidently intending to wreak their vengeance on the poor dumb animal.

It was at this point that Tom and Jem Ward decided things had gone far enough. Given a few more moments, and if nothing positive was done, it appeared certain that both the owner and jockey would be lynched. Accompanied by Baron Rothschild who happened to be nearby, the little trio went to the assistance of the two men. Tom burst into the thick of the fray like a tornado, both fists flying. Cleaving a path through the crowd, his auctioneer inflicted such hideous injuries on the two rioters attacking Charlton, eyewitnesses declared they would carry the marks to their graves. He next took on three or four of the ringleaders and sent them flying, before picking Charlton up in his arms, and carrying him safely out of danger.

Meanwhile Jem Ward and Baron Rothschild had fought their way through the mob to the badly shaken I'Anson. Shielding him with their bodies, they battled their way back through the rabble until they reached the safety of the weighing-in room.

There is little doubt that had it not been for the prompt action of Tom and his companions that day, the lives of both the owner and the jockey would have been lost. To express their gratitude for their rescue, William I'Anson together with John Scott (the owner of Imperuse) and several contemporary leading owners and jockeys, presented Tom with a magnificent silver tea service, comprising a teapot, sugar basin, cream jug, sugar tongs, and six silver teaspoons, all engraved with the monogram "T.S.".

The Yorkshire trainer never forgot Tom for all his bravery and personally made sure he was on many a winner for years afterwards. Much later, Charlton confessed to pulling Blink Bonny in the St Leger, claiming it had been at the instigation of one John Jackson, a bookmaker who specialized in the corruption of jockeys.

During Tom's tour of the northern counties a startling chain of events had been unfolding in London. For some unknown reason, Alec Keene, formerly a great friend and staunch supporter, switched his allegiance to Tom Paddock. Throughout the four months of Paddock's illness, Alec had paid him regular visits in hospital and helped with the maintenance of his wife and children.

Ben Caunt had also been busy. Since the fiasco of Tom's match with Jack Martin, Caunt had been harbouring a grudge, and he was now a leading activist and dedicated anti-Sayers campaigner. While Tom was in the north, he had issued a challenge to fight him for the championship, and had left a £10 deposit with Frank Dowling at *Bell's Life*.

The challenge read: "To the Editor of *Bell's Life* in London.

Sir, – Unaccustomed as I am to public challenging, long laid upon the shelf as I have been, it may perchance startle the sporting world to learn that Ben Caunt is once more a candidate for the championship.

Win or lose with Langham,* I challenge Tom Sayers for £200 a side and the championship, the contest to take place within six months of my forthcoming fight. My money is ready at your office, and I trust that this offer will be accepted, in order that the world may be as speedily as possible undeceived with regards to the merits of the much-vaunted new school of British boxing.

   Yours obediently,
   Benjamin Caunt''

   Tom had no hesitation in covering Caunt's £10, and announced that if the fight with Caunt did not materialize, then he was still prepared to meet his other challenger, Tom Paddock. Ben Caunt had wanted Tom to return to London to sign the articles, but as he was still making a substantial profit in the north he refused, instructing Ben to post the contract to him for his signature. In his flagrant hatred for Sayers, Caunt rejected the request until the fight with Nat Langham was settled. However, when he entered the ring against Langham, much to his surprise and chagrin he discovered that one of the seconds in Nat's corner was none other than his arch-rival, Tom Sayers. Caunt was easily beaten by Langham and, evidently having second thoughts about meeting Tom for the championship, he quickly recovered his £10 deposit and the whole affair fizzled out like a damp squib.
   Harry Broome was also jealous of Tom's achievements and categorically rejected the suggestion that Sayers was an outstanding fighter; not even the overthrow of the Tipton Slasher could convince him. He openly admitted he could see nothing astonishing about Sayers' victories, and thought it monstrous that this little whippersnapper should be allowed to call himself Champion of England.
   Broome had given up fighting after his ignominious defeat at the hands of Tom Paddock and he was now trying his hand at managing a string of pugilists in Portsmouth.
   Determined to bring about the downfall of Sayers, but honest enough to admit he was unable to cope with Tom himself, he said he 'knowed of a cove wot could.'
   In the autumn of 1857, he issued a communique stating: "I have an 'Unknown' who will put pay to Sayers and I am willing to match this mystery person for £200 a side and the championship belt."
   Tom replied to the challenge with the statement, "I am quite willing to meet the 'Dark horse,' whoever he is!"
   Immediately a wealth of speculation arose on the identity of this

---

* Nat Langham and Caunt were involved in a domestic squabble at the time, and were about to settle their differences in the ring.

Jem Ward, ex-champion of England, who together with Tom Sayers and Baron Rothschild, saved the lives of the jockey and trainer of Blink Bonny when the mob threatened to lynch them at Doncaster Races.

mysterious unknown. Some said it was Bendigo under a nom de plume, despite being in his forty-eighth year and not having fought in the last seven years. Others were quite sure it was Ben Caunt or Nat Langham. A large proportion declared it was Tom's arch-enemy Harry Orme, while scores believed it was Harry Broome himself. But they were all wrong and, to add to their astonishment, the "Unknown" was a young man named William Bainge, alias Bill Benjamin, a complete novice to the prize ring.

Bill Benjamin was the son of a farmer who lived near Northleach, a small hamlet in the heart of the Cotswolds. Since his boyhood, it had been young Bill's burning ambition to fight in the prize ring and now, having matured into a strong and sturdy young man, he had sparred

with the best of the up-and-coming young pugilists in his native Glou-
cestershire. Many believed him to be an absolute genius, but the
London Fancy were suspicious of these tales of prowess. They
suspected that if the Broome's were connected in some way, then the
chances were that this was nothing more than a contrived robbery, and
that Sayers had connived with their brother Johnnie, who was
notorious for his alleged manipulations in this field.

Tom was incensed at these unfounded allegations and emphatically
denied any participation in a swindle.

He said, 'I feel ashamed and disgusted that anyone would spread
such malicious lies, or think I would stoop to such a degrading proposition. I have always fought fair and square, and have never been guilty
of a dishonest act in my life. Should I ever be beaten in the ring, then
it will only be by a better man than myself.'

His faithful followers stood solidly behind him and were outraged at
the suggestion that he would be party to such a deception. They emphasized that they could not understand Broome's motives in pitting a
novice like Benjamin against the champion of England, especially at
this early stage in his career.

As the time for his encounter with Benjamin drew near, Tom began
the first phase of his training at his native Brighton and completed the
final stage of his road work at The Brown Jug, a small ale-house,
situated on the Hadlow Road, a few miles from Tonbridge in Kent. He
now engaged as his second the very capable Harry Brunton who for
many years had played an active role in the sporting calendar, and was
regarded as one of the best seconds in England.

Although his performances in the ring were neither sufficiently numerous, nor significantly important to raise him to notoriety, his tavern,
the George and Dragon in Beech Street, Barbican, was a favourite
resort of the Fancy and there were very few sporting men in London
who failed to recognize his short, squat, bull-necked figure. To those
who knew him well, and his little idiosyncrasies, it was a constant
source of amusement that whenever a stranger was present, he invariably called attention to the extraordinary muscular development in
his arms and legs. No matter what the topic of conversation, he would
somehow, in a fit of abstraction, double up his arms and pensively feel
his biceps.

The moment the stranger's eye caught his, he would say, 'Not so
werry bad a harm for an old 'un – eh, Sir? – feel it!' Or he would
stoop down and caress his calf muscles and, having drawn attention to
his leg, would remark with an innocent air, 'Not so werry bad a leg for
an old 'un – eh, Sir!'

It was a harmless piece of vanity his old pals loved to humour.

Harry was reputed to be deaf and was, by all accounts, a little hard of hearing, but he was probably not quite as deaf as he made himself out to be, especially when it suited his purpose. He had the uncanny knack of hearing things not intended to reach his ears, no matter how softly they were whispered.

His friends would often joke and say, 'If you offered Harry a fiver, he would hear it fast enough.'

He was exceptionally proud of having been born in the same year as his idol Tom Sayers and woe betide any man who ventured to insinuate that Sayers was not the greatest fighter who ever lived.

Harry was born at Bunhill Road, St Luke's, where his father ran a small though successful shoemaker's business. He had given Harry a good education and a deep bond of affection existed between father and son. Intensely proud of his father, Harry loved to relate the story of how a big, strapping sugar-baker had quarrelled with old Brunton and had given him a thrashing. Harry was absent from home at the time, but the moment he heard of the incident he stormed into the baker's shop and challenged him to a fight.

Almost twice the size of the seventeen-year-old stripling, the bellicose baker stepped out of his shop to thrash the son as he had the father. Undaunted, young Harry stripped off his hat, coat and waistcoat, and handed them to a sympathetic bystander. The sugar-baker laughed derisively at the impudent youth, and prepared to smash him to pulp. But the younger Brunton proved a task beyond the baker's capabilities. Unable to get within range of Harry, or guard himself against the youngster's blows, the baker's shirt front was soon drenched with the blood which flowed freely from his nose and mouth.

Finally, sulking and humiliated, he slunk back into his shop having had more than his share of Harry Brunton. But when Harry looked around for the bystander to whom he had entrusted his clothing, he found the gentleman had disappeared. Consequently, he had to walk home bare headed and in only his shirt and trousers, but he had avenged his father and that was some consolation for the loss of his garments.

Jemmy Shaw, who kept the Blue Anchor in Shoreditch, had followed Harry's amateur career with a keen interest and had predicted a promising career for the young hopeful. Shaw invited him to join his stable of pugilists and young Harry soon became one of his most promising pupils.

In his first professional contest at Hope Point, near the mouth of the River Thames, Harry had the misfortune to come up against the resilient Tom Hussey. Although Harry was undoubtedly the better fighter, he was cursed with a pair of "soft" hands, for no matter how brave a bare-knuckle fighter might be, if his fists could not withstand the repeated punishment against an opponent's hard bones, he could not aspire to championship standards. At the end of two and a half hours of fierce fighting, poor Harry's fists were swollen like balloons. Left with no other alternative but to wrestle, he was fortunate to win when he threw his stubborn adversary and knocked all the breath from his body.

Among the spectators who witnessed this battle was Jem Moore of The Old Rum Puncheon in Rose Court, Moorfields. Jem Moore was an excellent sportsman and one who had a keen eye for the finer points of a boxer. He teamed up with Harry and the pair developed a bond of friendship which lasted for the rest of their lives. It was the philanthropic Jem Moore who contributed the majority of the battle-money and paid all Harry's training expenses for his last, and only, great fight with Bill Cain. But regrettably, before the contest Harry foolishly accepted a challenge from a man named Duffyn (generally known as The City Bargeman) for £10 a side, an impromptu match, made on the Saturday and fought the following Tuesday. Although a sturdy and powerful man, Duffyn lacked scientific skills and Harry knocked him down repeatedly. There was not a visible mark on Brunton's body, but the succession of blows to the bargee's cast-iron head had seriously injured Harry's hands. Too late, he regretted his rash decision in taking on Duffyn when he should have been reserving himself for his encounter with Cain.

Bill Cain's fighting career began with great promise, and it certainly appeared likely he would follow in the footsteps of his famous brother Dick Cain, the celebrated Leicestershire pugilist. Although Bill Cain had been beaten by Alec Keene, his victories over two of England's leading pugilists, Tigser of Leeds and Homer Howden of Manchester, entirely vindicated his only defeat.

After his battle with Howden, however, he became addicted to alcohol and had led a dissolute existence, wandering around the country and ruining his health. When he returned to London, he was an undignified shadow of his former self – unkempt, demoralized, and virtually destitute.

Leading trainers were reluctant to help this wreck of a man, and the Fancy were quite sure his career was finished. However, he was extremely fortunate to have two very good friends in Tom Lockwood, who kept the White Lion in Drury Lane, and Joe Ellis of the Derby Arms in Turnham Green. They clothed him and fed him and it was through their vigorous efforts in restoring him to health that his match with Harry Brunton materialized. Their conflict was intensely brisk and exciting, lasting 3 hours and 7 minutes. For at least two of the three hours, Harry fought with hands so painfully swollen they had no effect on his adversary. The wily Cain would not give Harry the chance to wrestle and all he could do was to cuff with his wrists and forearms. By the time the engagement reached its climax, Brunton's right arm had become so stiff and inflamed from parrying Cain's repeated blows he was scarcely able to raise it high enough to guard himself. Despite his dreadful injuries, Harry fought on with dedicated courage until the 135th round, when Cain cross-countered with a tremendous right to the jaw.

Harry spun round like a top and fell flat on his face. At the call of "Time!" he lurched to the scratch. Cain calmly walked up to him, crashed his left full into his face and with a right to the jaw sent him tumbling senseless to the turf.

Harry Brunton never fought again. Eight years later, he teamed up with Tom Sayers in a partnership which endured until Sayers' last epic fight with John Heenan in 1860.

While Tom was in training, he received certain inside information from a sympathizer within the judiciary that a warrant would be issued for his arrest the moment he set foot in London, so rather than run the risk of capture he remained at The Brown Jug until the evening before the contest.

Bill Benjamin, who had been in training under the leadership of Harry Broome, arrived back in London with his entourage on the Saturday before the encounter. He took up residence at Jemmy Massey's where, over the next couple of days, he gave several impromptu boxing exhibitions, principally for the benefit of the curious, who were eager to catch a glimpse of him in action and to verify for themselves if he was really as good as he was rated.

Since the signing of the articles it had been the intention to lay on a special train but, at the very last moment insuperable obstacles were encountered on the intended battleground and it became necessary to change the venue. Consequently, instead of a rail journey of some eighty miles from London, the special was diverted to a waiting paddle steamer moored on the Thames. Considering the complexity of the last-minute alterations, everything worked exceedingly well and by half past nine everyone was safely embarked for their journey down the river. The ridiculously inflated price of tickets, combined with the early start and the piercing chill of the January morning had thinned the ranks of the supporters drastically, and the little company comprised less than a couple of hundred people.

Due to the ever constant threat of his arrest, Tom arrived in a closed carriage in the early hours of Tuesday morning and when

Benjamin embarked, long before any passengers were on board, he found him sitting downstairs in one of the cabins.

To catch the tide, the steamer cast off shortly before ten o'clock, but as it reached the open water an incompetent crew member allowed a hawser to foul one of the paddle wheels. The engineer and crew made concerted efforts to free the cable, but it was only extricated after having been cut into several short lengths. Although valuable time was lost due to the enforced delay, the steamer made good progress and reached the newly selected battleground, an island in the River Medway, soon after eleven o'clock. While the ring was under construction another steamer arrived in the estuary, filled to overflowing with supporters who, having learned of the affair early in the morning, had hurriedly organized an expedition of their own.

Billy Duncan and his ring constables did an excellent service, shepherding the spectators into their respective places and, thanks to their concerted efforts, not a single case of intoxication was reported.

Shortly before twelve-thirty, sounds of loud cheering echoed from all sides as Tom Sayers, accompanied by Bill Hayes and Harry Brunton, modestly dropped his beaverskin hat over the ropes and climbed through after it. Close on his heels came Bill Benjamin, escorted by his two seconds, Harry Broome and Jemmy Massey. Both contestants wore broad grins on their faces as they laughed and joked with their friends and supporters clustered in their corners. As they stripped for action in the bitter south-easterly breeze blowing off the sea, their colours were tied to the centre stakes; a French grey for Sayers and white spots on a blue background for Benjamin.

At fourteen minutes to one, the umpire called time and a hush settled over the audience as they gazed in awe at the physical contrast between the two men. Benjamin towered over Sayers and looked, as he undoubtedly was, the more powerful man. The rippling muscles beneath his skin were better developed than Tom's, and his attitude clearly proved he had been schooled by a good master. Sayers, by comparison, carried an excess of fat about his chest and shoulders, but in the freezing conditions that day it was a fault on the right side. Cool, calm and collected, he wore the same unmistakable gleam of confidence as he gazed at his adversary with his steady grey eyes. He had decided to let Benjamin make the first move and tried several times to entice him into an opening. Slightly apprehensive, the novice sparred and feinted like an accomplished boxer until he attempted to lead off with a left. Sayers nonchalantly parried the blow and returned with a sharp crack on the nose. Undeterred, Benjamin stood his ground and twice in quick succession blocked Tom and returned on the cheek. Then the champion stepped in and gave him a taste of real quality. He delivered two sledgehammer punches with lightning rapidity, the left on the cheek, and the right to the jaw, laying the novice prostrate on the turf.

His seconds entered the ring and carried him gently to his corner. As he sat on his bottle-holder's knee, he wore a look of utter dismay on his face, and he glanced around fearfully as if still at a loss to understand from where those two tremendous punches had emanated. The sheer velocity of their impact had sown the first seeds of defeat and had made it clear that he lacked the resources and experience to deal with a man of Sayers' calibre.

There was no smile of confidence on Benjamin's face as he came to scratch for the 2nd round. His eyes darted nervously about the ring as if desperately searching for some safe place to hide if Sayers came at him with his former ferocity. With a half-compassionate smile on his lips, Tom walked quietly up to him and led off with the left. To Benjamin's credit, he stopped the blow rather neatly, but missed in his return. Tom came in again and delivered a frightful left-hand punch to the novice's lips, instantly filling his mouth with blood and knocking him off his feet. For a few seconds he lay inert on the grass, the blood gushing from his stricken mouth then, rolling over on to his stomach, he gradually crawled into a kneeling position, gazing around as if undecided on whether to continue. His seconds did not hesitate; they picked him up and carried him to his corner, where he sat shaking his head, apparently having no desire to encounter another of Tom's deadly shots.

At the call of "Time!" Harry Broome had to physically thrust him forward into the ring. As he ambled reluctantly to the scratch, Jemmy Massey became so disgusted by his cowardly actions, he called him a "Yellow cur" and refused to have any further dealings with him for the duration of the contest.

Intent on making short work of it, Tom went in quickly. He planted another left on Benjamin's nose and landed again on his stricken mouth which was still bleeding profusely from the last round. The novice tried to rally with the champion but, beyond a slight touch on the lip, did no damage. Tom now registered two more devastating punches on the mouth and jaw and once again Benjamin found himself lying in the centre of the ring, gazing around in total bewilderment.

"Time!" was called, but nothing would induce Benjamin to return to the scratch, despite the repeated demands and threats from Harry Broome. As the seconds ticked away he wandered aimlessly about in his corner, clutching at the ropes until "Time!" was called for the third time. With a look of unsurpassed embarrassment on his face, Jemmy Massey turned his back on him and, with a shrug of the shoulders,

Harry Broome threw up the sponge. When he was quite satisfied that the fight was really over, a very subdued Benjamin slunk sheepishly back in his corner, amidst a chorus of loud hisses and jeers from the disgruntled spectators. His easy defeat, in just 6½ minutes, filled his followers with dismay, and the withering look of contempt he received from Jemmy Massey did nothing to ease his discomfort. No one could understand why Harry Broome had made such a tragic mistake in bringing out a novice like Benjamin as a candidate for the championship.

Among those who felt especially cheated was Jemmy Massey. He lost a considerable fortune that day in taking odds of 2 to 1. He readily admitted he had liked the look of the young contender, but he had been entirely misled by the glowing reports of Harry Broome. As for Benjamin, he confessed that he had been hit so hard by Sayers it had made him feel quite sick.

The middle weight champion, Nat Langham, was the only pugilist to beat Tom Sayers with bare knuckles.

# 14

## ALEC KEENE'S THREAT

On Sunday January 10, 1858, five days after Tom's battle with Bill Benjamin, *Bell's Life* reported that Tom Paddock had recovered from his illness and was once again ready to substantiate his claim to the championship for £200 a side.

Tom readily accepted the challenge, which he considered was long overdue, and at Owen Swift's on Wednesday January 13, when he was again adorned with the belt and presented with his battle winnings, the articles were drawn up for his match with Tom Paddock. However, almost immediately after the contract was signed, Paddock found he could only raise £150 of the prerequisite sum of £200, the lowest stake Sayers was bound to accept. On the brink of destitution after his four-month illness, he begged Tom to grant him a favour in waiving his rights and not let £50 stand between them. Although each held a fervent dislike for the other, Tom gracefully acceded to his request, and two days later a second meeting was called to amend sections of the contract which now stipulated:

"Articles of agreement entered into this 15th day of January 1858, between Tom Paddock and Tom Sayers.

"The said Tom Paddock agrees to fight the said Tom Sayers for £150 a side, according to the rules of the ring of the Pugilistic Benevolent Association, by which the said Tom Paddock and Tom Sayers hereby mutually agree to be bound. The said fight shall take place on June 15th 1858, within 100 miles and 25 miles from London. In pursuance of this agreement, £25 a side are now deposited in the hands of the editor of *Bell's Life*, who shall be the final stakeholder and name a referee and place of fighting. The second deposit shall be made of £10 a side at Alec Keene's, Three Tuns, Moor Street, on Wednesday January 20, and the remaining deposits of £10 a side shall be named at each preceding deposit, when the money is staked. The last deposit shall be made of £25 a side on Wednesday June 2nd, 1858. The deposits shall be made between the hours of eight and ten o'clock and the party failing to take any deposit to the house named, shall forfeit the whole of the money then staked.

The men shall be in the ring between the hours of eight and ten, or the man absent shall forfeit the battle money. The expenses of the ropes and stakes shall be shared equally by the combatants.

In pursuance of this agreement we hereunto attach our names.

'Alexander Keene.' for Paddock

'Tom Sayers.' (X)''

A few days after these amended articles were signed, Paddock became involved in a bitter quarrel with his benefactor, Alec Keene. An argument had arisen over Paddock's vindictive attitude and his ingratitude over the financial assistance Alec had extended to him and his family during his confinement in hospital. Declaring he was finished with Paddock, he swore he would put a stop to the contest by informing the authorities. Furthermore, in his indignation, he stormed into the offices of *Bell's Life* and demanded the immediate return of the money he had deposited to bind the match.

This sudden desertion of his principle backer left Paddock in a dilemma. With time fast running out, it now seemed certain he would be forced to forfeit the match. In his desperate search for a financier, he persuaded a bookmaker friend to lend him the money for the first deposit, and he approached Lord Drumlanrig to seek his help and advice in raising the required deposits. After listening to Paddock's tale of woe, his Lordship promised to give the problem his urgent attention and said he believed he could offer some assistance after consulting with his sporting colleagues.

The Fancy were now posed with the questions of would Paddock raise the remainder of the capital for his deposits? – Or should they take Alec Keene's threat seriously, and call the whole thing off? But as nothing further developed over the next couple of weeks, Tom returned to his native Brighton to commence training. A few weeks later, he chanced to meet Lord Drumlanrig on the steps of Brighton's prestigious Bedford Hotel. John Gideon relates how they had an ounce or two of conversation, for his Lordship had helped Paddock raise quite a substantial sum for the battle money. The noble lord asked Tom what weight he thought he should be on the day of the fight.

'Why,' Tom answered, 'you see my lord, the weather is very warm, and I'm very well now, but to keep so and be fit when I go into the ring, I shall not be more than ten stone eight pounds.'

This was precisely what his lordship wanted; thinking that by keeping Tom's weight down he could not possibly be big enough to lick Paddock, whom he knew would not be less than twelve stone four pounds.

Lord Drumlanrig then said, 'If you are less than ten stone eight on the day before fighting and weigh in at Alec Keene's, I will give you fifty pounds.'

'Thank you my Lord,' answered Tom. 'The fifty will do to back myself.'

Tom's training had necessarily been intensively strenuous, and at eleven o'clock on Monday June 14, dressed in his full fighting outfit of boots, drawers, stockings and colour for the waist, he weighed in at exactly ten stone, seven and a half pounds. On the announcement of his weight Lord Drumlanrig, true to his word, handed Tom the fifty pounds. This transaction eventually cost his lordship a total of £100, for he accepted Tom's fifty pounds as a bet, to return a hundred if he won.

Tuesday June 15 dawned with the promise of a glorious sunny day. The early morning mists had lifted from the river, and as the sun beamed down on the tranquil serenity of the Thames there was scarcely a ripple on the water, a welcome sight for the bad sailors. When the steamer slipped its cable, more than 400 excited passengers packed the decks, watching the flotilla of small boats sailing in their wake, each filled to capacity with a varied array of supporters.

Anchoring at Canvey Island, everyone disembarked safely and made their way towards an excellent piece of pasture-land specially chosen for the purpose. The ring was pitched and the paying members safely settled, but one nagging doubt still persisted in everyone's mind: was Alec Keene's threat to inform the police genuine? Any depressing thoughts, however, were quickly dispelled when a roar of cheering greeted the arrival of Tom Paddock. Sending his hat spinning into the arena and waving gaily to his supporters, he was escorted into the ring by Jemmy Massey and Jack Macdonald. The little party had only a few moments to wait before they were joined by Tom Sayers, Harry Brunton and Bill Hayes. As they approached the centre to shake hands, Paddock, although big and burly, still looked somewhat pinched about the face after his recent illness and there was also a certain dullness about the eyes which had not been present in any of his former fights.

Sayers' condition contrasted starkly to that of his adversary. A beaming smile illuminated his face, his eyes were as clear and as bright as a hawk's and his dark brown skin glistened in the bright sunlight as he adopted his usual fighting stance. Both knew no liberties were to be taken by either side and hostilities opened with the utmost caution. In all his previous battles Paddock's tactics had been to rush at his opponent, both fists flailing, psychologically designed to demoralize an opponent by seeing twelve stone of solid bone and muscle boring down upon him. But contrary to everyone's expectations, he steadied himself and probed for an opening with the left. Sayers easily blocked the punch but, after a little tentative sparring by both men, Paddock succeeded in reaching Tom's brow. This led them into a set of heavy exchanges in which Tom left a crimson patch on Paddock's cheek, and he received a slashing punch over the right eye, removing some skin and giving Paddock the first event.

As the midday sun blazed down fiercely on the arena, both men were perspiring profusely from their exertions, so by mutual consent they lowered their arms and retired to the corners for a drink of water and a sponge down.

Feeling refreshed, Paddock tried one of his characteristic rushes, but Tom was ready for him and stood his ground. He blocked the blows and in retaliation inflicted a deep cut on Paddock's left eyebrow. Unable to see anything clearly through the steady trickle of blood running into his eye, Paddock swept in again. Tom ducked under his arm, came up behind him and, as Paddock turned around in search of his elusive opponent, Sayers hammered him again over the left eye. An angry scowl crossed Paddock's features as he charged again at Tom, but the champion ducked and twice in quick succession planted his famous double on the cheek and nose before escaping scot free from the return. In a fit of blind rage, Paddock dashed after him and brought him down in a flying tackle.

The round had lasted 15 minutes, and on its conclusion, the Sayers' backers were freely offering odds of 2 to 1, an offer totally unacceptable to the Paddock party who were giving the opposition some very black looks. But it was patently obvious that Paddock lacked the vigour and dash of former days, and after the fight he confessed that long before the first round had ended he knew his chances of beating Sayers were extremely slim.

Both came to the scratch for round 2, grinning all over their faces. Again Paddock rushed in, delivered a stunning blow to the top of Tom's head and, in the exciting exchanges which terminated the round, the champion caught Paddock with a well-measured blow from the auctioneer and knocked him to the ground.

Round 3 was excessively arduous and punishing, with Sayers repeatedly aiming for Paddock's injured eye before slipping away each time unmolested. Again he danced under Paddock's arm, waited for him as he turned, and delivered a left-hand punch to the cheek, drawing fresh blood from a new cut. Intent on revenge, Paddock made several determined attempts to reach the champion, but he was effectively countered on every move. In the final moments of the round the Redditch boxer dashed in, struck Tom on the side of the head, paused for a second, hit him again on the mouth and forced him down.

As each man sat on the knee of his bottle-holder, a tug was observed a few hundred yards away, heading for the shore. When the boat grounded, a small group of figures were seen scrambling ashore, and instinctively a cry of alarm was raised;

'It's the police!' A wave of gloom and despondency swept the crowd; so Alec had kept his promise after all. But as the figures grew more distinct through the shimmering heat haze, several familiar faces were recognized, amongst them Alec Keene's.

A tremendous roar rent the air as the penitent Alec forced his way through the crowd and made his way towards Paddock's corner, holding out his hand in a gesture of welcome. Not a word was spoken as Paddock grasped the outstretched hand in his vice-like grip and stared intently into the face of his former enemy. Alec coughed and blew his nose loudly in an attempt to hide his emotion and the suffused tears brimming in his eyes. Those spectators who were close and witnessed the incident, declared they also saw a couple of bright sparkling tears well up in Paddock's eyes.

Seeing that in his absence Paddock had been getting the worst of the engagement, Alec whipped off his coat and took his place in his corner. This spontaneous act of loyalty evoked prolonged cheering and applause from everyone present, who were delighted to see that the two men had, at last, settled all their differences.

From this moment on the Redditch fighter gained renewed confidence and made many determined efforts to get at his slippery opponent, but it was all to no avail, for the "Little Wonder" as he had become known, was much too nimble and clever on his feet, indulging in all sorts of acrobatic feats, repeatedly dodging under Paddock's arm and coming up behind him in a most unconventional manner.

There was scarcely a breath of wind and, as the hot sun glared down on the arena, beads of perspiration glistened on the bodies of the two boxers. After having removed a fragment of skin from Tom's nose, both men stopped fighting for a few minutes to take a drink and a breather. So far it had been a tremendous round of give and take, Paddock receiving most of his punishment to the side of his head and Sayers taking his share on his cast-iron face. The round ended when Paddock went down amidst vociferous cheers from the Sayers contingent.

In round 6 Tom bestowed a pulverizing punch on Paddock's nose. With blood streaming from both nostrils, Paddock swept in wildly, intent on retribution. Swinging his right with tremendous force, he missed Tom completely and struck one of the stakes. Clutching at his injured hand, he grimaced at the intense pain. Lashed into a fury, and shaking his hand violently, he began chasing Tom around the ring. During the pursuit, the champion slipped and fell rather questionably. Instantly Paddock's umpire appealed to the referee who, without compunction, cautioned Sayers to be more careful in future.

Slow to the call of time, Paddock came out very cautiously for the 7th round. He repeatedly endeavoured to lead off, but on each occasion Sayers danced away or ducked under his arm, nailing him incessantly on the nose and cheek until he fell.

In Paddock's corner, Jack Macdonald and Jemmy Massey worked diligently on Paddock's battered features and successfully staunched the steady stream of blood, but when he came up for round 8 his left eye had closed completely and his nose and cheek were fearfully swollen. Nevertheless, regardless of his injuries, he consistently launched his ferocious onslaughts, but Sayers was still too quick for him and danced away each time unharmed. However, the round ended when Paddock knocked the champion down with a particularly vicious right, inflicting a deep cut inside his mouth and drawing a great fountain of blood. Although there were loud cheers for Paddock, so far in the conflict he had only scored two events.

The last blow had evidently shaken Sayers, who came up with suspiciously puffed lips. Paddock tried to pursue his advantage, but he imprudently came into the attack with his guard down and walked into a straight left to the nose which sent him reeling about the ring and put an end to his rushes for the moment. The brief respite enabled Tom to regain some of his composure, and when Paddock came in again he paid him another visit on the cheek before sprinting away from the return. Some good exchanges led them into a clinch, and the round concluded with Paddock getting down, narrowly escaping a terrific swing from the champion.

By the 12th round, Paddock's mouth hung open as he gasped for air in the oppressive and stifling confines of the ring. At the close, in the brief struggle to trip each other, Sayers threw his adversary and fell across his stomach. One hour and two minutes had now elapsed.

Paddock's face was grievously distorted as he approached the scratch and his one remaining eye glared menacingly at Sayers. As he launched himself at the champion, Tom slipped and fell as he back-pedalled from the attack.

Instantly there came a cry of 'Foul!' from both Massey and Macdonald, who ran protesting to the referee. The fall had been purely accidental and there should have been no grounds for an objection, but uproar ensued as the customary condemnations were lodged by the cardsharps and other dubious characters whose only concern was, perhaps, the value of a jug of beer, or those proportionately anxious to win, draw, or argue, rather than lose their often meagre investments. For several minutes the referee was subjected to a torrent of abuse from the restive mob, who swarmed into the arena demanding retribution. Amid all the confusion and din, the ring-keepers cracked their whips menacingly over the heads of the discordant rabble until they succeeded in driving the undesirables away from the ringside.

Eventually, after much coaxing and cajoling by the referee, Macdonald and Massey were induced to calm down and return to their duties. The referee having said 'Fight on', the battle proceeded but the short delay had afforded a welcome respite for Paddock, who now dashed in and punched Sayers on the cheek.

It was becoming clear by the 16th that Paddock was failing fast. At the instigation of his seconds, he raced in to turn the scales of victory, but woefully short in his reach and leaving himself wide open. Tom smashed home another terrible blow on Paddock's swollen nose, causing him to shake his head vigorously to clear his scattered senses. The round ended when Paddock forced Tom against the ropes and brought him down.

During the struggle for supremacy in round 17, Paddock sustained two deep lesions on his leg when he appeared to fall on the spikes of Sayer's boots. Massey instantly lodged an objection and declared the injury had been committed deliberately. But eyewitnesses refuted his preposterous claim and were quick to testify that the wounds had been inflicted by the heel of Paddock's other boot as he rolled over on the turf. To settle the controversy, the referee called Paddock over to inspect the spikes. Finding them much longer and sharper than those of Sayers, he had no hesitation in overruling the objection. It would have been extremely foolish of Tom at this point in the battle to have jeopardized his chances of success, when victory was almost within his grasp.

The aggressive infighting from round 18 had left Paddock's normally florid features covered in red welts and frightfully swollen. He went straight into a grappling hold and, after a long struggle, both fell, with Paddock underneath. Massey now made another spurious claim that Sayers had fallen with both knees on Paddock's stomach, but it proved merely another stratagem in which to snatch a verdict.

Paddock tried one last resolute effort in the 20th, but again was short in his delivery. Sayers countered heavily on the damaged cheek, before repeating the dose with even greater severity. Paddock's supporters were groaning with despair as he now stood waiting for Sayers to come to him, too exhausted himself to make an effective attack. Tom walked towards him and dealt him a savage blow on the nose followed by a right to the cheek. He then forced him against the ropes where he hammered away at close quarters until they both fell.

Paddock cut a pathetic figure as he staggered weakly to the scratch for the 21st and last round. His knees wobbled beneath him and, only able to distinguish a blurred figure before him, he made one last despairing rush. As he came lumbering forward, Tom sidestepped, and met him full on the right cheek. The devastating power behind the punch stunned Paddock. On the point of falling, he reached out as if to catch hold of Sayers to try to support himself but Tom, who had already drawn back his right fist to deliver the last smashing blow full into Paddock's face, restrained himself and seized the outstretched hand instead. Shaking it warmly, he conducted him back to his corner.

Massey and Macdonald could see it was pointless to continue the struggle, and the sponge was tossed high into the air. Amidst the tumultuous cheers and applause, the referee pronounced Sayers the victor in a time of 1 hour and 22 minutes.

Utterly exhausted, and totally confused by having been led to his corner, it took Paddock several minutes to fully understand that it was all over and he had been defeated. He became so upset by the verdict, he broke down and shed tears of disappointment at his humiliating defeat. He had no reason to feel ashamed, however, for not once did he allow his normally fiery temper to get out of control nor did he flinch from the severity of his punishment, taking everything Sayers could administer with apparent indifference. Even the unfortunate accident of hitting his hand against the stake did not prevent him flooring Sayers with the same fist. But sadly, all the former dash and determination had gone and he had been almost as slow and ineffectual as the old Slasher. In all fairness, following his serious illness he should not have been induced to try conclusions with one so much faster and younger than himself.

Soon after the affair had ended, the men dressed and returned to the steamer where Tom made a collection among the passengers for his fallen opponent. When the donations were handed over to Paddock, they amounted to £30; a clear indication of the gallantry and esteem in which he was still held.

A few days after his victory, Tom was again decorated with the championship belt and presented with his battle-money on the stage of the Victoria Theatre. As a further honour, he received Tom Cribb's superb lion skin champions belt and the magnificent silver cup presented to Cribb for his victory over Molineaux in 1811. The cup bore an engraving of the crest of Cribb's native Bristol; representing in the first quarter, the coat of arms of the city and the British lion looking down with stern regard on the American flag flying at half mast. The second quarter depicted Cribb in his coal barge; illustrative of his trade. The third quarter defined the combatants in action, and in the fourth quarter, the beaver, symbolic of America hiding its head under its folds, alluding to Molineaux's defeat. The supporters represented the champion looking with an eye of commiseration on his vanquished opponent, and inscribed underneath the motto:

"And damned be him who first cries, Hold! enough!" – SHAKE-SPEARE.

The itinerant Tom Paddock, beaten by Tom Sayers on Canvey Island in 1858.

# 15

## A TRIP TO JERSEY

Having disposed of the last of the big men, Tom naturally assumed he would now have a little respite in which to relax and enjoy his hard-earned honours, but Harry Broome, up to his old tricks again, declared he had found someone who would crush the champion once and for all. Fresh speculation swept the Fancy who were at a loss to know just who this unknown might be, for at this precise period of time there appeared to be no one of any importance left who could wrest the title from Tom Sayers.

After keeping everyone in suspense, the sporting public were astounded when Broome announced that his unknown protégé was none other than Tom's old adversary, Bill Benjamin. Broome's lame but plausible excuse was that in his last encounter with Sayers, Benjamin had attributed his defeat to an attack of nerves induced by having to strip to the skin before an assembled audience on a bitterly cold day.

Since his ignominious defeat, Benjamin had suppressed a smouldering hatred for all the derisive and sarcastic innuendoes he had endured in that time. Convinced they were totally unjustified and he was not the coward he had come to be dubbed, he wanted to meet Sayers again to vindicate his defeat and clear his name of the stigma of cowardice. He told his principle backer of his new-found confidence, and pleaded with him to stake him for a re-match. He evidently possessed great persuasive powers for his backer acceded to his request and agreed to finance him for the £200 stake money.

Both sides met soon after to speed up the settlement of the pre-liminaries and the articles were signed, sealed, and delivered for their second engagement on April 5, 1859. Tom was profoundly conscious that the contest would bring him six months nearer to the retention of the belt as his own property and, after the result of their last meeting, felt equally confident of another easy victory.

With his reputation at stake, Benjamin now set about gleaning every scrap of useful information relative to Sayers and his training techniques. His first priority was to engage a highly experienced manager and trainer, so acting upon the advice of an old and trusted patron, he sought the services of Nat Langham, whose managerial qualifications and intimate knowledge of Sayers would be of immeasurable value.

Nat was offered a substantial sum of money to supervise Benjamin's training programme, but unfortunately his current personal and business interests prevented him from accepting this highly lucrative offer. He did agree, however, to pay an occasional visit to Benjamin's training quarters to instruct him on some of his own unconventional training methods, but recommended that he send a retaining fee to Bendigo and engage him as his trainer and manager. Although Bendigo was devoting himself to his religious studies at this time, he needed very little persuasion to leave his meditations and join forces with Benjamin.

Meanwhile, Tom was occupying himself by touring the country, giving an exhibition here, or taking a benefit there, and showing off his trophies to hosts of admiring fans.

During his travels through the southern counties, he arrived in Dorset at the beginning of December. Deciding he had earned a short vacation, he thought it would be an ideal opportunity to catch the Channel Islands steamer from Weymouth, and visit his old friend and fellow-townsman Harry Phelps who, with his wife, managed a small boarding house in David Place, St Helier, Jersey. Quite possibly, nothing would have been known of his visit and the following incident had it not been for a letter written by a certain "Mr Brown,"* who was also visiting St Helier at this time. Mr Brown had sailed from Weymouth in his friend Captain T.M. Leir's yacht *Fennella*, and its crew of Jack, Joe and Jem (Captain Leir's 3 sons), a cabin boy and a cook.

Having landed at St Helier, they were met by some friends from the army garrison who invited them to a luncheon at Fort Regent, then a large barracks above the town. Later, in the course of a stroll through the streets, they came upon a quaint little public house called the Prince of Wales Tavern in French Lane where they were introduced to Harry Phelps.

Mr Brown goes on to relate: "We had a smoke and a long chat with our host, a most agreeable and pleasant-mannered young man, who seemed a perfect dictionary or encyclopaedia regarding the annals and traditions of the prize ring. Phelps informed us that he gave lessons in the noble art of self-defence to the nobility and gentry and to the

---

*A favourite pastime for many influential Victorian gentlemen was to travel incognito, or under various *noms de plumes*. Charles Dickens for example often used the pseudonym of "Captain Brown."

officers of the island. We saw much of Harry Phelps, who was always a welcome guest at Fort Regent and the other barracks on the island.

"A pressing invitation from some other Jersey friends was accepted by our *Fennella* crew and, after spending one glorious evening at Lionel's Cafe and Billiard Saloon, my friend Lord Lurgan said to me as we lit our cigars and buttoned our overcoats before mounting the hill to Fort Regent where we were to dine, 'I have asked a friend to meet you tonight.'

'May I ask his name?' said I.

'His name is Captain Smith' replied Lord Lurgan, 'and you'll find him a very jolly fellow.'

"Captain Smith was waiting for us when we arrived. He was a well-built, able-bodied personage, apparently in his late twenties, of stout build and medium height; about five feet eight inches, in a pair of neat high-lows, and worsted socks, with a compact well-put-together frame calculated to stand a deal of hard work. A round cropped, bullet head which is so seldom seen outside of our little island; a fresh, healthy mahogany-tinted skin, brown and clear as a glass of old ale, which painters would indicate with a mixture of madder brown and burnt sienna. His shoulders, chest, and back, square and substantial as a tower, deriving their proportions from good English beef and floods of nut brown ale; an honest-looking somewhat bulldog face with a square jaw and light grey eyes such as denote an energetic and persevering temperament.

"Such was our arrival; and as I took in these details at a glance, Captain Smith struck me as a gentleman with whom I would rather drink than fight. The 'get up' of our distinguished guest was a check suit of the 'Stunner Tartan,' with a preternaturally short coat and a hat of the 'Five-to-one-bar-one down the road' shape which invariably suggested an amount of astuteness bordering on dishonesty.

"The usual introductions were performed by our host: 'Mr Smith, my friend Mr Brown. Brown, my friend Captain Smith. You should know each other, and now you do.'

"We were indeed a merry party as we asked the mess-room waiter if supper was ready.

"Captain Smith was the principle guest of Lord Lurgan, and occupied the place of honour, sitting on the right of 'my lord' the founder of the feast. The Captain received marked attention from the rest of the party and everybody took wine with him, who, not to be outdone in politeness, returned the compliment by challenging each in return. As our supper party consisted of fifteen, the number of bumpers of champagne thus consumed in interchanging compliments would make a nice arithmetical problem.

"The conversation soon became general, and as each man lit his cigar, the wreaths of smoke curling upwards gave a cloudy appearance to the room, so that it became difficult to distinguish one face from another. Every possible subject was discussed – politics, racing, hunting, prize fighting, cockfighting, the opera, wine, women and scandal. There were lots of songs, heaps of cigars, uncounted bottles of wine and spirits, plenty of chaff, fun and laughter and, had it not been for the morning parade at 7 a.m. I believe we should have seen 'twice round the clock.' But at length the jovial meeting came to an end, and, amidst a volley of invitations all round, we took our departure from our hospitable host.

"As our road was the same, Captain Smith, who was staying at the Prince of Wales, Harry Phelps, the Leirs (who always slept aboard the *Fennella*) and I, who lived in lodgings, went off together and should no doubt have reached our destination in safety had it not been for the larking propensities of Jack Leir, who would insist on chaffing some drunken sailors who were standing on the corner of the market square.

"Words led to blows, and Jack was knocked down by an iron bar which one of the fellows had wrenched out of some railings. We dashed to the rescue, and found ourselves assailed from front to rear by a score of stout ruffians who, luckily for us, were 'half seas over.' Our party consisted of the four Leirs, Captain Smith, a Yankee Captain and myself; and it would have fared ill with us had not our military friend been with us.

"Just as we managed to get our backs to a wall and floor a couple of the leaders, the Captain commenced by suddenly catching the biggest of our assailants, an enormous Dutchman, by the collar and seat of his breeches and literally flinging him into the crowd of his friends, and then dashed in and let them have it right and left, a man going down like a ninepin at each straight one he delivered. The odds were, as I have explained, three to one less a fraction against us; but encouraged with such a commencement, we all went at it in a manner which considerably flummoxed our foes who were sent down one after another and then, I am ashamed to say, we made a clean bolt for it.

"As it was considerably more than daylight, and the sea looked inviting, we accepted an invitation to breakfast on board the yacht, and afterwards took a short cruise in her, returning to St Helier in time for dinner.

"Captain Smith stayed about a fortnight and, with Phelps, was a frequent visitor to Fort Regent. There he often gave me lessons in the 'noble art' and considerably astonished everybody who put the gloves on with him. All the time he stayed in Jersey after that memorable night, I noticed how singularly abstemious he was and, when asked the reason, he informed me he was in training for a little match he had on. More than this he would not say, nor could I get information from Lurgan or Phelps, and not until I returned to London and called at an address the Captain gave me, did I discover he was Tom Sayers who had run over to Jersey incognito to spend a week or two with his pal Harry Phelps."

Tom returned to London in the middle of January, a fairly wealthy man. Afraid he might fritter it all away, his friends advised him to invest the money wisely, knowing he had provisionally resolved to retire from the ring in June 1860 when the belt would become his own property. But the dramatic sequence of events which were to unfold over the next few weeks nearly cost him his title and the coveted belt.

At the end of January, he began the initial phase of his seven week training programme at the Brown Jug near Tonbridge. All went well for a couple of weeks until he received the distressing news that his mother, who had been suffering from cancer of the womb for the past year, was dying and not expected to live more than a few days. Abandoning everything, he set off immediately for Brighton and took up lodgings at the Plough Inn, in Rottingdean, a small village on the outskirts of Brighton. (Although extensively altered, the Plough Inn still stands on the corner of Whipping Post Lane.) Every day he rode into Brighton for his daily sea bath and cold shower at Brill's Bath in Pool Valley (now the site of the Cannon cinema) before spending the rest of the day with his parents.

On February 16, his mother Maria finally succumbed to her illness and died at the age of seventy-one. Tom had intended to resume training after the funeral but, within a few days of her death, he received another disturbing message that his wife Sarah was pregnant with the first of her three children by James Aldridge. The news came as a bombshell. Secretly, he had always expected she would return to him, but now, realizing that his marriage was finished, he finally dispelled any thoughts of a reconciliation.

Faced with the dilemma of breaking the news to his two children, he lost complete control of his emotions and reason. He started going to bed late and rising late and, instead of his usual walking and running exercises, he hired a horse from Sam Ridley's stables in North Street and joined the Brighton Harriers.

Over the course of the next few weeks he was often to be seen careering madly across the downs in full pursuit with the hounds. But regrettably, however competent he might have been as a prize fighter, he was not very proficient as a horseman and his frequent falls became a constant source of worry to his friends. They were gravely concerned about his safety, for should he have the misfortune to fall and sprain an ankle or wrist or, even worse, break or dislocate a limb, he would have cursed not only his foolishness in putting his backers money in jeopardy, but also for leaving himself in the invidious position of losing everything he had strived so hard to achieve over the past eleven years. Even as late as the Saturday before the contest, he was out riding with the Harriers and was seen to come to grief twice.

He had always sought to protect his private life from the glare of publicity for the press, as now, were only too quick to latch on to any underlying sensationalism, especially if it involved someone as news-worthy as the champion of England. The sportswriters were at a complete loss to understand his motives, for this was the first time in his whole career he had ever neglected his training to this degree. His irresponsible conduct, they complained, was unconductive to the supreme condition expected of the Champion of England. But they were unaware of his personal problems, and wrongly assumed that the reason he regarded his present contest with such cool indifference was due to the easy victory over Benjamin in their last meeting.

He certainly looked in poor shape when he arrived at Owen Swift's on the Sunday before the engagement and it was plain for all to see that he had taken very few pains with his training. Almost at once rumours began circulating of deep-laid conspiracies designed to defraud the public, and unfounded claims were rife that the Broomes had reached a secret arrangement with Sayers and that the fight was most certainly "fixed."

For the first time ever, many of Tom's loyal followers still remained to be convinced that he was not connected in some way or another, despite all his protestations that the accusations were a complete tissue of lies. There were whisperings about Benjamin too, as reports began filtering through affirming that he really was the exceptional fighter he claimed to be and Sayers' victory in their last match was a pure piece of good fortune.

On the morning of the contest, despite the flood of handbills adver-tising the fight, only a small minority of supporters assembled at London Bridge Station to take their seats on the half-empty train, a clear indication that the majority still believed the fight was a swindle.

It proved an uneventful, but pleasant journey to a secluded location, about a mile from Ashford station in Kent. The ring was formed in an adjacent field and, a little after 11 o'clock, amidst as much loud and enthusiastic cheering as was possible from such a small assembly, Tom Sayers made his way towards the ring, accompanied by Harry Brunton and Jerry Noon. Modestly dropping his hat over the ropes, he just as modestly climbed through them himself.

After an interval of about five minutes, flanked by Bendigo and Jack

Macdonald, Bill Benjamin made his entrance in an equally un-pretentious way. He looked the perfection of health and fitness. Standing proud and upright, the smile of confidence on his face presented a vivid contrast to his debut on the former occasion. In comparison, Tom looked decidedly overweight and much too fleshy. Nevertheless, he still retained an air of self-possession about him which denoted the more accomplished boxer.

Moving about the ring in a calm and businesslike manner, his ex-pression carried no fears for the forthcoming encounter but, seeing Benjamin standing before him in such superb condition, he must, for a fleeting moment at least, have regretted his lack of training; the new-look Benjamin was a very different man to the one he had thrashed with such consummate ease just fifteen months before.

At 11.20, amidst a most profound silence, the seconds delivered their charges to the scratch. They shook hands cordially and smiled as if each were greeting an old friend. The colours were then tied to the stakes, Tom sporting a richly brocaded pink and white striped hand-kerchief, with Benjamin adhering to the old-fashioned blue and white spot.

Benjamin cautiously inaugurated the proceedings, sparring to test Tom's reactions. Sayers dodged in to try his famous double hit, but Benjamin stood ready and waiting and easily sidestepped out of harm's way. Again Tom lunged forward and delivered a stinging left to the cheek. Benjamin recoiled from the shock and retaliated with a beautiful counterpunch which fractured Tom's nose. This quite un-expected success so early in the conflict evoked loud and prolonged cheering from the Benjamin contingent as the referee awarded "First blood" to their hero.

Reeling about the ring, the blood gushing in torrents from his broken nose, Sayers immediately dispelled any thoughts of an easy victory. Trying desperately hard to regain his self-composure, he realized he now had a fight on his hands. Until his dying day, Tom always insisted that this was the hardest spank on the nose he had ever experienced, and from that day onwards he always knew when it was going to rain from the pain which invariably occurred when the weather was about to change. The rebuff had clearly riled Tom and, hungry for revenge, he made a quick stab to the body followed by a slashing crack on the left cheek, laying the flesh open and knocking Benjamin off his feet.

Both men were steadily oozing blood as they came to the scratch for the 2nd round. Unconcerned after his knockdown, Benjamin feinted and let fly a tremendous swing with his left. Tom saw it coming and deflected it easily, but some heavy infighting followed as each gave and received repeated punishment to the nose and mouth. Finally, as they broke from a clinch, Tom planted a massive blow on Benjamin's head and forced him down close to the ropes.

Benjamin opened the action in the 3rd round with the utmost caution but Tom, anxious to begin, attacked with a straight punch on the nose. With an exceptional burst of speed, Benjamin countered with a smarting blow to the champion's cheekbone. This led into a series of turbulent exchanges until Sayers, catching Benjamin around the neck, held him tight and pummelled at his face. Then, with a simply Herculean heave of his shoulders, he threw Benjamin with prodigious force headfirst into the post.

Benjamin delivered several tremendous punches in the 5th, but they appeared to lack the same weight and precision as the champion's.

Tom was showing signs of exhaustion in the 6th round, and he became extremely erratic in his deliveries. Finally, when they came into a grappling hold, both fell headlong through the ropes.

There was a savage gleam in Benjamin's eye as he came to scratch for round 7, and with a new resilience literally launched himself at Sayers. This malevolent attack signalled a portent of what was to become one of the toughest and fiercest rounds anyone had witnessed for a very long time. In their battle of attrition, each disputed the ground inch by inch; Benjamin astonishing everyone with his cool and decisive manner and the timed perfection of his punching.

Breaking off occasionally to survey each other for a few moments, they would return to the fray, oblivious to the pain, each doing everything they knew to turn the tide of battle. Blowing freely from their exertions, and blood gushing in a deluge from each man, Sayers rammed home a left to Benjamin's eye as he returned with a demoralizing blow to the champion's mouth.

Benjamin's backers were beginning to regain some of their flagging confidence, feeling sure that if he continued in the same vein over the next few rounds, he stood a remarkably good chance of winning. The fighting was fast and furious and the courage and fortitude with which Benjamin stood up to his antagonist won the highest acclaim from everyone. Occasionally Sayers was wild with his punches and appeared to be tiring rapidly, but his greater hitting power was slowly taking its inevitable toll as hit succeeded hit. Benjamin's face was swelling ominously, but he continued undaunted, having decided to do or die in the attempt. Coming to close quarters, some incredibly hard punches were swapped and, as the blood cascaded over their bodies, the champion fell on Benjamin, expelling the last drop of air from his lungs. Benjamin had lost his chance and Sayers would never allow him another.

As they came out for round 8, the huge bump on the side of Benjamin's head and the frightful bruising around the eye clearly indicated the dynamic power of Tom's deliveries. But the champion was not having it all his own way. His face was flushed to a deep shade of crimson and he appeared quite distressed. Seeing him in this exhausted condition, Benjamin believed the time was now ripe to finish the task before him. Pulling himself together, he made ready for what he thought would be the final onslaught. The series of rapid exchanges which followed were all in his favour until suddenly, and for no apparent reason, he broke off the engagement and retreated.

A look of blank disbelief crossed Tom's features; why should Benjamin back off when he had him on the defensive? Quick to seize the advantage, Tom began to pursue him about the ring. Suddenly Benjamin stopped in his tracks, turned, and swung a left hook, but the champion countered swiftly with his auctioneer and knocked him unconscious.

It required the concerted efforts of both Bendigo and Macdonald to restore him to his senses before time expired. Still badly shaken from the last tremendous punch, he marshalled his energy and came out resolutely. He attempted to spar a little, but Sayers timed his next punch to perfection and sent it crashing full into the middle of Benjamin's face. As he stepped forward to counter, Tom returned with even greater speed to his damaged eye, and sent him hurtling to the ground.

Poor Bill Benjamin presented a pitiful spectacle as he staggered out for round 10. Despite repeated requests from his seconds to submit, he still struggled valiantly to hold up his hands. With comparative ease, Tom delivered another crushing blow to Benjamin's good eye and knocked him down again. During the half-minute intermission, Bendigo and Macdonald were seen in heated discussion on whether he should be allowed to continue, and after a few seconds threw up the sponge.

But Benjamin insisted on returning to the scratch in spite of his horrendous injuries. He wanted to prove beyond all questionable doubt that he was not the coward he had come to be dubbed and was far from being beaten. Breaking away from his seconds, he made his way to the centre of the ring for the 11th and last round. He tried to lead off but, well short of his target, he stumbled forward into a punch on the nose which sent him to grass for the last time.

As a gesture of sportsmanship, Tom walked over to his corner to shake his hand, but Benjamin, almost totally blinded, still refused to submit. Resisting the restraints of his seconds he said he wished to commence another round, but they were uncompromising and vigorously denied his demands. He struggled violently with them in a bid to

Bill Benjamin nearly wrested the title from Tom Sayers in their second battle.

Bob Brettle was forced to submit to Tom Sayers after he dislocated his shoulder.

return to the centre but they bundled him out through the ropes and away from the ring.

As Tom was proclaimed the winner in a time of 22 minutes, the entire arena erupted with a crescendo of cheering. Smiling broadly, he waved gaily to his supporters, but on this occasion he declined from vaulting the ropes in his usual fashion. He was totally and utterly exhausted, not so much from his heavy punishment, but more from the strenuous efforts and neglect of condition in a battle, disputed in several rounds with unwarranted speed and desperation.

Benjamin's punishment had been as heavy in eleven rounds as might have been expected in a conflict of twice the distance. Although defeated, he was by no means dishonoured. He could now hold his head high with pride, for in his dogged determination to undergo this second ordeal, he had succeeded in redeeming his tarnished character. As he was led away he received loud applause for his courage and tenacity in absorbing all the heavy punishment Sayers could administer, without ever flinching or complaining.

This second encounter with Benjamin taught Tom a lesson never to be forgotten. In future, under no circumstances must he ever enter the ring in such a deplorable condition, against any opponent, regardless of his experience. Throughout the course of history many a brave man has suffered for his recklessness by losing a position in life he was never able to regain.

The 12½ stone Harry Paulson, beaten by Tom Sayers at Appledore in Kent.

# 16

## SHADOW ACROSS THE ATLANTIC

With defeat of Bill Benjamin, the sporting public were sure there was no one left in Britain capable of disputing Tom's right to the championship, but to their amazement they now learned that shortly after his match with Benjamin was ratified, another challenge had come from Bob Brettle of Birmingham and he was engaged two-fold.

This second match was made under rather curious circumstances as John Gideon narrates: "I was fairly staggered one night at Owen Swift's when Dougald Patterson, the baker of Jermyn Street, offered to stake £400 to £200, that he had found a Scotsman who would enter the ring a lighter man than Sayers, and beat him. We there and than staked a tenner each in the hands of Jack Percival to bind the bargain, and settled the evening when we would meet again to draw up the articles.

"Now, in 1859 I thought I knew every fighting man in existence, as well as their country, weight and form and, cudgel my brains how I would, I could find no trace of any Highland man good enough to grass the champion. As to the result I had no fear, but when I knew who the Scotsman was, an offer of any part of 3,000 to 1 on Sayers was refused by the supporters of the lad from the land o' cakes.

"On the night of the appointed meeting at Swift's, much to the surprise of all present and myself in particular, Alec Keene produced Bob Brettle who brought with him the certificate of his birth to prove he was a Scotsman, born at Portobello near Edinburgh, but brought up in Birmingham, having lived there with his parents."

Bob had been apprenticed in the glass industry, and first became connected with the prize ring while employed as a glass-blower in one of the larger establishments. In February 1854 he made his debut against Malpas of Birmingham and ten months later encountered the veteran Jack Jones of Portsmouth. Darkness forced an end to their conflict and the referee ordered them to fight the following Saturday. On the appointed day Brettle failed to show up and the stakes were awarded to Jones. Subsequently it was discovered that Bob had been apprehended by the police but it was never established whether his arrest was caused by his own negligence, or by that of his friends who, fearing for his safety, had informed the authorities.

He defeated Roger Coyne in November 1855 and Sam Simmonds suffered a similar fate the following June. A little over a year passed before his next contest with Job Cobley. Finding the going too tough, Cobley resorted to dropping and lost the engagement by falling without a blow. In 1857, Brettle met Bob Travers at Appledore in Kent but, after 65 minutes and 42 rounds, the police arrived and stopped the proceedings.

The next day, after fighting another 100 rounds in 2 hours and 5 minutes, Travers found the earth the safest place and dropped without a blow. This last encounter was understood to be Bob's final appearance in the ring, but the overriding temptation to have one last crack at the championship was an opportunity he could not resist. The London Fancy could hardly believe he was serious for, as far as they were concerned, he stood exceptionally little chance against Sayers. Bob's opinion differed. He and Tom had been friends for several years and, in that time had engaged in many sparring contests together. Consequently, as a result of these sessions, Brettle genuinely believed he had always had the best of these encounters. Perhaps he did but, as George Sims had found to his cost, Tom Sayers was more at home with bare fists than with his hands muffled in gloves at a sparring contest.

Brettle said he wanted to meet Sayers in the prize ring, but only on the understanding that Tom put down £400 to his £200 and throw in the championship belt. The Sayers' backers were highly amused at the suggestion and were only too willing to comply with the odds Brettle was asking. But Tom was a little more reticent. He agreed to the stake money but said he could not justify adding the belt as well against such preposterous odds.

At first Brettle begrudged the opportunity of passing up the belt but, on further reflection, concluded that the extra £200 Tom was prepared to stake was more than sufficient to purchase a new belt of double the value. So, waiving all pretensions to the trophy, he agreed to Tom's terms and closed the bargain.

At Owen Swift's on the night of the meeting to ratify the articles, Tom's supporters, implicitly confident he would beat the Birmingham champion, were offering odds of £100 to £10. John Gideon, who still regarded the affair as quite ridiculous, ventured to suggest that in all probability, Brettle would be vanquished in ten minutes. Bob's eyes flashed with anger at the suggestion and, in the heat of the moment, offered to bet £100 to £10 against such an eventuality.

'Make it £200 to £20 and it's a bet,' said Gideon.

'Done,' replied Bob as he handed his money to Alec Keene.

The articles were then signed and the date for the contest confirmed for Tuesday September 20, 1859. This suited Tom's plans admirably, for it left him ample time for another moneymaking tour before settling down to serious training. Curiously his last meeting with Bob Brettle had been on his tour of the northern counties at the time of Paddock's illness. Bob was then managing a circus at Dale End, Birmingham and they had arranged to stage a sparring exhibition in the circus ring. Bob had asked a colleague if he would care to meet the champion of England when he arrived at the circus that evening.

Tom evidently made a deep and lasting impression on Bob's anonymous friend, who wrote an evocative and graphic account of the meeting:

"The performance began at 8 o'clock in the evening and Sayers had promised to be there but, at 9.30 he had failed to put in an appearance. However, a few minutes after this time, Bob Brettle touched me on the arm, causing me to turn around and, before I scarcely knew, I was being introduced and shaking hands with the champion of England. In front of me stood a man about 5 feet 8 inches in height, dressed in an old-fashioned coachman's topcoat: one of those with any quantity of small capes hanging from the neck down over the shoulders. On his head was a kind of skullcap and his face was not improved by the three or four day's growth of hair which so thickly covered his cheeks and chin.

"I had scarcely time to express the pleasure I had at seeing him and the fear I had been in that, by his non-arrival, the pleasure would have been denied me, when Brettle hurried him off to introduce him to the public from the sawdust arena. Before moving away Bob told me they were going to have a quiet supper upstairs at his home and invited me to come, an invitation I accepted readily.

"Two minutes later, Tom Sayers was introduced to the Birmingham public who cheered the champion most lustily, a cry, however, being raised that Tom should set to with their hero. To the applause Tom bowed his acknowledgements, and to the demands for him to set to with Brettle, he explained that he had just come off a long journey by rail, which had been aggravated by a stoppage on the road, so he was not in the condition he should like to be when sparring before a Birmingham audience. He, however, begged to assure them that, as he intended taking a benefit in the town before long, they would then have the opportunity of seeing him and his friend set to.

"I may state that Tom in the rough, as I had seen him, had not made a very favourable impression upon me. In fact, his whole makeup reminded me more of a stage highwayman than of what he really was. In short, he looked more like Jerry Abershaw*, to my fancy, than the champion of England. But when I got to Brettle's pub, the White Lion at Digbeth, and walked up to Brettle's private sitting room, Sayers was quite another man. The barber had removed all surplus hair from his face. He had got on a clean shirt, a black coat and waistcoat and a pair of dark elastic cord inexpressibles which set off his well-shaped legs to advantage. Sayers was now not only presentable in appearance, but fairly good-looking.

"In his manner he was quiet and unassuming, saying very little, but what he did say was to the point, and what I also noticed was his language being quite free from oaths. I believe that, had it not been for the unmistakable fighting-looking mug, so far as conversation went, he might have passed for a Bishop. As to fighting, very little "shop" was spoken. After supper we stuck to the bottle very close, but I remember Sayers drank very sparingly."

Tom returned from his latest tour at the end of July and began his training at Newmarket under the guidance of Joey Jones, a little-known but clever pugilist. The excitement of the forthcoming contest caused enormous interest amongst the jockeys and racing fraternity of Newmarket and Tom soon became a distinguished celebrity in the district.

Soon after the articles were signed, Bob Brettle went into training at Ashbourne in Derbyshire under the supervision of his old adversary Bob Travers. Under Travers' intensive discipline and coaching, Brettle succeeded in reducing his weight to 10 stone 4 pounds, about 5 pounds lighter than Sayers.

For at least a month prior to the engagement, John Gideon had been seeking to procure a suitable location for the venue, out of reach of the undesirables, easily accessible by train and tolerably safe from the all-prying eyes of the authorities. Although it eventually cost him a considerable amount of time and effort, plus a sizeable amount of expenditure in bribing the railway officials, he had good reason to be satisfied with his arrangements. His remunerative proposals to the railway company were certainly very tempting when he estimated that as the train would be carrying in excess of 1,000 passengers at thirty shillings a head, everyone connected with the management of the excursion could expect a handsome share of the profits when the money was equally divided between the railway executives and the backers of both men.

* The notorious highwayman.

Meanwhile, as the day of the engagement drew near, the excitement in London reached fever pitch, especially when the Birmingham supporters began turning up in force, their pockets well lined with cash. Great was the pity that many of these wide-eyed, gullible travellers who, never having seen anything comparable to the great metropolis, stood exceedingly little chance against the professional con men and cardsharps. In their naive innocence, they were soon tricked into losing every penny they possessed and many were forced to make the long and dangerous journey home on foot.

To the consternation of many travellers, when they reached the station early on the morning of September 20, they found the entrances and platforms seething with a multitude of supporters. On seeing the vast assembly, the majority had serious misgivings that there would not be enough room on the train for everybody, but their fears proved groundless for, when the huge train pulled into the station, it comprised of no less than thirty-six carriages.

At 7.45 the engine emitted a shrill blast on its whistle and, amidst the clouds of thick black smoke permeating the station, the train steamed slowly out of the terminus aided by two powerful engines attached to either end. The travellers settled back in their seats to enjoy the pleasant journey to the picturesque little village of Etchingham, situated on the main Tunbridge Wells and Hastings line. Shortly before 10 o'clock, when the train pulled into Etchingham's tiny station, the carriages appeared to erupt as the doors flew open and the vast concourse of people swarmed out into the adjacent fields. Marshals instructed everyone to assemble into one large body in preparation to be escorted to the field of battle, and a few minutes later they were joined by an intermediary who had travelled down to Etchingham the previous evening. Placing himself at the head of the column, he led them off on their short journey to a meadow, about a quarter of a mile from the station.

The sergeant and two constables of the East Sussex Constabulary who witnessed the arrival of the train found themselves completely overwhelmed by the huge army of supporters. Outnumbered by about 400 to 1, they quickly realized there was nothing they could do to prevent the fight taking place so, deciding discretion was the better part of valour, they joined forces with the company and marched off to watch the fight unmolested.

While the preliminaries were being concluded, a brisk business began for the sale of refreshments and inner-ring tickets. The relatively high proportion of upperclass spectators may be gauged from the sale of the ringside seats which totalled £54. 10s.

Billy Duncan and his ring constables cleared the ring of the customary inquisitive spectators and, when everyone had been comfortably settled, a mighty roar rent the air when a cap was observed flying high over the dense mass of people.

Escorted by Alec Keene and Jem Hodgekiss of Birmingham, Bob Brettle elbowed his way through the tightly packed crowd, a broad smile illuminating his face at the warm reception. Tom Sayers followed a few seconds later, attended by Jack Macdonald and Harry Brunton. As the little trio pushed their way through the vast throng they too were greeted with the same tremendous ovation, Tom acknowledging the response with a wide grin and a cheerful wave to the crowd.

The spectators now began to make their last-minute investments. Several large bets of 3 to 1 caused a stampede among the betting fraternity and there were many calls of '£25 to £10 on Sayers!' as eager punters rushed to lay their bets before hostilities commenced. Brettle went over to Tom's corner and offered to take £150 to £50 from him but Tom tactfully declined; all his bets had been invested earlier and at much better odds. Bob then held up the promissory note and offered to take the same odds from anyone present, but all he received for his efforts was a sullen stony silence. With a glum look on his face, he walked slowly back to his corner and handed the note over to his friends.

The only formality remaining to be completed was tying the colours to the stakes. As Tom knotted his handsome blue and white striped handkerchief with a blue border, and Brettle his dark blue with a white star, a heated discussion broke out in the Sayers' corner and people began pointing and staring in the direction of Brettle. Harry Brunton and Jack Macdonald hurried over to Frank Dowling, the referee, and lodged an appeal that the spikes on Brettle's boots were too long.

The umpires and referee called Bob over to examine the offending spikes. Signalling for a ruler, they found them well beyond the regulation length and, nodding their heads in agreement with the Sayers' seconds, they declared their objection valid. A file was produced and work began filing down the points but, despite the concerted efforts of Harry Brunton and Jack Macdonald, the spikes still remained too long for their intended purpose. It was the prerogative of Brunton and Macdonald to show the spikes to the referee, who doubtless would have insisted they be taken down even further but Tom, anxious to begin, told them he was not unduly worried and thought the problem of little importance.

As they threw off their blankets, Brettle's fresh complexion and healthy appearance contrasted starkly against the full and blemished features of Sayers. Although Tom was in superb condition, his bronzed face was now showing the wear and tear of his years of dedication to the ring.

At the call of "Time!", both walked to the centre, their faces wreathed in smiles. Bob made the opening gambit by walking round his adversary with a crablike, sideways shuffle. Slowly his former smiling countenance faded and he began leering at Sayers, evidently goading the champion into launching an attack. But, after his lengthy experience in the ring Tom was quick to perceive his ambiguous motives and kept in step with his circling movements, shifting his position and constantly presenting a square front to his adversary. At length, finding Sayers wise to his little game, he dashed forward swinging his left.

The punch caught the champion on the nose, but Tom simply smiled at him as if to say, "Just wait a minute, your turn will come."

Bob continued his pedestrian wanderings while Tom remained facing him and calmly awaiting his next attack. Abruptly Brettle rushed in again and, after a spate of heavy exchanges, Tom left a bump the size of a pigeon's egg on Bob's forehead. Having received the worst of the treatment, Brettle slowly retreated in his attempt to draw Tom forward and create an opening. Hoping to catch Tom unawares, he lunged out with his left but miscalculated his distance. Tom countered with a magnificent punch full on the mouth, and "First blood" was instantly visible.

Encouraged by his success, Tom now intensified the pressure. He feinted for an opening and, as Bob ducked his head, the champion delivered another crushing blow on the forehead. As Brettle slumped to the ground, so an air of despondency descended over his backers. "First knock-down" was registered on Tom's behalf but, after some deliberation between the umpires and the referee, the claim was disallowed on the grounds that Brettle was getting down when the blow was delivered.

Round 2 opened with a series of heavy exchanges, Tom landing on the left eye and Bob mainly to the body. Brettle broke away and once again resorted to his cunning circling routine, flexing his muscles and taunting Sayers as he strutted around the ring, trying to lure him into an opening. But the wily Tom simply walked around with him, persistently facing him and refusing to be drawn out. Unable to provoke a reaction, Brettle struck out with a swinging left and, in the exchanges which followed, landed a slashing punch on Tom's cheek as he was falling back.

Instantly a claim of "First knock-down" to Brettle was registered, but again the referee vetoed the demand and declared the blow had caught Sayers at the same instant he was slipping down.

As Tom approached the scratch for round 3, there came a loud burst of cheering from the Brettle supporters, who noticed the abrasion their hero had left on Tom's cheek. This boost to Brettle's ego encouraged a renewed sense of confidence but, as he dashed in to dictate the fighting, Tom stopped him in his tracks with a straight punch to the mouth. There now followed a burst of wild and savage infighting, each man hammering his adversary unmercifully. Ultimately, after having suffered the worst of the punishment, Brettle went down on his knees.

It had been anticipated that in his anxiety to win the bet of £200 to £20, the champion would leave himself open to Bob's dangerous righthand counters. But those who knew of Tom's proficiency in ringcraft were confident he would not be influenced into making any rash indiscretions and, when Brettle came to scratch for round 4, it was discovered that the vital ten minutes had elapsed.

Bob lost no time in getting back to business. With a couple of sideways steps, he flung himself at Tom and planted his right on the ribs. This assault was followed by several counter hits from either side and, while Tom was busily dodging and sidestepping, the extra long spikes on Brettle's boots raked down his shin, tearing his stocking and inflicting a deep wound. Bob instantly apologized, and assured him it was quite accidental, promising to be more careful in future. But his excuses were unacceptable to Macdonald, who rushed over to Solid Coates, Brettle's umpire, to claim the fight on a foul.

As Frank Dowling called the seconds over to discuss the incident, Tom limped over to assure them he was all right. He insisted, despite all Macdonald's objections, that if he could not win the fight on its merits then he would rather throw up the sponge. His outburst averted any further dissent and eased the tension between all parties. By now his stocking and drawers were drenched with blood and, when his seconds removed his boot and rolled down his stocking, they found to their consternation that the lacerations were excessively deep. Bandages were wrapped tightly around his leg, and he limped back to the scratch to continue the battle. Still hobbling painfully around the ring, he successfully landed on Bob's nose and mouth, but in the return he received a tremendous crack on the jaw which bowled him over.

"First knock-down" was awarded to Brettle amidst the vociferous cheering of his fans.

On coming to scratch, although Tom's cast-iron face bore no visible marks from the last blow, Bob's nose and left eye were fearfully swollen and blood was still trickling from his cut lips. Instantly assessing Brettle's condition, John Gideon shrewdly offered £40 to £10 on Sayers, but the only taker was Bob Travers who invested a tenner on his pet. In the next series of exchanges, the champion's auctioneer landed like a battering ram on Bob's shoulder. The impact sent him spinning round and he collapsed in a heap.

Brettle's expression was deadly serious as he came to scratch for the penultimate round and, in the thrilling climax of the rally which ensued, Tom smashed home a frightful punch on his neck. Bob's knees crumpled beneath him and he pitched over on the ground.

In the 7th and last round, Brettle resumed his peripatetic walkabout, occasionally striking out with his left, but invariably out of distance, almost as if he was terrified of encountering Tom's devastating right if he came too close.

The end came with Sayers piling on the pressure. Bob's last major effort came with a swinging left but, as his fist sailed over Tom's shoulder, the champion countered with a mammoth right on Brettle's left shoulder. His face contorted in pain, Bob grasped at his arm and tried to prop himself up against the stake in his corner. The expression of intense agony on his face made it quite clear that something was drastically wrong and as Tom approached, more in consternation than hostility, he went down on his knees.

Solid Coates hurried over to investigate the cause, and found he had dislocated his shoulder. Unable to move his stricken arm or to shield himself from further punishment, Brettle's downcast seconds reluctantly threw up the sponge and resigned the victory to Sayers. When Jack Macdonald learned the extent of the damage he promptly went over to render his assistance and, together with a doctor who was present among the spectators, reset the arm into its socket. Tom went across to shake hands and offer his help but, finding there was little he could do amidst all the frenzied activity taking place in the corner, changed into his clothes and soon reappeared among his friends.

Many of Brettle's followers believed he was equally as good as Sayers until his untimely injury terminated the battle. But Bob's personal opinions did not correspond with those of his friends and, shortly after the contest, he called at the offices of *Bell's Life* to notify them of his intention to retire from the ring. He said he knew of no man in his own category likely to try conclusions with him and would never again overmatch himself as he did on this occasion. He had a good business in Birmingham and could well afford to leave prize fighting alone.

But things did not end there. Legal proceedings were instigated against the railway company for its involvement in the affair.

In his summing up, the magistrate at Maidstone Quarter Sessions told the company's representative Mr Beattie, 'The character of the railway company was at stake in a matter of this importance and in future the railway should not facilitate itself in such disgraceful scenes as were witnessed within sight of the Parish Church, with half-naked men bruising and mutilating one another for ruffians to applaud.'

With the defeat of Bob Brettle there really was no one else left in Britain capable of disputing Tom's right to the championship. John Gideon had been hoping for one last major contest, whereby Tom could end his career on a note of triumph and retire a substantially wealthy man but, with only eight months remaining before his proposed retirement, he could see few prospects for another match in the near future. However, while the fights with Benjamin and Brettle had been keeping Tom busy in England, another event, of far greater significance than anyone could possibly imagine, was looming across the Atlantic and casting its shadow over the British prize ring.

# 17

## THE AMERICAN SCENE

The first tangible evidence of any involvement between the English and American prize rings was in 1837 when James Burke, or Deaf Burke, unable to find anyone in Great Britain willing to fight him since his fatal clash with Simon Byrne in 1833, paid a visit to the United States to see if he could find someone there who was not afraid to meet him. Professional pugilism in America was still in its infancy at this time, having been introduced some twenty years earlier when Jacob Hyer, the acknowledged father of the American prize ring, fought Tom Beasley in the first recorded ring battle in 1816.

In his mission to New York, Burke found little success and he had serious misgivings of having made the right decision. Then, in April, he received a challenge from Sam O'Rourke, the renowned Irish brawler, to meet him in New Orleans. So, with nothing to detain him in New York, he packed his few belongings and headed south.

In the saloons and gambling halls along the banks of the Mississippi, excitement had steadily heightened among the Irish immigrants at the prospect of a match between the English champion and their Irish hero. At around one o'clock on the afternoon of May 5, the two men met to do battle at the forked junction of the Bayou Road. For the first three rounds Burke had the best of the engagement, but trouble erupted in the 4th when Mick Carson (O'Rourke's second) pushed Burke from behind into the arms of O'Rourke. Spinning around, Burke raised his fist as if to strike Carson but, restraining himself, warned him that if he did it again he would knock him down.

Carson, who had come armed with a knife and a pistol tucked in his belt, replied with a sneer that if Burke attempted to lay a finger on him, he would, 'split his gizzard.'

Outraged at his humiliation, the repugnant Carson then called upon all the Irishmen present to, 'Get Burke', but, before he could utter another sound, the Deaf-'un felled him with a sledgehammer punch to the jaw.

For a few moments, Carson's fellow Irishmen were stunned and shocked at Burke's unorthodox action then, snapping out of their stupefaction, they began assailing him and his companions with their shillelaghs, whips and fists or anything which came to hand.

Burke and his party did the only sensible thing: they took to their heels and bolted. Sprinting down the road, the yelling crowd in hot pursuit, they came upon a small group of men standing by the roadside. Seeing their desperate plight, one member of the party gave Burke a bowie knife to defend himself against the angry mob and another gave him a horse on which he made good his escape. But the frenzied supporters of O'Rourke were out for blood and, incensed that Burke had eluded them, fell upon the unfortunate man who had supplied the knife and killed him.

When the blood-crazed rabble eventually returned to New Orleans, a full scale riot erupted as bands of armed and drunken Irishmen, brandishing an assortment of weapons, battled it out with other groups of armed rioters. Gangs of toughs, bent on destruction, began congregating in the vicinity of Union House while others, who had assembled outside the theatre, went on the rampage, smashing property, looting and committing acts of indiscriminate violence against any individuals who had the misfortune to be in their way. The police compensated by making a number of arrests, but they were numerically deficient to deal with a full scale riot and, at eight o'clock in the evening, the National Guard were called out to restore order and quell any further disturbances.

After his narrow escape from almost certain death, Burke beat a hasty retreat back to New York. However, shortly after the New Orleans riot, he agreed to fight another Irishman named O'Connell, but the New York sheriff's department, fearing a repetition of the New Orleans violence, promptly banned the contest. Nevertheless, despite the forbidden restriction, the fight took place without any disorder on Hart's Island, where Burke soon made short work of his less experienced adversary.

When Burke returned to England in 1838, Tom Hyer, Jacob Hyer's son, entered the scene as America's champion. Although he was destined to make the sport of pugilism popular in the United States, it was really the Irish settlers who assumed the predominant role with their champion "Yankee Sullivan", alias James Ambrose, who had fought several battles in England before making New York his home town. Consequently, with two champions contesting the title, a division was created between the American-Irish who supported Sullivan and the all-American party who stood by Hyer.

At this time, Hyer kept a respectable sporting house in Park Row, New York, patronized then by the more reputable sportsmen, whilst Sullivan owned what can best be described as a "den of vice" in Division Street, situated in the heart of New York's slum quarter.

A deep sense of rivalry existed between the two champions and, when Tom Hyer issued a challenge to fight any man in America he naturally assumed Sullivan would respond. He was not prepared, however, for the shock he received when one of Sullivan's friends, a man named George McChiester, better known as Country McClosky, a big, husky, hulk of a man who terrorized the city, walked into his saloon and offered to fight him there and then. Hyer treated the whole thing as a joke and flatly refused to consider his absurd demands. He did, however, agree to fight him in the ring and their battle took place at Caldwell's Landing, Albany, New York, on September 9, 1848. By all accounts, it proved a truly desperate conflict. For 101 rounds, lasting two hours and fifty-five minutes, Hyer knocked McClosky all around the ring. At the end, Yankee Sullivan, finding his man could not win, threw up the sponge, oblivious to all McClosky's pleas to continue.

Shortly after the engagement, Sullivan stormed into Hyer's bar, shouting abuse and threatening all and sundry with violence. Words soon led to blows and the two men began fighting in the saloon, smashing tables and chairs over each other in the traditional bar-room brawls usually seen in the movies. The violence ended when a fragile truce was called and an appeal made for an official match.

The contest was fought on January 7, 1849, at Rock Point, Kent County, Maryland. Sullivan received a terrible beating and was admitted to Mount Sinai Hospital in Baltimore. Hyer was arrested for causing grievous bodily harm and thrown into jail until Sullivan was out of danger.

With Sullivan out of the running, Hyer took over a saloon in Chatham Street, a place renowned for its regular nightly brawls. A frequent visitor to this establishment was one John Morrissey, a young, tough Irishman who had arrived in America when a boy with his destitute immigrant parents. During his formative years, he suffered a life of extreme hardship and deprivation but, by the time he reached maturity he had developed into a tall, strong and athletic young man with a formidable reputation as a bar-room brawler.

Morrissey's friends had wanted to match him against Yankee Sullivan but, just before the articles were due to be ratified, Morrissey left New York in his hurry to join the great Californian gold rush.

While he was working his claim he met George Thompson, alias Bob McClaren, an English prize fighter who had previously trained under the supervision of Peter Crawley. By coincidence, Morrissey discovered that Thompson was the man who trained Tom Hyer and for that reason took an instant dislike to the Englishman. As the weeks passed, the uneasy tension which simmered between the two, ultimately culminated in a bitter quarrel.

They decided to settle their differences in the ring for a stake of $4,000 (£800) according to the rules of the London Prize Ring. The battle proved a terrible affair. Morrissey's supporters had come armed with knives and revolvers and when Thompson began to get the better of the Irishman (having knocked him down six times in ten rounds) the hoodlums around the ring threatened to shoot him if he won. Thompson wisely dropped without a blow and forfeited the fight. Morrissey's next match was with Yankee Sullivan at Boston Corners, on the boundary between New York and Massachusetts. Again this was another disgraceful debacle. In the 38th round, Sullivan became involved in an argument taking place between the seconds and the umpire. A free-for-all broke out among the spectators and Sullivan started fighting with the seconds. When at last order was restored, the fight was awarded to Morrissey on the grounds that while Sullivan was busily engaged against the seconds and supporters, he had left the ring during the melee, and did not heed the call of time. Morrissey returned to New York in triumph, with the formidable reputation of having beaten both Thompson and Sullivan.

Of all Morrissey's fights, probably his most savage was that with Tom McCann over the favours of the latter's mistress, Kate Ridgely, a fashionable brothel owner. During their pitched battle in the saloon, Morrissey was hurled to the floor, where McCann held his head pressed against a hot stove. Very soon the acrid smell of scorched hair and burning flesh drifted through the bar-room. Anxious spectators rushed to his aid and poured water over Morrissey and the hot coals. The clouds of rising steam and smoke choked McCann just long enough for Morrissey to scramble to his feet and win a fight he seemed almost certain to have lost. It was from this brawl that Morrissey earned the title of "Old Smoke," a nickname he carried for the rest of his life.

He was soon, however, to have the worst of a ferocious struggle against Bill Poole at Amos Street Dock, New York City. Poole won the fight almost unmarked, except for a gaping gash in his cheek where Morrissey had bitten him. Morrissey deeply resented the fact that Poole had thrashed him and allegedly took his revenge by hiring a gang of thugs to give him a beating. But things went terribly wrong: Bill Poole was shot and died a few days later. Although political pressures were brought to bear at Morrissey's trial, there was no concrete evidence he was implicated in any way and the charges against him were dropped.

Morrissey was next matched to fight Tom Hyer, but he withdrew and forfeited $100. They were matched again shortly after and fought at The Abbey, New York. Here, Morrissey's gang outnumbered the followers of Hyer. To avert a potential bloodbath, Hyer produced revolvers for Morrissey and himself and proposed fighting it out with a duel, but Morrissey wisely declined.

By now the great American public were disgusted with Morrissey and everything he stood for. His backers, ashamed to be associated with his name, deserted him and began a search for a less abhorrent hero who would whip, as Morrissey had now become, the most detested man in America.

While these events were taking place in America, on the other side of the Atlantic, Aaron Jones could see very few prospects of making his fortune in England following his recent defeat at the hands of Tom Sayers. Jones had no intention of ever encountering Sayers again and had resolved to look further afield to see what other country could offer him the chance of a successful career. After giving the matter a great deal of deliberation, he settled upon the United States as his next port of call and, in the late spring of 1857, set sail for New York.

He was warmly welcomed by the Americans who were delighted with his charming manners, good looks and quiet disposition; a vast difference from the brawling fighters they had been forced to endure over the past few years. He soon became a great favourite in New York, captivating the imagination of the younger generation with his anecdotes on British sporting activities and, more particularly, those in which he had been associated.

Aaron had only been in America a short time when John Morrissey received a challenge from a group of sportsmen who had selected a young and aspiring pugilist named John Camel* Heenan as contender to the title. Heenan at this time was working in the Californian gold mines where he had figured in many sparring contests for the entertainment of the mining community. His sporting friends had wanted to match him in a contest with Yankee Sullivan at the time he had been in California but Sullivan, having heard of young Heenan's formidable reputation, had backed out and refused to fight.

Morrissey accepted Heenan's challenge and agreed to meet him at Long Point, Canada, on October 20, 1858 for a stake of $5,000 (£1,000). By a strange twist of fate, Morrissey chose as his trainer, Sheppard, alias Jack Hamilton, an old friend of Tom Sayers. On learning this vital piece of information, Heenan's backers thought the most appropriate trainer for their fighter should be Aaron Jones who,

*Pronounced Carmel.

John Camel Heenan, "The Benicia Boy," shaved off his moustache for his fight with
Tom Sayers on April 17, 1860.

having recently fought Sayers, would be well acquainted with all his
training and fighting techniques. Their decision presented Aaron with
a golden opportunity for fame and fortune. He jumped at the proposition, and promised Heenan's backers he would devote all his energies
to getting Heenan ready for the ring. But unfortunately, at this precise
moment of time, Heenan was lying in bed in California nursing an
injury to his leg, caused by a blow from a pickaxe while digging for

gold. From this moment on, in spite of all his efforts, nothing seemed to go right for Aaron. The first phase of Heenan's training had to be delayed due to his injury and later, in the final weeks of his preparations, when he was attacked by a virus infection. This put an end to the remainder of his work and consequently, when he entered the ring against Morrissey, he was more than a stone over-weight.

During the early stages of their fiercely contested battle, Heenan had the misfortune to strike his fist against one of the stakes, which seriously injured his hand. This accident gave Morrissey an overwhelming advantage, and he slowly but surely wore Heenan down until he capitulated. The victorious Morrissey was now fully justified in claiming his right as champion of America, but Heenan was dissatisfied with the decision and challenged him to a second engagement, maintaining that had it not been for the injury to his hand, he would most assuredly have won. Morrissey had found it difficult enough to beat an injured and untrained Heenan and he had no intention of agreeing to a return match so, rather than face the possibility of a humiliating defeat, he nominated Heenan as the new champion and announced his retirement from the ring.

Towards the close of 1858, following his unhappy saga with Heenan, Aaron Jones began having second thoughts about returning to England. During his stay in America, with time being a good healer, plus a few thousand miles of ocean, he had gradually come to believe that the legendary Tom Sayers was not such a formidable customer after all and, thinking he would like to have another crack at the title, made up his mind to return to his old country.

At precisely the same time, rumours began reaching England that "Uncle Sam" was about to send over one of his champions to humble the pride of Tom Sayers.

Early in 1859, these rumours became a certainty when a letter arrived at the offices of *Bell's Life* from George Wilkes, the editor of *Wilkes' Spirit of the Times* in New York, enquiring on what terms John C. Heenan could be placed on the rota for a match against Tom Sayers. At first the British sportsmen were astonished at the idea of a defeated man being selected to represent America and considered it a gross insult to their champion but, upon further investigation, it transpired that Morrissey was an Irishman by birth and not a native American; therefore, Heenan was recognized as the legitimate representative for the United States.

Frank Dowling replied to George Wilkes' letter, intimating that upon the immediate receipt of a deposit from Heenan he would be placed on the list for a match against Sayers, but stipulated that in the event of him winning the fight, under no circumstances would he be permitted to take the belt back to America without leaving its equivalent in value in England, or, remaining himself in England for three years to contest its possession against all comers on the usual terms.

A second letter arrived from George Wilkes by the very next mail, dated New York, March 28, 1859.

"Dear Sir,

Enclosed please find a draft for £200 Sterling, drawn in your favour on the Bank of Liverpool, which I have been requested to forward to you on the part of Aaron Jones, in order that you may deposit of him the necessary sum for a meeting with the champion of England, within six months of the date of the battle of the 5th of April between Sayers and Benjamin; and in case the winner of that fight does not accept, you will please hold the money subject to my order."

The language with which Jones accompanies this draft is as follows:

"I Aaron Jones, hereby challenge the winner of the coming fight for the championship, to fight me within six months from that time for two hundred pounds and the champion's belt. The fight to take place near London and to be governed by the rules of the London Prize Ring.

"Jones also requests me to say to you that he would prefer having the forfeit or first deposit to be as much as fifty pounds, as he does not wish to be at the trouble of crossing the Atlantic for nothing, though he is willing to pay his own expenses over and back to get the fight. He also hopes that Sayers will, for old acquaintance sake, give him the first chance; but this is a consideration which I have no right to press, after having previously consented to lay before you the wishes or the claims of Heenan. Your sense of propriety will find a law for the matter, and will, I hope, likewise permit me to remain,

    Yours, very truly at command,
    Geo. Wilkes.

P.S. I am also desired by the backers of Jones to say that the stakes will be increased to five hundred pounds a side, if the champion wishes it.

                                          G.W."

Tom was summoned to the offices of *Bell's Life* where Frank Dowling informed him of the conditions set out in the letter. Tom had no hesitation in reaching his decision and declared he was quite prepared to place Jones first on the list of candidates after his second battle with Benjamin.

Hardly had the second letter been dispatched before another arrived from George Wilkes, enclosing the sum of £50, which he had been instructed to stake on behalf of Heenan, and the request that if it was not contrary to the rules, the stakeholder, Frank Dowling, give Heenan's claim first preference as he had been the first to challenge Sayers and he was afraid that if he was not placed on the list of candidates, his chance of meeting Sayers might be lost through some unforeseen development.

In making his initial approach to *Bell's Life*, Aaron Jones had shown sufficient foresight to send his deposit. In consequence, this now left Frank Dowling obliged, in accordance with the recognized practice of the prize ring, to give him first priority and leave Heenan to curb his impatience.

Shortly after the defeat of Benjamin, Tom was called upon to meet Jack Macdonald, delegated by Jones to act as plenipotentiary on his behalf. At the conference, many arguments emerged from both parties, but in the end £50 a side was deposited and the articles were duly signed, sealed and delivered, under which Jones was bound to fight the champion for £200 a side.

Within a very short space of time, and to complicate matters even further, another communication was received from George Wilkes, requesting Frank Dowling to return £50 out of the £200 he had sent for Jones to pay his passage to Europe and transfer £100 to the account of the match between Heenan and Sayers. He concluded that if Jones intended to proceed with the match, then he would have to find the remainder of the money himself, as his American friends, having some reason to be dissatisfied with him, were now desirous of transferring all their interests to Heenan.

Another letter arrived on the next mail packet with the reassuring message that Jones would be able to find all the necessary money himself, and therefore to consider the match to be definitely on.

There the matter rested until the following October, when renewed interest was stimulated by the arrival of another startling communique addressed to:

The Editor of *Bell's Life*, 5 Norfolk Street, Strand, London
Office *Wilkes' Spirit of the Times*, in New York.

October 7, 1859.

"My Dear Sir,
I take pleasure of informing you that Aaron Jones, conceding to the common desire on this side of the Atlantic to see Heenan have the first chance for the championship after the unknown (Bob Brettle) has

desired me to have forfeited the £50 which now remains staked for him in your hands against Sayers. Enclosed I send you Jones' letter authorizing me to take this course and, as I represent the money of his backers, your authority for declaring the match off will, I suppose, be considered complete.

"I forget as I write, whether Sayers had already covered a deposit of Heenan's for the championship; if not, please let the same deposit be made and covered in his case (£50) as was made and covered in the case with Aaron Jones. I am very solicitous about this point as, for special reasons, I want Heenan regularly upon the record at as early a moment as possible. I send with this a note to Sayers, directed to your care, in which I apprise him of Jones' forfeit.

Please preserve the note of Jones to me and believe me to be yours, ever truly at command.

Geo. Wilkes.''

When the letter was published in *Bell's Life*, it came as a bombshell to the sportsmen of London. Tom was notified of this latest communication almost as soon as it arrived, and having no business on hand to delay any arrangements, it appeared certain the way was now clear for the first "World International Boxing Contest."

Tom's backers, anxious he should finish his career as quickly as possible, covered the £50 of Heenan and signed the articles for Tom to fight him on or about the day originally fixed for the fight with Jones, on the supposition that it was Heenan's wish to step into his shoes. But it was clear from George Wilkes' reply that the English managers had misinterpreted the details concerning the arrangements. He had been shocked and surprised to find that the contest was to be fought on the terms dictated by the English, and immediately sent another communique to *Bell's Life*, dated November 23, 1859.

"My dear Sir,
Your letter of 3rd inst., enclosing copy of articles for a fight between Heenan and Sayers, and signed by the latter for our acceptance, reached me yesterday, and has been communicated to Heenan.

We are all, however, taken by surprise at the proposal that the fight should come off in February next, instead of at the expiration of the regular six months, as was stipulated in the original proposition and I am requested on Heenan's part to say that he expects the usual preparatory term will be granted to him. By reference to his cartel you will find he challenged Sayers to fight near London for £200 and the champion' belt, in six months from the date of his (Sayers) reception of that challenge, or the date of the first deposit under it.

"This challenge, having reached England during the pendency of the engagement between Sayers and the unknown, was kept in abeyance in your hand, and having been further kept back by the next succeeding engagement of Sayers with Jones, was not recognized or received by Sayers until after he had accepted forfeit from Aaron Jones. Being thus left free of all engagements, he responded to the challenge of Heenan, and on the 26th of October (I believe) covered the £50 deposit, which you had for months held in Heenan's name. The articles for this new match, however, were not signed by Sayers until the 3rd of November inst., and consequently Heenan claims that he is entitled to six months preliminary time from either one or the other of those dates.

"He, however, desires me to say that if there is anything in the rules of the Prize Ring Benevolent Association which entitles the champion to reduce the term for meeting on his acceptance of a regular six months challenge, he will conform to those rules and fight Sayers at the indicated time, even though it will leave him deficient of the due pre-paration; but he utterly repudiates the idea (which the selection of February by Sayers perhaps infers) that his match with Sayers is a con-tinuation of the match with Jones.

"With this explanation he desires me to state that he will be ready to put up the second deposit of £50 at Owen Swift's in London on the 15th of December next, and if he is not represented at that time by any agent from this country, he begs you will continue your past kindness and again put up the money for him. Waiving no right, but conceding to all rules, he remains your obedient servant, through very respectfully yours,

George Wilkes."

At first, it was feared this would cause a further hitch in the ar-rangements and force another delay but Tom, convinced in his own mind there was no one to beat him either in England or America, asked Frank Dowling to write a letter confirming that as he had promised to give Heenan a chance, he would not disappoint him. He was quite agreeable to let the affair take its course, and proposed to extend the time to the end of March. The stakes should be for £500 a side, or as much more as Heenan could raise.

Before the letter reached its destination Frederick Falkland, the advance representative of Heenan, had already left America prepared to make the necessary arrangements on Heenan's behalf immediately he arrived in England.

Early in December, he presented his credentials at the offices of *Bell's Life*, where he was introduced to Frank Dowling, and several advocates of Sayers, but as Tom was not present at the meeting they formally agreed to meet again at Owen Swift's on the evening of December 15, when the second deposit should be made.

Tom was an early arrival on the appointed evening and he soon cemented a congenial relationship with Heenan's ambassador. When the meeting was brought to order, Frederick Falkland stated that he had been given implicit instructions not to make the match for more than £200. Sayers, he said, would undoubtedly be the favourite, and as the odds would be against Heenan, he could lay out the remainder of the money to more advantage in bets. The English managers agreed to Falkland's terms, and the following day the articles were drawn up in the approved form and a copy dispatched to Heenan with the request that his presence was required at once in England.

Meanwhile, the series of unforeseen developments taking place in America nearly destroyed all George Wilkes' delicate negotiations of the last few months. John Heenan and his quondam opponent John Morrissey had been involved in a clash of personalities, and Heenan had been provoked into making a rash agreement to fight Morrissey a second time, before his meeting with Sayers. Thankfully, the timely intervention and diplomacy of George Wilkes saved the situation when he implored Morrissey to postpone their dispute until Heenan's meeting with the English champion was resolved.

Morrissey complied with the request, but his contemptuous parting words to Heenan were, 'Go and fight Tom Sayers for the championship of the world; if you win, then I will fight you for ten thousand dollars.'

Heenan now began his final preparations for his visit to England, but once again there was nearly a hitch when he was wanted in connection with a serious breach of the peace. He had been attacked by several members of Morrissey's gang, and in the ensuing melee had almost killed a couple of the ringleaders. Intent on revenge, the remainder of Morrissey's accomplices set the law in motion by issuing a writ against Heenan for assault and battery. Should the warrant have been served, it would most certainly have prevented him from sailing for England. But once again George Wilkes came to the rescue and hid him until his ship was about to sail. On New Year's Eve, with the aid of several trusted accomplices, he was smuggled aboard the steamship *Asia* which brought him to Liverpool on January 16, 1860.

He was accompanied on the journey by his trainer Jim Cusick who, immediately upon landing, secured the services of Jack Macdonald as Heenan's second and deputy trainer in England.

Macdonald's contract with Cusick was barely two weeks old when Captain William Peel informed John Gideon of certain rumours he had heard that Macdonald was to second Heenan. Gideon told him he must be mistaken. He had personally enlisted Harry Brunton as principle second and, through the intercession of Owen Swift, Jack Macdonald had been engaged as Brunton's assistant for the sum of £100 if Sayers won and £25 if he lost. Gideon taxed Macdonald on his breach of contract, but he was unrepentant and claimed that whatever the result he would be paid much better by the other party. With the vacancy left by Macdonald's desertion, Gideon now began a search for a reliable replacement. Fortunately there was no shortage of proficient seconds in England and he soon engaged the services of the very competent Jemmy Welsh.

Within a couple of days of his landing, John Heenan had completely entranced the British public. His glossy curly hair and pleasant manner won instant affection from all who met him. Wherever he went, crowds of curious people flocked to catch a glimpse of him in his long, fashionable overcoat, bordered with an astrakhan collar and deep cuffs, American-style patent leather boots, silk top hat and gloves. He became the universal topic of conversation among all classes of society who passionately debated his chances against England's champion, and his origins in America.

John Camel Heenan was born on May 2, 1835 at West Troy, New York, where his father Timothy Heenan was employed as a munitions technician in the laboratory of the Ordnance Department of the Watervliet Arsenal. According to his biographer, young John was a great favourite among his fellow school friends, and highly exalted for his sporting capabilities and natural aptitude for boxing. During his adolescence, he belonged to a small gang of boys who were constantly engaged in free fights with the other local gangs.

Curiously, one of the rival ringleaders was a young lad, about fourteen years older than Heenan, named John Morrissey. At this time in their lives, they could not have guessed that when they grew up they were to become famous as two of America's top professional prize fighters, who would meet each other for the championship, or that one of them would become the first American to fight for the championship of the world.

At the age of seventeen, and having completed his apprenticeship as an engineer at the Troy arsenal, John Heenan set out for San Francisco to make his fortune on the Pacific coast of California. He arrived at the town of Benicia, where he found employment in the engineering section of the Benicia Workshops, a subsidiary of the Pacific Steamship Company. Swinging a heavy sledgehammer all day helped to develop his broad shoulders, deep chest and muscles like steel. Standing 6 feet 1½ inches, his fine powerful frame, dark hair, good looks and dashing smile attracted a lot of attention, particularly among the ladies.

After a few months with the company, he inevitably fell foul of the factory bully who, for a prolonged period had terrorized all his fellow workers and, more especially, the young apprentices and new employees. One day he singled out young John for some misdemeanour and threatened to hit him, but big John Heenan, having grown up in the tough environment of New York, was not one to be intimidated and he told the belligerent oppressor that he was ready to fight him at any time.

Surrounded by a cheering crowd of engineering workers, the two fought a long and aggressive battle. Gradually, young John established his superiority over the tyrant and administered some particularly heavy punishment. His fellow workers, delighted that their long ordeal of domination was over, now regarded him as "champion of the weak," and dubbed him "The Benicia Boy," a nickname he carried throughout his life and fighting career.

With the lure of unlimited wealth in the Californian gold fields, Heenan left Benicia and went to work in the hostile environment of the mining camps where any man had to be of a tough disposition to survive. Enduring untold hardships and deprivations, his excellent physique and fitness earned him the proud title of "The strongest man on the slopes of California."

During the time he was panning for gold, he was involved in countless sparring exhibitions. One day, having impressed a group of visiting sportsmen with his fighting skills, he was persuaded to return to New York and throw down the gauntlet to John Morrissey, the man he had known in his juvenile days at Troy.

A few weeks after their battle at Long Point, Canada, and having acquired the title on Morrissey's resignation, Heenan met and fell in love with a young and vivacious actress named Adah Isaacs Menken. Adah had first appeared on the stage as a child dancer in partnership with her sister, performing under the name of the "Theodore Sisters." At the early age of fourteen, she became the principle dancer in the Opera of New Orleans. At the farewell benefit which ended her engagement, reports indicate that her ardent admirers showered her with presents worth an estimated $3,000.

According to her own account (undoubtedly to impress the theatrical world) her real name was Dolores Adios Furtes and she was the daughter of a wealthy Spaniard. But this was pure fantasy, for her father was a Scotsman named McCord and her Christian name was Adelaide.

Another of her unsubstantiated claims was that at the age of fifteen

The tempestuous American actress Adah Menken, the wife of John Heenan, took America by storm when she appeared on stage as "Mazeppa," stripped naked and tied to the back of a horse.

she experienced one of the most romantic escapades ever to befall a young and impressionable girl. One day, while on a hunting expedition in Texas, she was surprised and captured by a party of Indians. Captivated by her beauty, they took her to their camp where they worshipped her as a kind of princess. After three weeks as their prisoner, she was rescued by a squadron of Texas Rangers who carried her off in triumph to their fort. Her gallant rescuers brought her back to their commanding officer, General Harvey who, feeling sorry for the young girl after her terrifying ordeal, adopted her into his family. She exerted such a strong influence over this officer that he not only allowed her to accompany him everywhere on horseback, but actually gave her command of her own troop of horse.

In 1856, Adah married one Alexander Menken at Livingstone, Texas and resigned herself to becoming a loyal housewife. But it was not to last. Her fiery temperament and capricious moods could change in a few moments from one of childlike pleasure, to one of violent anger and icy contempt. One day, in one of these fits of pique, she stormed out from her husband to seek a divorce.

Adah still yearned for the bright lights of the theatre, and after a series of small-town engagements all across America, she arrived in New York in 1858. Unlike her former pampered life in Texas, she soon found the sidewalks of New York bleak and hard, for the rowdy saloons were full of budding young actresses, all too willing to trample over any girl to obtain the smallest part in an equally small production. But the male residents of the East Side found her extremely attractive and were enchanted by her brash manners and bold make-up. Her oval face, straight nose, full sensuous lips and large liquid violet eyes were framed by a mass of crisp dark curls. A little over 5′ 1″ in height and about eight stone in weight, her stocky figure was heightened by her full bosom and trim waist.

Eventually, she secured the starring role as the widow in "The Soldier's Daughter", but the critics of the *New York Tribune* tore her acting to shreds.

One reporter wrote: ". . . the new actress Adah Menken needs taming down."

She was furious at their offensive comments and nothing could silence her resentment. She stormed into the offices of Edwin Jones, a contributor to the *Clipper*, and delivered a tirade of abuse against all the newspaper men who had been so unkind to her acting abilities. Jones appeared unsure of what to say to pacify her anger, but the tall dark man sitting with him burst into laughter at her fiery outburst. The man was John Heenan who, after a whirlwind romance, asked her to marry him.

After their marriage, and when the first flush of passion had subsided, Adah's thoughts turned once more to her theatrical career. She played in serious drama with enormous success, but the role which made her an international star was her impersonation of Mazeppa. An enterprising impresario named Captain John Smith intended to stage a production based on Lord Byron's romance of Ivan Mazeppa, a Tartar prince, taken prisoner by his enemies. In the play, Adah would star in the principle role of the prince, and in the scene which was to shock the whole of America, she was to appear stripped naked, and tied to the back of a horse which would carry her across the stage.

On the opening night, dressed in silk fleshings, and spreadeagled across the mare's back, Adah was breathtaking. The show was an instant success, and the "Naked Lady" became the talk of America. Crowds flocked to catch a glimpse of the exposed female body in an age when even the sight of an ankle was considered provocative. To increase the eroticism, Smith enlarged the set by building a zig-zag ramp, lengthening the time Adah was seen on stage. The American press tore her act to ribbons.

One disgusted editor wrote: ". . . Menken's exhibitions are unfit for the public eye . . . degrading to the drama whose temples they defile . . . a libel upon women whose sex is hereby depraved, and whose chastity is corrupted . . ."

But Adah was now in the position to ignore what the critics said; she had achieved her lifelong ambition. New York's Broadway was paying her the colossal sum of $500 a performance, and with an apparently limitless expense account, her extravagant tastes allowed her to wear the most elegant dresses and expensive jewellery money could buy. But even greater riches lay overseas in the cities of London, Paris and Vienna. She caused a sensation when she appeared as Mazeppa at London's Astley's Theatre, and when she took her daily ride in Rotten Row she was surrounded by hoards of devoted admirers. In France, the Parisians stood spellbound at the spectacle of her driving her gilded chariot to the Gaité for her nightly performance.

While Adah spent most of her time in the pursuits of the arts, Heenan, unable to accept her dedication to the stage and her violent tantrums, sought refuge amongst his innocuous sporting friends.

So far in her career Adah had preferred to be billed as Adah Menken, but now, with mounting interest in the forthcoming fight, she was quick to capitalize on her married name, and in New York huge placards and billboards proclaimed "The appearance of Mrs Heenan."

Meanwhile, in Texas, Alexander Menken now discovered that his missing wife was allegedly married to America's leading pugilist, but as far as he was concerned, Adah had walked out on him and there had been no divorce proceedings. A curious fact emerged that at a later date when Adah sued John Heenan for divorce, Judge Isaac Wilson dissolved a marriage which, it would seem, had never been legalized.

Adah married four times in her short life, but as her health began to deteriorate, she would often revert to her black moods of depression. Her former admirers, who once had pursued her with unabashed ardour, now treated her with contempt. She developed breast cancer and died in Paris on August 10, 1868, leaving behind memories to those who knew her of a passionate woman with singular powers of fascination, both physical and intellectual. But needless to say, with her volatile temperament, she was not at the dock to see Heenan off to England on December 31, 1859.

# 18

## PREPARATIONS FOR BATTLE

Within a few days of landing in England, The Benicia Boy was whisked away to his training quarters at Salisbury, where Frederick Falkland was waiting to supervise the first phase of his preparations. The destination was supposed to have been a closely guarded secret, but the anti-pugilist lobby, actively campaigning to ban the contest, soon discovered his whereabouts. Fearing the impending battle was to take place in their neighbourhood, they approached Heenan with the request that he withdraw from the contest but, having spent nine months in detailed negotiations and lengthy correspondence, he was in no mood to listen to their pleas. Tempers flared and their anger mounted at his intransigent attitude.

They threatened that if their demands were not met, they would create trouble for him and Sayers if there was a breach of the peace anywhere within the vicinity of Salisbury. Afraid he had overstepped the mark, and that their threats could jeopardize the contest, Heenan and his party decided the risk was too great in prolonging their stay at Salisbury, so they moved their quarters to The Round Table in St Martin's Court, close to Ben Caunt's The Coach and Horses.

During his stay in London, Heenan nearly landed himself in trouble again; this time with the authorities. On February 21, attired in his smart astrakhan trimmed overcoat and a fur-lined cap as protection against the chill winter weather, he took a trip down the Thames with Jack Macdonald to see the fight between Bob Travers and Jem Mace. Shortly after the ring had been pitched, the entire company found itself surrounded by a large force of the constabulary who had been lying in ambush. Sporadic fighting broke out between the police and groups of supporters, and there came a mad scramble to return to the safety of the steamer. In the melee, Jem Mace grabbed Heenan by his long overcoat and dragged him aboard the vessel as it was putting out to

Tom Sayers' training quarters at Brighton where he began his initial training for his great battle with John Heenan.

sea. Meanwhile, those unfortunate passengers left stranded on the shore were quickly overwhelmed and apprehended by the police.

After a short journey to the other side of the river, another landing was made on the Kent coast, but no sooner had the fight commenced than an even larger contingent of police arrived and began rounding up the principle parties. Bob Travers narrowly evaded capture by deftly manoeuvring out of a burly policeman's grasp, while Jerry Noon, closely pursued by a huge constable, made his escape by running into the sea. Waist-deep in the freezing water, and with the officer slowly gaining on him, he discarded his heavy overcoat and dived into the icy sea, striking out strongly to the middle of the river where he was hauled into a waiting boat.

Jack Macdonald was deeply concerned over Heenan's safety, for should he be discovered or captured, the consequences could be disastrous. Turning the American's coat collar up around his face and pulling his fur cap well down over his head, he hurried him back to the steamer amidst the general confusion of the passengers fighting a rearguard action.

John Heenan's training quarters at Salisbury. The persecution by the local anti-pugilist campaigners forced him to abandon his stay in the area.

Dusk was falling as the last of the stragglers clambered aboard and, with nowhere else to go that day, the only course lay in abandoning the fight and reassembling the following morning.

The next day was more successful. There was no sign of any police activity along the river, and the contest reached a satisfactory conclusion despite Travers' constant resort to falling on every conceivable occasion. He blamed the turf for his falls, but his tumbles were so blatantly obvious the referee could not equivocate and Travers was disqualified.

Heenan and his entourage did not remain long in London. For a short time they stayed at the home of Jack Macdonald in the little hamlet of Oldford, near Frome in Wiltshire, but here once again, the anti-fight campaigners were quick to track them down and another move became necessary. In one last desperate attempt to throw the "kill-joys" off their scent, the little party went by train to Box, a secluded little village near Bathampton. But here too, they were soon in trouble when someone informed the local magistrate that a fight was to be held at Bathampton. As a result of all the unwelcome publicity, the anti-fight campaigners learned of their whereabouts and asked the magistrate to issue a warrant on a proposed breach of the peace. Fortuitously Macdonald received a timely warning from one of his friends, and before the writ could be served they had packed their belongings and were off to a different locality, far away from the wretched troublemakers of the west country.

Their next rendezvous was reputed to be a safe hideaway at a place near Bedford, but here too they received further threats, and yet another move became necessary.

This time the new location was on the borders of Nottinghamshire, Derbyshire and Leicestershire where, given a few moments notice, they could slip over the border into either of the other two counties. They made their headquarters at Mr Rice's, Navigation Inn, nestling on the banks of the river Trent. In his wisdom, Jack Macdonald believed this to be a safe haven, for it was reputed that several of the local constabulary were not above a little bribery and corruption. Moreover, there was also a certain tailor by the name of Cook who, it was claimed, was credited with unlimited powers in squaring the local police force. Macdonald hastened to engage him to handle the delicate transactions of the back-hand payments to certain officers of the law and kept him well supplied with funds for that purpose.

For a while they rested in peace, but disturbing reports began filtering through that Cook was an audacious rogue who could not be trusted. A close watch was kept on his handling of the cash payments and it soon became obvious that instead of bribing the police as agreed, he was pocketing a large percentage of the money for himself.

It was never fully established whether Cook double-crossed Macdonald, or the police double-crossed Cook, but what is known for certain is that just before Easter Cook introduced an undercover policeman into the select little circle of friends.

Soon after dawn on Good Friday, three plain-clothes policemen arrived at the Navigation Inn, intending to take the inmates by surprise, but fortunately Heenan had been awakened a few minutes earlier by one of his party who had glanced out of the window and saw the suspicious movements of the policemen. Jumping out of bed, he had only time to don a shirt and a pair of breeches before making his escape from the back door of the inn. Still in his bare feet he ran to the lock house, about a quarter of a mile away, and begged the lock keeper to give him shelter and bar the door against any intruders.

Unaware he had escaped from the rear of the premises, the three policemen forced their way upstairs and demanded to know which was Heenan's bedroom. They burst through the door but, to their intense frustration, found he had gone. In their search for clues to his whereabouts, they found his clothes hanging in the wardrobe and the bed covers still warm. Unable to find him anywhere in the bedroom, they concluded that he must be secreted somewhere about the inn. While they were busily interrogating Macdonald, Cusick and Falkland, a young boy arrived at the door with a note for Macdonald. In his naive innocence, the lad was about to hand the message over, when one of the constables snatched the piece of paper from the boy's hand and read the contents:

Am safe at the lock house. For God's sake, bring my socks, boots and something to wear. – J.C.H.

Overjoyed at their unexpected discovery, the officers set out immediately for the lock house. On their arrival they banged loudly on the door and demanded admittance "in the name of the law." But the lock keeper was unyielding and refused to comply with their commands, claiming that as they were not in uniform, he had only their word that they were police officers; therefore if they wanted to gain entry, then they would need a search warrant. Infuriated at the man's stubborn defiance, they held a hurried conference to decide their next move. Among the many alternatives, they proposed to send one of their number back to Derby to obtain a magistrate's warrant, while the other two maintained surveillance on the lock house.

As the minutes ticked slowly away and the morning wore relentlessly on, Heenan began to find the strain of the siege intolerable. Sitting quietly in the solitude of an upstairs room, he found time for reflection. Since his arrival in England, it seemed that almost everyone's hand had been turned against him. Disillusioned by the attitude of the Fancy and the British public in general, he was convinced that certain so-called sportsmen, who had invested large sums of money in bets, were doing everything in their power to protect their interests.

At last, after three long hours of seclusion, he found the pressure unbearable, and in a fit of depression decided to make his break. Quietly opening an upstairs window, he climbed out on to the roof, dropped down into the garden below and set off across the fields as fast as he could run. With nothing covering his feet, he lacerated them severely on the stony ground as his pursuers gave chase.

In all probability he might have evaded capture if he had been wearing his boots, but he gave his hunters a good run for about two miles, leaping over hedges with remarkable agility, until they ran him down in the corner of a meadow where he became hopelessly trapped between a deep pool and a thick thorn hedge. With his feet bleeding profusely and a look of abject despair on his face, he had no option

The bare-foot Heenan, trapped between a deep pool and a thorn hedge, is captured by two plain-clothes policemen on Good Friday, April 5, 1860.

but to surrender. He was then handcuffed to one of the policemen and marched off in triumph to the magistrate's court in Derby.

Amazingly, nothing serious developed from the arrest. The magistrates were quite content to bind him over in his own recognizances for £50 and two sureties of £25 each, to keep the peace in that county.

There was tremendous consternation in the sporting world when news of his arrest became known, and Jack Macdonald was severely reprimanded by Frank Dowling over his choice of locality. Everyone, he said, knew the Derby magistrates were notorious in their persecution of prize fighting.

With the police forces of the three counties now on full alert, it became necessary for yet another move. The party returned once more to Salisbury, where they had originally started out in January. Heenan continued his training, but now took the precaution of moving from village to village, whilst Macdonald continued his subterfuge against the spoilsports and the relentless anti-pugilist campaigners.

Heenan had every reason for believing there was a conspiracy against him, for while he was being harassed and hunted throughout the country, Tom Sayers had continued with his preparations completely undisturbed. In early February, he returned to his home town of Brighton to commence three weeks preliminary training. While there he took the opportunity to see his father again and pay his respects at the grave of his mother, and that of his grandmother, Elizabeth Butcher, who had died shortly before Christmas 1859 at the grand old age of ninety-eight.

His second phase of training, consisting of two weeks road work, was undertaken at the Brown Jug near Tonbridge, and the last four weeks of sparring practice at Newmarket.

Tom was an avid believer in the old and traditional methods of training recommended by Captain Barclay, the man who had trained Tom Cribb back in 1811. To the great majority of prize fighters, training was an irksome necessity, looked upon as sheer deprivation and self-denial. But Tom Sayers was the exception; he loved every minute of it. From the moment the articles were signed, he conformed to a rigid diet, totally abstaining from all high cholesterol foods, dairy produce and tobacco.

His first morning repast, taken at four or five o'clock in the morning, consisted of two egg yolks (well beaten), and some thin bread toasted the previous evening. At eight-thirty, he would partake of one small cup of very weak, fine roasted Mocha coffee without milk or sugar. For dinner at one o'clock, he would slowly sip half a pint of old ale through a straw and in the evening, for either late tea or early supper, a meal consisting of chicken or fish and a glass of old port.

He seldom deviated from his strict rule of being in bed between eight and eight-thirty every night, and no matter what the season or weather, always slept with his bedroom window open about six or eight inches. During the summer months, he rose at 4 a.m. and in the winter, it was common practice to be out running or walking at least an hour before dawn. He frequently competed against many well-known contemporary athletes, often out-distancing the famous Charley Jenkinson, better known as the London Stag and Bob Fuller, the equally famous long-distance walker.

'Every mile I cover in my exercises, is another round in my favour,' was his favourite phrase.

Regardless of his condition he took his medicines regularly. Every twenty-eight days it was a blue pill and a draught of black laxative, and every Sunday morning without fail, two teaspoons of Carlsbad Salts and one of Epsom Salts taken in water as hot as he could swallow. He also had many weird and wonderful superstitious beliefs associated with all his fights and rarely deviated from the same procedures. The strengthening plaster he wore around his loins was always prepared by one particular chemist in Compton Street, Clerkenwell. For his part in the melodrama the chemist always insisted he would not accept payment for his services, but merely regarded a handkerchief in the colours of the fight as his only reward.

The colours, too, were always designed and printed by another of his recognized suppliers: David Evans & Co. of Wood Street, Cheapside. In the preparations for his fight with Heenan, a contract was signed for the production of over six hundred of these handkerchiefs; all intended for sale at the fight, priced at one guinea each.

Another of his mystical superstitions was connected with the astringent he used to harden the skin on his hands and body. Five or six times a day, he rubbed in a tepid solution of the liquid compounded from Essence of Turpentine, saltpetre, lemon juice, scraped horseradish, bay-salt, vinegar and whiskey. This mixture was a concoction of his own invention and nothing on earth could shake his faith in the efficacy of this lotion.

In addition to the above, during the last three days of training, his hands would be rubbed with a solution of dissolved hydrated sulphate; 'To pickle the mauleys' as he would say.

Throughout the winter months, a steady stream of leading American sporting personalities and journalists had been arriving in England for the fight. Mr Bergman, and Dr Rawlings of *Frank Leslie's Illustrated News* had arrived, so too had George Wilkes and John Morrissey. Morrissey was obviously impressed with Tom's record, and from the moment the two met, a special bond of affinity was formed. Morrissey turned his allegiance to the English champion and remained with him at Newmarket, giving him sound advice on American training methods and imparting valuable and important information on Heenan's fighting capabilities.

When his training was almost complete, *The Sporting Life* reported: "Tom Sayers' condition is perfection. During the week he has been taking his breathings on Newmarket Heath, where the indefatigable Bob Fuller never loses sight of him. Harry Brunton has, as usual, been with the champion, giving him the finishing touches. Tom looks superb. His eye is as bright as a star; his complexion as clear as alabaster. Stripped, he looks better than ever in his life and the muscles are as hard as iron. Last week he visited the racecourse at Newmarket and was admired by everyone. Dressed in a fashionable suit, he strolled about the Heath with Fuller, Morrissey and Brunton. The champion is as confident as if Heenan's sponge was already thrown up."

Meanwhile, the managers and organizers of the fight had set themselves a daunting task, for theirs was the responsibility of putting the whole show together against insuperable obstacles, and the ever present threat of magisterial interference. John Gideon had held secret talks with top executives of the South-Western Railway, discussing timetables and routes and, probably the most important of all, the names of those who needed to be bribed.

Acting upon their recommendations, Gideon and Tom Oliver went to inspect a prospective piece of pasture land near the small town of Farnborough, on the Hampshire and Surrey borders. Strategically situated amidst a wild heathland of prickly gorse and bracken and screened from the road by rows of tall slender birch trees, the ground was reasonably flat and well-drained and they were close enough to escape over the county boundary should the police arrive to put a stop to the proceedings. The nearest town of any real significance was Farnham and they were too far away to be threatened by the county constabulary headquarters at Winchester.

With their first objective successfully accomplished, their next assignment required the combined assistance of both camps; synchronized to precise and accurate timing for the articles stipulated that "both contestants must arrive in London on Sunday, the 15th of April."

Although Tom had been free from all the troubles Heenan had experienced, he was not altogether free from danger.

*The Times* for April 2 reported: "Colonel Archibald Robinson, Chief Constable of the Hertfordshire Police Force, made application to the justices assembled in petty session for a warrant to apprehend Thomas

Sayers, champion of England and John Heenan, pugilist, in order that they be bound over to keep the peace."

The Newmarket magistrates had also been persistently badgered by the anti-pugilist campaigners to issue a warrant to prevent the fight taking place, but their sympathies lay with the champion and they declined to sign the document until mandatory instructions were received from London, forcing them to take the appropriate action. Consequently, a few days before Tom and his companions were due to return to London, Scotland Yard detectives were sent to Newmarket with express instructions to keep a close watch on Sayers, with powers to arrest him should he attempt to make his way to London. Tom soon discovered he was under observation, but considered it would be futile to attempt to hide or slip away from his vigilant guards.

He was still under close scrutiny on the Saturday before the fight when he walked boldly down Newmarket's High Street before taking some gentle exercise on the Heath. Later that evening, still shadowed from the distance by plain-clothes policemen, he paid a visit to his old horse-racing friend Sam Rogers, to discuss the problem of how he might evade the determined law enforcement officers and get to London on time. Sam Rogers sat for several minutes, deep in thought, contemplating a possible solution. Suddenly his face lit up and, wreathed in smiles, he said he had hit upon a brilliant and daring plan. He asked Tom to give him a little time in which to co-ordinate the intricate details, and invited him to lunch the next day.

Tom returned to Sam Rogers' stables on the Sunday morning to be weighed in before leading officials of the prize ring, sporting dignitaries and principle backers. On mounting the scales amidst the applause of the excited onlookers, he drew the beam at 10 stone, 8 pounds.

Now came the time to put the first stage of Sam Rogers' plan into action. Immediately following the weighing-in ceremony, Jem Handley, one of Tom's sparring partners who was about the same height and build as the champion, dressed himself in Tom's flannels and cap. Accompanied by Harry Brunton, he strolled nonchalantly on to the Heath while the watching detectives, believing he was Sayers, followed at a discreet distance. But Tom had already slipped away. He had joined Sam Rogers, Farmer Bennett and John Gideon, and was now dining on boiled leg of mutton with all the trimmings, washed down with a tankard of White Hart old ale; the first time in nine weeks of tough and arduous training he had allowed himself the luxury of a whole pint of alcohol.

Despite the warrant out for his arrest, Heenan arrived safely in London on the Sunday morning and went to stay at the Cathedral Hotel in St Paul's Churchyard. There was great commotion among the

Tom Sayers was officially weighed in at Sam Rogers' stables, Newmarket, on Sunday
April 15, 1860, for the first "World Championship fight."

hotel staff when they learned the identity of their distinguished visitor, but they were told he was to have as much rest and quiet as possible and that the need for secrecy was imperative.

At Sam Rogers' stable early on Sunday evening the second phase of the escape plan was now implemented. Having disguised himself as one of the stable lads, Tom mingled among the other grooms and jockeys who were to accompany a number of racehorses to the train waiting at Newmarket station.

Amid all the general bustle and confusion of "boxing" the horses, Tom slipped quietly into one of the wagons and climbed inside a small compartment at the rear of one of the stalls. Once safely hidden, a groom locked him in and carefully covered the trap door with bundles of hay and straw.

All along the railway line from Newmarket to London, small groups of policemen waited at every station and whenever the train stopped they carefully scrutinized the face of every passenger who boarded or alighted from the carriages.

At Shoreditch station late that night, an enormous crowd had gathered to await the arrival of Tom, despite the threat of his instant arrest the moment he set foot on the platform. Dozens of plain-clothes policemen mingled among the great host of people, and when the train pulled into the station they intently studied the faces of everyone in the crowd, confident there would be at least one person in the vast throng who would recognize the champion the moment he emerged from his carriage. But Sam Rogers' ruse had worked beyond all expectations, for while the search continued among the passengers, the wagon containing the horses was shunted into a nearby siding.

As midnight approached the great crowd, expressing their disappointment at not seeing their hero, slowly dispersed from the station. The police concluded that as Sayers had not arrived on the train, (the last from Newmarket that day) then he must have reached London by some over devious route. At last, their patience exhausted, they marched off in sections back to their respective stations.

In the early hours of the morning the Station Master, who was an accessory to the whole plot, opened the wagon door and released Tom from his hiding place. As he emerged from the wagon, still stretching after his long confinement, he was hurriedly bundled into a waiting cab and driven off in the company of Nat Langham and Bob Ware, to the Castle Tavern on Hampstead Heath.

# 19

## MORNING AT FARNBOROUGH

Throughout the whole of Monday, the eve of the great battle, London literally seethed with excitement as rival factions argued the merits of their particular hero, the latest betting forecast, or whether the champion's belt would remain in England or be carried away across the sea to America.

Although *Bell's Life* had published a detailed list of the principle sporting taverns where tickets to the fight would be obtainable on Monday evening, a proliferation of rumours still abounded. To circumvent the peddling of forged tickets, an embargo had been enforced, prohibiting their sale until darkness had fallen and, as evening approached, crowds of voracious fans gathered outside the taverns advertised in *Bell's Life*, eagerly awaiting their chance to buy their railway tickets at the exorbitant price of £3 each; about six times greater than the current face value of a third class ticket.

The Fancy had been under the misapprehension that this prohibitive cost would deter the unwelcome and lower element of society, but even the poorest of London's labourers had somehow managed to scrape together enough money in their determination not to miss this once-in-a-lifetime experience.

From the moment the sporting taverns opened their doors, they were inundated with sportsmen of every description, clamouring for a ticket. At Alec Keene's, Nat Langham's and Owen Swift's, the noise was deafening as supporters, many in near panic for fear they would be left behind, shouted, pushed and jostled in their desperate bid to obtain their precious little piece of card from the distributors, with veiled instructions to be at London Bridge Station before four o'clock in the morning!

No one knew, or even cared where they were going; all they wanted for their three gold sovereigns was a simple ticket which read: "FROM LONDON BRIDGE TO . . . . . . . . AND BACK AGAIN.

The biggest crush of all was at the George and Dragon, where John Morrissey was staying as a guest of Harry Brunton. As the evening wore on, it became almost impossible to break through the press of bodies and, as more people arrived to swell the throng, those who stood on the fringe of the gathering found themselves pushed relentlessly into the crowd until they became part of the living middle. Many of the early arrivals had become hopelessly trapped at the back of the suffocating mass and were unable to force a passage out into the street again.

Most of the wiser and prudent supporters bought their tickets immediately they went on sale, before going home to bed for the early start and the gruelling day ahead. But the younger and more impressionable fans scorned the idea of bed, for they fervently believed that this night would be recognized as one of the most memorable occasions in the annals of sport. They were resolved not to miss a single minute of this unique moment in history and could see nothing daunting in sitting up throughout the night, discussing with their friends the thrilling excitement of the approaching battle.

By ten o'clock, virtually the whole of London was in a state of feverish tumult; the names of Tom Sayers and John Heenan were on everybody's lips and the contest was the sole topic of conversation. Many had already decided to continue their merrymaking into the early hours of the morning, for London held an unlimited range of entertainment and nightspots. Some preferred a visit to the music halls while others, perhaps more intellectually minded, enjoyed an evening at the legitimate theatre. Many sought the company of the females who frequented the area in and around the Haymarket, but the majority spent the evening singing and carousing in the taverns.

With the approach of midnight, the noise slowly subsided as the streets gradually emptied. The last toasts to the contestants had been drunk and most took the opportunity for a quiet nap before the dawn. One or two late-night revellers still roamed the narrow gas-lit streets and alleyways, singing the latest ballads or bawdy music-hall songs, while others, who perhaps had imbibed a little too freely in the gin palaces, lay in a drunken stupor where they had fallen.

Brilliant stars sparkled in the black, cloudless sky and only the flickering gaslamps cast their glow in the cold frosty air of the now deserted streets. Shortly before two o'clock, the distant sounds of jingling harness and the clatter of horses hoofs on the cobbled streets could be heard as companies of armed and mounted policemen made their way to their appointed stations along the main railway lines leading to Dover and Brighton.

At around three o'clock the first of the travellers emerged from their homes and began wending their way towards the railway terminus. Gradually, the echoing clatter of hoofs and the rattle of iron-clad wheels over the cobblestones grew increasingly louder as horse-drawn vehicles of every description converged on the station.

The scene rapidly became one of continuous bustle as coaches, complete with liveried servants in shining riding boots and top hats, lowered the steps for their occupants to alight. Carriages with gilt crests and coronets painted on their gleaming doors mingled with battered Hansom cabs and carts of every shape and size. Hundreds arrived on foot, wrapped in warm overcoats, mufflers and furs to combat the chill morning air. The midnight revellers slowly drifted in, some still singing their music-hall ditties, while for those who had made a night of it the effect of their excesses was still plainly visible on their drawn and haggard faces. Almost everyone seemed to know someone else but occasionally, anxious and threatening glances were cast in the direction of certain strangers, as whispered questions were asked about who was, or was not, a plain clothes detective.

At a quarter to four, and after what felt like an eternity to many, the gates were opened and the crowd, now numbering in the region of a thousand, poured through the station's entrances. Despite the enormous number present, a strange air of secrecy prevailed along the gas-lit passages and platforms where whispers were heard rather than voices. Everyone seemed to be creeping around on tiptoe as if they were trespassers on the railway's property and about to run off with the rolling stock.

Two gigantic trains stood waiting in the station; the larger consisting of thirty-three carriages and the smaller of thirty. The Fancy did not demand luxury, and many wry glances were cast in the direction of the odd assortment of four and six wheeled coaches, many of which had been pensioned-off years before.

By four o'clock the first train had steam up and was ready to leave, but there was still no sign of the two fighters or their retinue. Typically, rumours spread rapidly through the coaches that both Sayers and Heenan had been arrested, and the whole thing looked like being called off.

This unforeseen delay created an anxious ten minutes for the passengers. Then, at 4.15 a loud cheering was heard from outside the station, which steadily swelled into a mighty roar as Tom Sayers appeared on the platform, dressed in a flashy type of suit more usually to be seen at the seaside. His fresh, stylish appearance clearly indicated a good night's rest, and that he had taken extra special care with his grooming. He walked smartly down the platform, flanked by his father, Harry Brunton, Jemmy Welsh, Farmer Bennett and John Gideon.

Almost five minutes had elapsed since Tom's arrival and there was still no sign of Heenan or his party. Fresh rumours swept the carriages; was it true? Had he been taken after all? But at 4.20 another great shout rent the air, proclaiming the entrance of The Benicia Boy. Escorted by Jack Macdonald, Frederick Falkland and Jim Cusick, he strode briskly down the platform to a compartment reserved for him and his seconds, his coat collar turned up and his hat pulled down over his face as if he wished to avoid recognition. With both men and their companions now present, it only remained for the tickets to be collected.

At four-thirty precisely a bell sounded as the signal to proceed. Jets of steam hissed from the valves and there came a reverberating roar from the two engines in tandem as thick choking smoke, soot and sparks were emitted from the smokestacks, blackening the station roof. As the couplings snapped and the carriages gave a lurch forward, everyone gave a sigh of relief. They were on their way at last.

Everything was going according to plan as the first train steamed out of the station, followed a minute or so later by the second, both destined for a place in the country known only to the driver of the first engine and a very select company of individuals.

The citizens of London were still sleeping in their beds as the trains rattled along at a good pace through the metropolitan districts which, in 1860, extended for about eight miles from central London. As they cleared the last of the buildings and came out into the country, the first pink tints of dawn illuminated the eastern sky. But, as the first rays of the sun fell across the fields and lanes, the hearts of the passengers sank at the sight of uniformed police officers, in countless numbers, lining both sides of the railway track.

The metropolitan police forces, under the command of Sir Richard Mayne, had stationed officers, mounted and on foot, every few hundred yards along the main line and on all the small country stations. Groups of three or four constables, each armed with a cutlass, stood stern faced and silently shivering in the chill morning air, watching the trains as they sped past. Occasionally, a small detachment of mounted officers would canter their horses alongside the trains but, once satisfied the fight was not to take place in their neighbourhood, they would slow down or gallop away out across the fields to report the latest movements to the senior officers of their division.

Only John Gideon and his associates were amused by all the activity, for this was all part of a carefully contrived plot to distract the authorities on the intended destination. Certain false information had been allowed to leak out that the contest was to be fought in Sayers' home town of Brighton, or somewhere along the line to Dover. In consequence, special security precautions had been implemented by the county police forces further down both lines to prevent the Mill taking place. But sadly all their well-laid plans were in vain, for when the first train reached Reigate Junction the signalman, who was in the pay of the organizers, switched the points from the main south-bound line, to the track running westwards. Instantly there came a buzz of speculation and surprise from those travellers familiar with the geography of the railway and the direction they were now heading.

The police patrols, utterly confused by this unexpected development, still waited patiently in puzzled groups further down the line, wondering what had happened to the two trains and their occupants. The passengers, meanwhile, elated that no more police were to be seen, settled back in their seats for what now promised to be a pleasant and relaxing journey.

The trains sped along in peaceful serenity until reaching Guildford, where they stopped to take on a supply of water for the engines. Fresh speculation mounted over their eventual destination, and while waiting for the watering to be completed, many could not resist the temptation to make a few bets on the exact location of the venue.

Resuming their journey westward, it was not long before they entered the wild, heathland district near the military camp at Aldershot. Only now, in this final stage of their journey, was the message relayed through the carriages that their destination was Farnborough.

By the time the second of the two trains pulled into the tiny Farnborough North Station, they far exceeded the length of the short platform. As the carriage doors swung open, about 1,200 people poured down the grassy embankment and into the surrounding fields, illuminated now by a glorious sun in a blue and cloudless sky. The Fancy were highly delighted with the choice of location and heartily congratulated the organizers on their excellent decision.

Frederick Locker Lampson, the English writer, recalled, "For several weeks I had been confined to London pavement and the dead wood of the office desk. How well I remember the strange delightfulness of the green trees, the fresh grass cool beneath my feet and the gracious April air as it played upon my face! A lark was soaring and singing far above our heads, rejoicing in his glorious privacy . . . ."

They clustered around Tom Oliver and his son Fred, gazing at the ropes and paraphernalia with a kind of wondrous fascination until father and son, slinging the ropes over their shoulders and tucking the stakes under their arms, set off across the fields closely followed by the multitude who fell into step behind them. It was a magnificent sight as people from all walks of life, young and old, lords and commoners, strode along, their coat tails flying, clutching at top hats and bowlers. With about half a mile of difficult terrain to negotiate, it rapidly came to resemble a steeplechase, as ahead lay a constant succession of wide ditches and double hedges; formidable obstacles everyone would have to overcome. Almost half the company who attempted to leap the ditches, either fell headlong into the stagnant foul-smelling water or slipped backwards into them on reaching the opposite bank. Many of the humbler classes, quick to recognize the chance of earning a few pennies, ferried the more wealthy passengers across on their backs. As everyone trudged relentlessly onwards, clothes became tangled and torn on the sharp thorn hedges and shoes frequently became stuck in the thick cloying mud of the fields.

Suddenly the vanguard came to an abrupt halt at the Blackwater, the narrow stream which divides Hampshire from Surrey. A few venturesome ones tried to leap across but, largely unsuccessful in their attempts, landed in the middle of the stream. Those who did manage to scramble to the opposite bank only had to jump back again when they found the ring was to be formed on the Hampshire side.

Tom Oliver now began the task of measuring a square of twenty-four feet on the grass and, swinging their wooden mallets with vigorous energy, he and Fred hammered in the stakes and adjusted the ropes.

Meanwhile the crowd continued to roll onwards like some gigantic tidal wave. Never before had such a representative cross section of the public assembled to witness a prize fight. There were Lords, Dukes and Marquises, Members of Parliament (including Lord Palmerston, the Prime Minister), high ranking naval and military officers, barristers and lawyers, merchant bankers, civil servants and clergymen. Scarcely an art or profession was unrepresented. There were editors with their artists and reporters, poets, doctors, authors, actors, singers, publicans, leaders of fashion, jockeys and trainers, thieves and pickpockets (who had rich pickings that day from the Americans), horse dealers, costermongers, navvies and bricklayers. The pugilists were easily recognizable by their high cheek bones, broken noses and cauliflower ears. There were fathers who brought their sons to witness the art of self-defence as it should be performed, and the different nationalities were represented by a sprinkling of Scotsmen, Welsh and Irish and about 200 Americans.

The appearance of the trains and the hundreds of people who alighted from them was a signal to the local inhabitants to barricade their doors but later, when it became clear they had nothing to fear, they ventured from their homes and cautiously joined the throng. Farnborough's lone constable hurriedly telegraphed an urgent message to the constabulary of the nearby towns, telling them of the invasion and requesting immediate reinforcements.

Having completed this part of his duty he boldly made his way across the fields to the vast congress of people, but there was little he could do except to keep up appearances. Estimates vary on the number who attended, but the figure must have been well in excess of 1,500. There were the occupants of the sixty-three carriages which, according to railway figures, held about 1,200 passengers. There were the inhabitants from in and around Farnborough, many were soldiers who came over from the garrison of Aldershot Barracks, and there were a great many other individuals who materialized by various other unexplained sources.

The gigantic task now began of settling this multitude into place. The cost of an inner ring ticket was ten shillings, but this only entitled its holder to sit on the damp grass so, for the comfort of the paying guests, Billy Duncan, the enterprising ring inspector, had brought along a large supply of canvas chairs and stools which he rented out at one sovereign each.

To obtain a grandstand view of the action, a considerable number of the more agile visitors had swarmed up the slender birch trees lining the meadow, but their clowning activities only served to antagonize the more sedentary and less active spectators who grumbled that they looked more like grinning apes sitting up in the branches than responsible human beings.

There was one very old and timid gentleman present who, rather than find himself pushed to the back of the crowd, had hired the services of two professional fighting men to protect him. Others had climbed on wagons and carts which had miraculously appeared, while many of the spectators on the extreme edge of the crowd had either to stand on tiptoe, or climb on the backs of others to obtain a glimpse of the proceedings.

When everyone within the inner enclosure was comfortably settled, twenty of London's leading pugilists were recruited as ring constables and, armed with whips, sticks and cudgels, took up their positions along the ropes of the outer ring.

With everything in readiness, a signal was given and a burst of tumultuous cheering heralded the appearance of Tom Sayers, flanked by Harry Brunton, smartly dressed for the occasion in a loose-fitting smock buckled about the waist, and Jemmy Welsh, resplendent in a short coat and a peaked sea-captain's hat on his head. Tom was full of smiles as the little trio pushed their way through the vast crowd. On reaching the ropes, the champion modestly dropped his hat into the ring and ducked in after it; his gesture of defiance evoking renewed cheering from the assembly.

He was followed almost immediately by Heenan, wearing an overcoat draped over his shoulders. He too received an equally rapturous reception, not only from the American contingent, but also from the British. He elbowed his way through the dense throng chaperoned by Jack Macdonald, who sported a pillbox hat and a pair of braces over his shirt, and Jim Cusick, immaculately attired in a bow tie, "bumfreezer" jacket and bowler hat.

Heenan smiled broadly as he stepped into the ring and turned to face Sayers. This was the first time the two had actually met, and they stood staring intently at each other for several seconds before advancing and shaking hands in a sincere and cordial manner. The warmth and feeling of their introduction was transmitted to the crowd, who again burst into loud cheering. For about half a minute the two men stood in the centre of the ring talking quietly, enquiring after each other's health and exchanging some pleasantries about the weather. A coin was then tossed, with Heenan winning the choice of corner. He elected to take the slightly higher ground, giving him the advantage of having the early morning sun behind his back, and leaving Sayers in the unenviable position of facing the full dazzling glare.

There now came a general movement of supporters to each corner. Among the friends gathered around Tom were Bob Brettle; Alec Keene; Jem Ward; Jerry Noon; Jack Grant; John Morrissey; Tom's father; Joe Goss and his future opponent, Jem Mace; Harry Orme; John Gideon; Tom Oliver; Bob Travers, the negro pugilist; The Tipton Slasher; Bob Fuller; Fred McCabe, the well-known contemporary entertainer; "Pony" Moore, of Moore and Burgess Minstrels; F.E. Beckwith, the champion swimmer; Fred Lillywhite, the celebrated cricketer; Robert Chambers, the new champion of the Thames and his former opponent, Harry Kelly. Seated on the ground, notebook at the ready was George Wilkes, and furiously sketching everything taking place were the journalistic illustrators, anxious to complete a drawing of the proceedings in time for the next edition of their publications.

The baskets containing the water bottles were now placed by their respective posts, the colours tied to the stakes, and the two umpires appointed. Frank Dowling was assigned the task of referee and the seconds and officials formally introduced.

During the transactions of the formalities, the crowd had gazed in wonder at Heenan's American-style elastic-sided boots, contrasting strongly against the traditional English lace-up variety worn by Sayers. As Heenan shrugged off his overcoat, a gasp of unrestrained admiration escaped the lips of the spectators. Standing a little under six feet

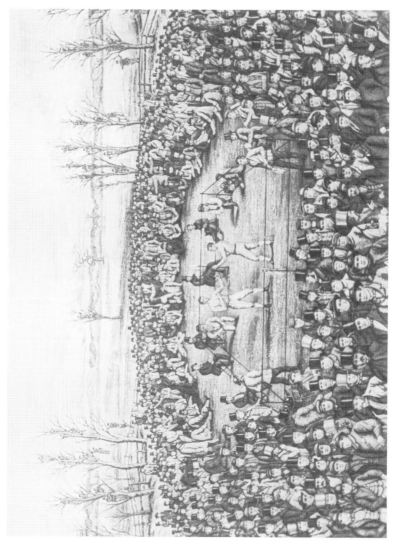

The great contest between Sayers and Heenan at Farnborough, Hants, on the morning of April 17, 1860.

two inches, with extraordinary long arms, deep chest and wide powerful shoulders, he appeared a truly formidable opponent. His physical
exercises and long hard training had developed immense muscles in his
arms and shoulders. There was not an ounce of superfluous fat on the
bone structure of his rib cage, which was crossed by powerful tendons
and sinews rippling beneath the skin. Swinging his arms in a circular
motion, loosening up his joints and muscles, every movement of the
thews and sinews worked like finely oiled machinery beneath the flesh.
Each gesture he performed was made with the natural grace and
freedom belonging only to those men who have attained the highest
peak of fitness. He had shaved off his moustache and his hair had
been cropped close in the traditional fighting style.

In all, he looked extremely fit and handsome, and as Bob Brettle
mused, 'Well, Tom may beat him, but I'm beggard if he'll eat him.'

Tom gazed at Heenan long and earnestly, as one who saw in his
every movement an extremely dangerous adversary. As he too began to
strip, the contrast between them became even more marked for Tom
was five inches shorter, some twenty pounds lighter in weight, and
shorter in reach. His only real advantage appeared to be his strong
shoulder muscles which, as everyone knew, were capable of tremendous hitting power. Although he looked as hard as granite, it was
becoming more obvious by the minute that not only would he have all
his work cut out by having to contend with Heenan's height and
weight, he would, moreover, have the disadvantage of the sun shining
full into his eyes. But the older and wiser disciples among the Fancy
were not unduly worried about their champion; they knew he had a
hide as hard as leather, unlike Heenan, whose skin, as fair and as
white as marble, would bruise much more easily.

At exactly 7.29 a roar of cheering and applause heralded the fighters
and their seconds as they walked to the scratch and shook hands. The
atmosphere suddenly took on an air of tension and breathless anticipation as an eerie hush descended over the crowd.

Many described it afterwards: 'It was as if the whole world stood
still for a few moments; the slight breeze stopped blowing through the
trees, and the spectators who had climbed them fell silent. Even the
larks in the bright sky stopped singing as everyone held their breath.'

As the strange tremor passed and life returned to normal the
seconds returned to their corners, leaving the antagonists face to face at
last. Heenan flexed his gigantic shoulder muscles, and the hard sad face
of Tom became intent at the umpire's shout of ''Time!''

# 20

## THE FIRST WORLD CHAMPIONSHIP FIGHT

The great battle to decide who should be the first man to claim the title of Champion of the World began very slowly indeed. For a full minute each man stood perfectly still, studying his opponent carefully, their seconds peering intently at them from opposing corners and the spectators watching with bated breath for the onset of hostilities.

Each began by tapping his left foot lightly on the grass before commencing a series of weaving and bobbing movements, their bodies swaying from side to side after feinting or preparing to dodge from some imaginary blow. So cautious were they that after about five minutes of these ridiculous movements they lowered their arms and burst into laughter.

Tom was still smiling as he raised his fists again and squinted his eyes against the low, dazzling orb of the sun. Quick and constant now, their arms working like well-oiled pistons, they continued to feint and weave, each trying to find the other's weak spot and neither prepared to take the slightest risk. Tom fired a left and a right, but was completely out of range. Heenan shook his head and grinned as he too put out a feeler, but the elusive Englishmen was far too quick for him, playfully shaking his head as he danced gracefully away from the muscular arm and its tremendous reach. Heenan now changed his tactics and retreated into his corner as if to seek the support and encouragement from the large body of Americans gathered there and to lure the champion into facing the brilliant sunshine.

At length, after an exchange of lefts about the body, Tom's hard brown fist shot out and registered a tremendous hit full on Heenan's nose, drawing "First blood." When it was seen that Tom had scored the first event so early in the battle, a great shout of approval rent the morning air. As the uproarious applause and shouts of congratulations slowly died away, Tom landed again on The Boy's sore nose, but as he was ducking from the return, Heenan hammered home a vicious blow on his forehead which instantly raised a lump. Cautious sparring progressed until Heenan seized Sayers around the neck and held him tight in his vice-like grip. Refusing to be restrained, Tom twisted his body slightly and began pounding the back of Heenan's neck. Finding his hold to be ineffectual, The Benicia Boy released his grip and Tom fell to the ground chuckling with laughter. This piece of lighthearted levity eased the tension and the crowd broke into loud and animated conversation.

When the two protagonists stood up for the 2nd round it was plain for all to see that the punching had been extremely severe. The back of Heenan's neck displayed the crimson marks of Tom's handiwork, whilst the Englishman bore a scarlet bump on his forehead. As Sayers neared the scratch, Heenan slowly backed away and stayed close to his corner. Tom went over to him in a fearless endeavour to entice him out but, on coming within striking distance, The Boy lunged at him with his left. As Tom deflected the blow Heenan rushed headlong into the attack, his long arm traversing backwards and forwards like a huge piston. Closing in, he grabbed Tom firmly and, with consummate ease, lifted him high into the air. Loud yells of delight emanated from the American ranks as Heenan threw him bodily on the grass and dropped with his full weight across the Englishman's chest.

In his corner, Tom listened attentively to the sound advice proffered by Harry Brunton. He told him to keep his distance, and on no account should he attempt to wrestle with the American; he was far too big and powerful for a mere ten stone man.

Tom was still bothered by the sun in round 3 and, as he squinted against its brightness, he misjudged his distance and came within striking range of Heenan. Instantly the American shot out a straight left which caught Sayers on the bridge of his nose and sent him sprawling almost into his corner. The Benicia Boy smiled and looked extremely pleased with himself, but Tom regarded it all as a matter of course and appeared totally unconcerned as he rose to his feet.

There was intense excitement at the first knockdown, and aristocratic patrons peered with disdainful glances at the ring-keepers, mercilessly applying their sticks and whips to the heads and shoulders of the boisterous individuals jumping up and down and shouting in wild abandon near the outer ropes. The Americans were in a particularly jubilant mood and enormous sums of money were loudly offered on their fighter.

As the noise and excitement slowly subsided, Tom came to the scratch with a deep red weal just above his eyes. He still looked rather bewildered from the last crushing blow and blinked owlishly in the brilliant sunshine. Encouraged by his success, Heenan went up to Tom, dodged to one side and as he turned into the full glare of the sun, planted a terrific punch on his jaw and sent him down again. The spectators were stunned and for a few seconds total silence descended over the entire congregation. The stillness was suddenly broken by the American supporters who burst into loud cheering, confident that Tom Sayers had at last met his match. This opinion was also shared by some dispirited members of the Sayers party, who looked particularly depressed when the Americans offered odds of 6 to 4 on Heenan.

When Tom came out for round 5 his face bore the singular marks of Heenan's tremendous hitting powers and for a time he stayed well clear of his antagonist. As Tom cautiously backed away, The Benicia Boy advanced and let fly with a left to the champion's mouth. Tom deflected the punch beautifully and returned on Heenan's nose. The American's eyes blazed with fury. He tore in, and after dodging a swing from Sayers, delivered another terrific blow to the nose. As Tom went spinning across the ring with the blood pouring down his face, Heenan spun round to face his seconds and threw up his arms in exuberant jubilation. This gesture created tremendous excitement among the American supporters, who leapt into the air and threw their top hats high into the sky. Leaning across the ropes, they thumped their hero on the back and showered him with congratulations, confident that the champion's belt was going home to Troy.

As Heenan's seconds duly sponged his face and body, he was at this point relatively unscathed. But in the opposing corner things were not going so well for the English champion. His head and face, covered in blood, were held pressed between cold sponges to stem the flow of blood and keep down the contusions.

His seconds performed miraculous deeds in the allotted time for, when he came to scratch for round 6 the swellings had almost subsided. Perhaps feeling a little over-confident now, Heenan was rather wild in his next onslaught and as Tom skipped smartly back, he missed with his next two punches. He appeared dazzled by the sheer brilliance of Tom's remarkable footwork and the split second speed in which he was in and out of distance. During the next bout of heavy counterpunching, Heenan delivered the one vital blow which was to decide the whole course of the conflict.

In deflecting a dynamic blow from Heenan's ponderous left fist, Tom received the full force of the punch on his right forearm. The blow packed such stupendous force, it sent Sayers' own fist crashing into his face and rocked him on his feet. He winced at the excruciating pain, but steadying himself for a moment, retaliated on the American's right cheek with such awesome power he split the flesh wide open.

Heenan grimaced as he recoiled from the punch, and the searing pain in his cheek. Closing in, he struck the champion on the right cheek, and Tom grasped the opportunity to go down and end the round.

Heenan was unaware at this time that he had landed the most crucial punch of the fight, for Tom's right hand, the famous hand which had won so many battles was now quite useless. In a huddled consultation with Harry Brunton and Jemmy Massey, he described the dull numbness running through the length of his arm. His seconds made a careful examination to determine the extent of the injury and found to their consternation that a tendon in the forearm had been torn. Realizing his handicap must be concealed from Heenan for as long as possible, Tom returned to the scratch for round 7, endeavouring to mask his almost hopeless situation with a broad grin which, he sincerely hoped, would convince everyone he was thoroughly enjoying himself. But despite his pretence, it soon became obvious that he had sustained a serious injury to his arm, for he now held it close in to his body as if to give it support.

There were loud cheers as he went over to Heenan, still hovering in his corner, and delivered a thumping blow to the chest, the sound echoing across the meadow as if someone had smashed a box. He came in again, dodged Heenan's next deliveries, and let fly with another slashing punch on the right cheek, raising a bump of considerable proportions, enlarging the cut, and sending The Boy reeling backwards like a drunken man. Again Tom's left smashed into the lacerated cheek, lengthening the gash and enlarging the bump. The English champion was now anticipating the American's moves and, in the exchanges which followed, landed again on the injured cheek.

Heenan broke off the engagement and went over to his corner for a wipe of the sponge from his seconds, while Sayers stood in the middle of the ring, patiently awaiting his return. The American seemed in no hurry to leave his corner, and when he did decide to renew the struggle, he walked slowly up to Tom and aimed a punch. However, when he tried to repeat the same manoeuvre, he found Tom ready and waiting. Shooting out a left to the right eye, he then sent in a vicious uppercut which whistled perilously close to Heenan's face. As Tom danced away and came in from a different direction, a loud crack was heard as his fist connected once again on the American's damaged cheek. The Sayers supporters were now experiencing a renewed wave of optimism for here was the Tom of old, making his gigantic opponent appear as foolish as he did in his battles with Paddock and the Tipton Slasher.

Clearly irritated with his slippery antagonist, Heenan launched an aggressive assault, but he was stopped dead in his tracks when he received another resounding crack on the right cheek. The sound of the blow was audible all around the meadow and the force behind the punch instantly closed Heenan's right eye. The Benicia Boy retired to his corner for a wipe of the sponge and for his seconds to examine the extent of the injury. The noise and excitement reached a new level of intensity as Tom strolled over to Heenan's corner to inspect the damage he had inflicted and to whisper something to his adversary. In the early morning sunshine, Heenan's remaining eye glinted with savage fury at the Englishman's audacity in coming to the privacy of his corner. Tom beckoned to him in an endeavour to entice him out, but he shook his head and declined to be tempted.

Instantly, cries of, 'Two to one on Sayers!' were heard at the American's refusal.

Finding he was unable to lure him out, Tom retreated looking rather perplexed. Suddenly, as if a bull had been turned loose, Heenan stormed out of his corner and aimed a particularly vicious swing. The champion blocked the blow admirably, but it was at the expense of more acute agony to his injured arm. Tom's face was still contorted in pain when Heenan feinted and struck him on the bridge of the nose. Obviously losing his balance from the impact of the punch, Tom rolled over backwards on the grass. Rising to his feet, he looked at the American and burst out laughing. To the delight of the crowd, in a round lasting thirteen minutes, the English champion had exhibited all the old skills and stratagems which had made him so famous.

In the Sayers corner, Harry Brunton was now busily engaged in rubbing in a liberal supply of embrocation, and massaging the muscles in Tom's arm to ease the stiffness and inflammation.

When time was called for round 8, Heenan was already up and standing at the scratch but immediately Tom squared up to him, for no apparent reason, the American changed his mind and walked back to his corner. With a puzzled frown on his face, Tom followed in his wake. Suddenly Heenan spun round and let fly with a tremendous swing but, swift as ever on his feet, Tom jumped clear. The Boy missed completely with his next two shots, and as Tom bounded away from the third and presented his back to Heenan, the American hit him on the nape of the neck for good measure.

As Heenan continued to pursue him, Tom back-pedalled around the ring, grinning at the American and skipping nimbly away from every attack, his magnificent display of footwork eliciting loud cheering from the assembly. Heenan stepped in, landed a left on the nose which renewed the bleeding, and Tom countered on the mutilated cheek. The American again retired into his corner for another wipe from Macdonald, and once again Tom went over to inspect the latest damage. Heenan was becoming increasingly angry at the repeated incursions into his corner and, swinging round, delivered a vicious left full into Tom's mouth, splitting his lip against his teeth and instantly filling his mouth with blood.

Clearly shaken by the force of the punch, Tom stood for a few moments, spitting out great mouthfuls of blood on the grass. Surprisingly, despite his obvious advantage, The Benicia Boy now seemed to prefer his own corner rather than the scratch and Tom had a difficult time in persuading him to come out. Eventually, when he did decide to return, another bruising struggle ensued. In the exchanges, Tom's punches were certainly the heaviest, especially those he delivered on Heenan's right cheek, which was now tinged a deep purple and swollen to about the size of a pigeon's egg. Again Heenan landed on Tom's mouth and another great torrent of blood poured from his bloated lips. When Heenan attempted to repeat the same punch, Tom was forced to block him with his anguished arm. Although he winced at the agonizing pain, he refused to be intimidated and his hard brown fist delivered another pulverizing blow to Heenan's lacerated cheek, sending the American reeling around the ring. Shaking his head vigorously, Heenan swept in like a tornado to where Tom was standing, but the elusive Englishman was nowhere near where he expected him to be. His brilliant footwork had already taken him to the other side of the ring.

Annoyed at his humiliation, Heenan returned to his corner, sulking like a naughty schoolboy. With a sardonic smile on his face and rubbing his hands together, Tom strolled over to The Boy's corner and scrutinized him carefully. Resentful at the intrusion, he lashed out with a tremendous left, but Tom's reactions were like lightning and he was already several feet away, laughing at the American. Heenan angrily shook his head, but seeing how ridiculous the whole situation was becoming, laughed good-humouredly with Tom.

Sidling up to Heenan, Tom planted his left on the tortured cheek before retreating with a broad smile on his face. More first-class hitting and blocking followed until Sayers dispensed another thumping left on The Boy's anguished cheek. In a fit of blind rage, Heenan retaliated with a punch on Tom's nose, but he was brought to a standstill in the next onslaught when the champion hammered him again on the right cheek. Heenan tried repeatedly to take the initiative, but Tom stayed well clear of him until he delivered a thundering blow on the Englishman's forehead, staggering him for a few seconds and leaving an abrasion above the eyebrow.

Then came a truly savage exchange of counter punches in which Tom received a tremendous smack on the mouth, rattling his teeth to their very roots and opening the floodgates once again. It was a simply devastating blow which, for anyone of lesser calibre than Tom Sayers would, most probably, have ended the conflict at this point. With a copious torrent of blood pouring from his stricken lips, he stood for a short time, shaking his head as if to clear his senses. To everyone's amazement, he speedily recovered and returned to the fray, his knife-edged knuckles inflicting another slashing punch on Heenan's right cheek, sending the blood streaming down over his chin and on to his broad chest. Both men were bleeding profusely and, by mutual consent, they lowered their arms and returned to the corners for a wipe of the sponge and to rinse out their mouths.

Refreshed from their seconds' administrations, they stood toe to toe and exchanged a barrage of withering punches. Pausing for a moment, Heenan skilfully ducked under Tom's guard and delivered a fulsome uppercut which lifted the champion off his feet and sent him crashing to the turf. Heenan turned to his seconds as if to say something, but no sound escaped his lips; he could only open his mouth in a gesture of gasping satisfaction.

The round had lasted twenty minutes and was a splendid example of championship fighting at its very best.

In their corners, their seconds were now working frantically, administering to both fighters' wounds, sponging their faces and washing away the blood spattered over their arms and chests. Tom's arm, frightfully swollen, and horribly discoloured from the wrist to the elbow, lay helpless across his chest. Although his nose and mouth were bleeding copiously, and he was frequently spitting blood, both eyes were open and he was still strong on his legs.

Macdonald and Cusick looked particularly worried over Heenan's deep cuts, which were much too serious to be properly treated at the ringside. His right eye had long since closed under what was now a hideous crimson gash running through a monstrous lump of blue flesh. His swollen mouth had the abnormal effect of puffing out his upper lip; twisting his face into a grotesque mask and creating the impression he possessed several rows of teeth and gums.

Many of the journalists and spectators who had never before attended a prize fight, were sickened and appalled at the horrendous injuries and were amazed that the human body could withstand such tremendous punishment. A proportionate number who had gambled heavily on the outcome were now pacing nervously about the meadow, anxiously enquiring about the latest developments of a scene they could not bear to watch. Those perched up in the trees still shouted or cheered for their particular favourite as they clung precariously to the bending branches, while people on the fringe of the assembly were climbing on the shoulders of those in front to obtain a better view of the contestants and their condition.

Heenan came up for round 9 and attacked viciously. But the nimble-footed Tom was still too quick for him and skipped swiftly away. Again Heenan lunged in and this time landed a punch which burst like a bombshell on Tom's mouth. Drawing back to spit the blood from his mouth, he was loudly jeered by the Americans clustered around Heenan's corner. Stung by their taunts, he sprang at Heenan and delivered a crushing blow to the nose which sent him tottering backwards into his corner. Quick off the mark, he followed it up with another annihilating punch on the mouth which again sent Heenan reeling around the ring. If Tom could have used his fearsome right hand, the conflict would, most probably, have ended at this stage, but he dared not run the risk of trying to finish the fight with his left hand only, against an antagonist so immensely superior in height, weight, and strength. Deprived of his principle offensive weapon, he could only follow up his advantage with another destructive left to Heenan's mouth.

In answer to the Americans' contemptuous sneers, cries now came from the Sayers contingent of, 'Don't hurt him Tom, take him home to his mother!'

The last round had been quite an uphill struggle for Tom and he was still breathing heavily when he arrived at the scratch. Heartened by the support of his followers, he stood in the centre of the ring, calmly awaiting the next onslaught. Heenan swept in and, after some rapid counterpunching, the round terminated when Heenan lifted Tom bodily and hurled him with tremendous force to the ground.

At this point, a couple of uniformed police officers arrived to support Farnborough's lone constable who was still watching the proceedings with the keenest interest. But when the policemen saw the size of the vast assembly, and the threatening behaviour of some of the spectators, they quickly dispelled any thoughts of intervening and very prudently decided to await further reinforcements.

"Time!" was called for round 12, but neither fighter showed much enthusiasm in coming to the centre.

"Time!" came the second call, a little louder.

Both sauntered to the scratch and as Tom raised his hands and faced his adversary the American lashed out and caught him on the jaw. But Sayers was equally quick in responding and it was Heenan who dropped to the grass.

Round 13 proved unlucky for Tom. Heenan was first to leave his bottle-holder's knee, and he went directly across to Sayers' corner. After a feint and a dodge, he delivered a straight left to the nose and Tom's legs buckled beneath him.

Heenan returned to his corner, and looking at Frederick Falkland exclaimed, 'That's one for you Fred!' Offers now came to lay 5 to 4 on Heenan, but the takers were scarce.

The last massive blow seemed to have undermined Sayers' strength and he came up slowly and cautiously. Seeing his distress Heenan tried to force the fighting, but again Tom's remarkable footwork came to his rescue and saved him from further punishment.

In the 15th, the American sailed in and felled the English champion with two powerful punches; one on the nose and the other to the jaw. His seconds picked him up and dragged him to his corner, his heels trailing on the grass.

George Segor, the landlord of The Brown Jug, leaned across the ropes and yelled, 'It looks like he's got you licked Tom!'

A slight frown crossed Tom's normally good-humoured face as he growled, 'The man who licks me, will have to kill me first.'

The poignancy of this remark appeared to give the vital jolt he needed to bring him back to sober reality, and in the 16th he sparred defensively until Heenan hit him on the mouth and knocked him down again. Heenan's prodigious show of strength and skill inspired prolonged cheering from the masses, but the initiated ones among the Fancy had been correct in their assumptions that Tom's cast-iron face would not show the full extent of his punishment, despite his repeated knockdowns.

By comparison, Heenan was decidedly the more disfigured; his face gashed from the deep flesh wounds and the entire right side of his face, including his eye, nose and mouth, was one frightful lump of blue flesh, steadily oozing blood.

Both were slow to time for the 19th and neither seemed in a hurry to commence hostilities. Ultimately, Heenan went into a wrestling close, threw Tom, and fell on him.

On the outskirts of the meadow a small contingent of policemen had arrived, perspiring freely after their hurried march from Aldershot. On attempting to force a path through the cheering and screaming mob, they were met with such unwarranted violence and hostility they withdrew to regroup and await further reinforcements.

Closely pursued by the American, Tom was constantly on the retreat in the 20th and, after some exchanges at close quarters, both men went down beside the ropes.

Sayers was exceptionally slow in coming up for the 21st and only just made it within the allotted time. Taking advantage of his lethargy, Heenan swept in, shot out a left to the nose, and again floored the English champion. The fields re-echoed to the triumphant cheering of the American supporters at the continual falls of the Eng-lishman, but Heenan was also paying a heavy price, not only from the accuracy of Tom's punching, but also from his own painfully swollen knuckles.

Tom sensed Heenan's fists were causing him trouble, for his punches now carried less power and he noticeably winced whenever he dealt a blow.

Finding himself little the worse for wear at the end of each engagement, Tom acquired an additional vigour in the 22nd round. Heenan noticed the sudden change in his adversary and backed away into his corner. Tom trailed after him and tried to deliver a swinging left, but as he continued turning from the momentum of the punch, The Benicia Boy, quick as a flash, dropped him with another jab to the jaw. However, it did not go unnoticed that Heenan's hand was extensively swollen and the blow lacked any of its former power.

There were angry scenes at the beginning of the 23rd round. Time was badly kept by both contestants, and complaints were made by the Sayers' managers that Heenan was allowed the use of a stool in the ring. An appeal was lodged with the referee, who immediately ordered its removal as contrary to the rules of the prize ring. In a fit of intense rage, Heenan kicked the offending stool from the ring and into the crowd. Intent on exacting revenge after his humiliating rebuke, he bore down on the English champion. Tom tried a swing with his right, but the arm was completely stiff and useless and he missed entirely. When one hour and eleven minutes had elapsed, they closed into a grappling hold and both went down together with Sayers beneath the American.

Tom was still in considerable distress from the acute pain in his arm and when Heenan in his next attack landed a blow on his head, he slipped down.

Looking weak and tired, Tom walked slowly to the scratch for the 25th round. With a faint trace of a smile on his battered lips, he surveyed the colossal figure of his adversary. Despite everything he had thrown at the American, he still came back for more; nothing it seemed could wear him down. The only apparent benefit was that Heenan's tender fists no longer carried the power to inflict a lot of damage. As Heenan dealt a tap on the side of Tom's head, the English champion retaliated with a left to the nose and renewed the stream of blood. The American's countenance darkened, and rushing wildly at Sayers, he bowled him over like a ninepin and trampled him underfoot.

In round 26, it was Sayers who appeared the fresher of the two. After delivering another pile-driver to Heenan's open eye, they stood square on to each other, trading some tremendous punches, each drawing a fresh river of blood which flowed freely over both men. Heenan came in again, crashed his fist on Tom's nose and sent him floundering around the ring. Twice in quick succession Sayers blocked the American's ponderous right and, after a deluge of rabbit-punching from both men, Tom fell to his knees. Carried away by the excitement of the moment, Heenan dealt him a punch as he reached the ground. Instantly an appeal of "Foul" was lodged by the Sayers' managers, but the objection was overruled by the referee who dismissed the blow as purely accidental, because Heenan could scarcely see whether his antagonist was up or down.

Once again Sayers was slow to respond to time, and as he casually sauntered to the scratch, a look of complete amazement crossed his face when Heenan walked up to him and dealt a heavy punch on the top of the head. Despite the gnawing agony of his arm, he countered with remarkable effect on Heenan's left cheek and followed it up with a left to the nose, opening the floodgates once again to a fresh river of blood. The slight exchanges which concluded the round led them into a harmless tussle, and Tom slipped down.

On coming up for the 30th, a new portent was observed; Heenan's other eye was beginning to close.

Jemmy Welsh was quick to notice Tom's advantage, and above all the din shouted, 'That's it Tom, put up his other shutter and the show will be all over!'

Heenan needed no reminding; he knew he had no time to lose. His next attempt to lead off was thwarted when Tom met him neatly on the nose, and opened up a fresh stream of blood. Angry at his abortive attempt, and still smarting from the blow to his nose, Heenan spurted towards Sayers and literally running him over, fell across his body, crushing the air from his chest.

"Time!" came the call for round 31, but Heenan remained close to his corner, refusing to come to the centre. This short respite was most welcome to Tom for it afforded him valuable time in which to recover his breath. Eventually, when Heenan did decide to return, he sparred indolently until he retired again into the sanctity of his corner. Tom went over to see him, but only received a rap on the nose for his impudence. More desultory sparring ensued until Heenan retreated into the confines of his corner yet again.

Tom stood before him and examined him with the eye of a connoisseur but the American, deeply resentful of the derisive incursions, decided to put a stop to the Englishman's impertinence once and for all. But as he stepped forward to settle the score, Tom bestowed a spanking blow to his mouth instead. Once again Heenan retired into the safety of his corner and once again Tom flippantly went over to see him. In a paroxysm of rage, The Benicia Boy swung a left to the Englishman's nose, and laid him prostrate on the grass.

Summoning up some hidden resources of energy, Tom danced around Heenan in the 32nd, before leaping out and catching him a resounding crack on the chin. Heenan tried repeatedly to entice him into the confines of his corner where his unique footwork would be of little advantage, but Tom would not be lured into the same trap as in the previous round and he refused to be tempted. Finding he was not going to play into his hands, The Benicia Boy reluctantly returned to the centre where some rapid hits and stops were exchanged. Again Heenan went into his corner for a short respite, still hoping to tempt Sayers into making a rash move, but Tom stayed well out of range, refusing to be provoked. Having taken his rest, Heenan came out and walked into an annihilating punch on the right cheek which almost closed his other eye. Heavy counter punches were exchanged and Tom was floored yet again with a jarring right to the cheek. The betting was now evens: Sayers for choice.

Heenan's face presented a hideous spectacle and it was becoming increasingly obvious that however strong he might be, unless he could finish the battle within the next few minutes, he must surely lose his sight.

His vision fading rapidly, he made a rush at Sayers but only succeeded in reaching his chest. Both looked utterly exhausted as they stood waiting for the other to make his move. When at last they closed into a clinch, Tom held Heenan by the neck and beat a rapid tattoo on the great raw wound on his face before letting him slip through his arms to the ground.

The small police presence had now been reinforced by several larger contingents recruited from the neighbouring towns and a hurried conference was taking place on their next course of action. A big, burly sergeant was detailed to form a phalanx of about thirty constables and, with a superintendent at their head, they marched resolutely into the rear of the spectators. Scuffling and small-scale skirmishes broke out as they began forcing a pathway through the crush, intent on reaching the ring.

Oblivious to their presence, the two fighters came to the centre for the 34th round. His vision now reduced to a misty blur, Heenan was finding Tom no easy target. He lashed out with a right to the body, but his knuckles were now so tender the blow lacked any real destructive power. He had little success in the next series of exchanges and, after some rapid infighting, both fell with Tom under.

Hideously mutilated and with his one remaining eye almost closed, Heenan opened the 35th by dashing at Sayers and hitting him on the nose. The English champion now did what some considered a rather curious thing; he turned and ran. He knew Heenan would soon be blind and he needed just that little extra time to lure the American into chasing him about the ring – the same ruse he had adopted when he wanted to tire the Tipton Slasher.

The time was now 9.30. Two hours had elapsed, and the police were slowly threading their way through the crowd. Here and there kicks and punches were aimed at them, but there were also those who let them pass unmolested, perhaps to save their money or their man – a question on which the crowd was pretty evenly divided.

When Heenan came up for the 36th, there came a buzz of consternation at the ghastly spectacle he presented. His features had literally disappeared and he was totally unrecognizable as a human being. His head was fearfully bruised and swollen, the right side of his face completely misshapen and he was still bleeding freely from the deep cuts. Unable to see anything clearly, he rushed in, grabbed Sayers by the neck, and dragged him towards the ropes. He tried desperately to hold him there and force him into a submission, but Tom slipped through his grasp like a slippery eel, and rolled over on the grass.

Cries of, 'Ring-keepers, – Ring-keepers!' were raised as the vanguard of the police reached the ropes of the outer ring. Here, they became entangled with the two dozen pugilists who did their utmost to repel them by cutting left and right with their heavy gutta percha whips. It became a nightmare for those caught up in the middle of the disorder, as again and again the burly constables contrived to drive a wedge through the ring-keepers and into the crowd assembled within the inner ring.

Summoning up his last reserves of strength, Tom was first up and waiting for Heenan in the 37th and last official round. His nose and lips were extensively swollen and his right arm hung helplessly at his side. Bracing himself for the expected charge, as Heenan floundered towards him, he smashed his fist twice in quick succession into the slit of his remaining bloated eye.

Unable to distinguish anything clearly, Heenan's only possible salvation lay in wrestling his opponent into submission. As he groped his way around the ring, the shadowy figure of Tom Sayers loomed into his line of vision. With more luck than judgement, he grasped him around the neck, and for about a minute held him pressed over the ropes.

Tom made vigorous attempts to extricate himself from the hold until, getting one hand free, he dispensed a series of short jabbing uppercuts into Heenan's face, jerking his head back on his neck like a puppet. Through the darkening mist, Heenan could dimly distinguish the shadowy outlines of the ropes and stakes. With his right hand clutching a post for support, he forced Tom's head over the ropes with his other hand, and leaned on his neck.

Shouts of, 'Hold him Heenan!' resounded from his American allies, and frantic cries of, 'He's strangling him, he'll kill him!' echoed from the other side.

Tom's face began to turn a deep shade of purple, and his eyes started from his head as Heenan slowly began choking the life from his body.

At this point the police penetrated the cordon around the outer ring and the main body of spectators scattered in all directions, leaving a clear patch for the main force to link up with their comrades. Many constables were still engaged in minor incidents, and one small band of ring-keepers were still battling valiantly to hold a section of the police at bay, but under a hail of blows, and by sheer weight of numbers, they were relentlessly swept aside in the huge mass of struggling humanity.

As the crowd, maddened with excitement surged backwards and forwards, Frank Dowling and the umpires, caught up in the crush, were swept away from their posts and disappeared among the vortex of bodies. Having lost sight of the ring, and unable to call a halt to the hostilities, he sent an order with one of his subordinates, instructing the men to cease fighting. But in all the tumult and confusion, the message was either ignored or it never reached its destination.

By now, Tom had turned black in the face and, in the absence of the referee, his friends concluded that they must act quickly if they were to save him from almost certain death. Heenan was still leaning with his full weight across Tom's neck when someone in the crowd cut and lowered the ropes. As the tension suddenly gave way beneath them and they fell together on the grass, the mob surged into the ring itself, nearly trampling all over Tom who lay on the ground gasping for breath. Everyone seemed to be shrieking at the top of his voice for order, and as they all crushed relentlessly forward, so they all called upon everyone to stand back. To add to the confusion, the police had now fought their way into the ring and were busy pulling up the stakes. The Americans were loudly proclaiming that Heenan had won, while Tom's supporters were screaming that according to rule 28, Sayers was the victor and Heenan had lost on a foul.

For the time being the battle was over, having lasted 2 hours and 6 minutes. In accordance with the accepted practice, the men should now have been taken away but, having recovered his breath, Tom was on his feet again and ready to resume fighting. The crush of bodies in what had formerly been the ring was now so dense, the two contestants were left with an area of about six feet square in which to carry on fighting.

The close proximity of the spectators was a serious disadvantage for

Sayers, whose only real chance of survival lay in having enough space in which to avoid the long reach of Heenan. Surrounded by a small circle of spectators, Tom stood silently awaiting the next attack, his face, hands and body spattered with his own and Heenan's blood.

Amidst the tumult and shambles, shouting and screaming supporters urged their particular favourite to, 'Stand up and finish him off!'

Five more so-called rounds were fought, in which all attempts at timekeeping failed and intervals between rounds were arbitrary. Occasionally, cheers went up from those in the circle proclaiming Heenan had won after knocking Sayers down, only to be vehemently denied seconds later when Tom sprang to his feet and gave the American such staggering blows that he too was hailed as conqueror.

Still unable to distinguish anything clearly, Heenan stumbled forward to where Tom sat on his second's knee and let fly with a left and a right. Poor Jemmy Welsh collapsed under one mighty blow and Harry Brunton crumpled in a heap from the other. As they lay on the grass, Heenan kicked them viciously, unsure who they were, but hoping one of them was Sayers.

Intent on revenge at this unprovoked assault on his friends, Tom leapt at Heenan, and with what little strength he could muster, knocked him over.

Heenan staggered forward again, arms flailing wildly, aiming punches at anything that moved. Jim Cusick got in the way and he too was laid flat. Tom, now completely exhausted and virtually incapable of throwing a punch, took to hugging Heenan, leaning on him and trying to push him over. At this moment Frank Dowling reappeared, having fought his way back through the crowd to what remained of the ring. He reached out and, restraining them by their arms, ordered an end to the fight. Both seemed relieved that it was all over and neither raised any objections to his actions.

The police were now present in considerable force and, taking command of the proceedings, announced they were quite prepared to let everyone go in peace, providing no further action took place.

The officials held a hurried conference and agreed that due to the extent of the men's injuries and physical exhaustion, there was no point in moving to another location merely to reach a decision. So they declared the fight officially over after a total of 42 rounds, lasting 2 hours and 20 minutes.

Immediately Heenan heard the news, he rushed madly away, bowling people over as he forced a passage through the crush of spectators. As a final act of bravado, and to prove he was still as strong as ever, he sprinted across the fields, leaping a couple of low hedges as he went, but within the space of about five minutes, he lost his sight completely and had to be led by the hand back to the waiting train.

Despite Tom's absurd claim later that he could have fought for another hour if necessary, judging from his performance in the last round, it is highly improbable he would have lasted more than another ten minutes.

Screened by his supporters, and with his arms encircling the shoulders of his seconds for support, he too began the journey back to the train.

He had not long departed when the police, for reasons best known to themselves, decided to make an example of him and ordered his arrest. Setting off in hot pursuit, the column soon caught up with the stragglers. Although they eagerly searched the faces of the crowd, they could find no trace of Tom or his companions. The intentions of the police had quickly spread and a timely warning had reached the little party.

Still screened by his faithful followers, Tom, his seconds and John Gideon had set off across the fields to where a horsedrawn van waited by the roadside. Clambering aboard, they set off at a brisk trot towards the town of Farnborough. Once safely hidden in the back of the van, Tom changed from his fighting attire into a variety of clothing donated by his friends, and it was here that John Gideon received his most cherished possession – Tom Sayers' fighting boots. For many years after the event, he would proudly exhibit them, exactly as they were when Tom had taken them off, the traces of Farnborough mud and turf still adhering to the spikes.

Some time later, when the hue and cry had finally died down, the van was driven into the station approaches where Tom stealthily emerged masquerading as a supporter. Mingling with the spectators, who were still wandering aimlessly about, he subsequently resumed his seat on the train which was now considerably delayed on his account.

Throughout the morning and early afternoon hundreds of people had been assembling at London Bridge Station, anxiously awaiting the return of the two trains and their occupants. Their patience was rewarded shortly before three o'clock when the great crowd arrived back to a tumultuous welcome. The instant the passengers alighted, they were quickly surrounded by swarms of excited people who bombarded them with questions about the result and details of the great battle. The uproar was deafening as everyone yelled and shouted above the noise of the engines and the usual clamorous din of the station.

Both sides declared their man would have won if the police had not intervened, but all agreed unanimously that the referee could not defy

John Heenan, "The Benicia Boy", shortly after his fight with Tom Sayers.

the law and therefore had no other alternative than to stop the contest. The official welcoming committee were most disappointed to learn that, as a precaution against the possibility of their arrest at the London Bridge terminus, the two men and their companions had been set down a few minutes earlier at the Bricklayers Arms Goods Station, in the Old Kent Road.

When the small party had disembarked at the depot, Tom and his associates had been escorted across the road to his old friend Ned Elgee's hostelry, The Swan (now Gooseberrys), in the Old Kent Road. The moment he entered the tavern, he was greeted by a large group of cheering fans who had witnessed his arrival and had crowded into the taproom to slap him on the back and shower him with congratulations. Disregarding the euphoria taking place around him, Tom's physician, Dr Adams, was gravely concerned over the injury to his arm, and after giving him a thorough examination, checking for broken bones, torn tendons and contusions to the muscles, he bandaged the arm from the wrist to the shoulder. He advised Tom to go straight to bed and get some much-needed rest, but Tom stubbornly refused to heed his counselling, and for a while, sat slumped in a chair, nursing his injured arm. However, shortly after he was comfortably settled, he enquired rather wearily after Heenan's health, saying how concerned he felt over his lamentable condition. Gideon looked out of the window and saw Heenan and his friends were still in the station, so he suggested that it might be a good idea if the two heroes of the day met again and shake hands.

One of the journalists who had attended the fight, quick to recognize a potentially good news story, went back across the road to invite The Benicia Boy and his friends over for a drink and to meet Tom. But to his consternation, he found Heenan sitting in a closed cab, wrapped in blankets, blind, horribly disfigured and apparently unconscious. Shocked and appalled at his grievous condition, he recommended he should be taken immediately to see a doctor.

Later that evening, after a period of complete rest and quiet, Tom regained some of his former cheerfulness and, over a cup of tea with Ned Elgee, laughingly regretted his doctor's orders preventing him from sampling the bottles of champagne his friends were liberally drinking to toast his health, success and bravery.

# 21

## AFTERMATH

Early the following morning, two senior metropolitan police officers called at the offices of *Bell's Life* with implicit instructions from the Home Secretary, affirming that should Heenan and Sayers attempt to renew hostilities, a warrant would be issued and the two men arrested. They also warned moreover that an order would be given to the proper authorities to indict all other persons connected with the breach of the peace already committed. Fully conversant with the implications of the law, Frank Dowling agreed to comply with their instructions and assured them there would be no further negotiations between either party for another contest.

Later that morning, Tom called at *Bell's Life* to discuss the possibility of another meeting with Heenan. Frank Dowling informed him of the visit by the police and told him quite categorically that any request for a re-match was completely out of the question, and that a meeting would be held the following Monday with the backers of both parties to discuss an amicable settlement.

The news that Tom Sayers was visiting the stakeholder's office quickly spread through the streets of London and an immense crowd began to gather in the Strand. When he emerged from the building, he was greeted with a spontaneous burst of enthusiastic cheering and applause. In spite of all the terrible punishment he had sustained just twenty-four hours earlier, he looked in remarkably good condition. Although his right arm was bound up and in a sling, only his swollen nose, the cuts on his lips and a few bumps on his hard forehead remained visible.

When questioned by reporters who had hurried to the scene, he admitted the knock-down blows at the beginning of the battle had been dreadfully severe, but for the last hour of the conflict, the American's hands were so badly swollen the blows did little more than actually knock him down and had only inflicted superficial damage. He said he bitterly regretted that the contest had been stopped and was quite confident he would have won if only the fight had lasted another ten minutes. It certainly appeared to many that with the general air of confidence he assumed, it was quite possible he had not underestimated his powers in this respect.

Heenan on the contrary, despite the absurd declarations issued by his American friends, was in no condition to see, or be seen. For at least forty-eight hours after his return to London, he was confined to a darkened room, unable to see through his swollen eyes and, for almost three days lay in a critical condition, totally incapable of making an appearance at the referee's office.

For the next few days, the big fight was the major topic of conversation. In Parliament, the Stock Exchange, in the clubs, taverns and sporting houses, even in the pulpit, the talk was of nothing else. There may have also been a grain of truth in the rumour that Queen Victoria had asked to be informed of the result immediately it was known. Never in the annals of the prize ring had the British press given so much editorial coverage to a championship fight, and the newspapers were full of graphic reports.

Two tons of newsprint packed in thirty-five bales, the largest quantity of newspapers ever shipped abroad, left Southampton bound for America in the race to be first across the Atlantic with the news. *The Times* carried an extensively detailed account, occupying two and a half broadsheet columns. The article, a masterpiece of journalism, reputedly earned for its writer, Nicholas Woods, the princely sum of one hundred pounds. *Blackwood's Edinburgh Magazine* published a long article, so too did the *Saturday Review*. Punch devoted a poem written by H. Chalmondley Pennell entitled, "The Combat of Sayerius and Heenanus," a parody of Lord Macauley's "Horatious" in his Lays of Ancient Rome.

The continental journals, generally cynical and ludicrously ill-informed on English sporting affairs, were especially liberal in their admiration of the insular bravery and fortitude of the English champion. The *Debats* devoted nearly five columns to a description of the fight.

Although most of the narrative was taken from the leading English newspapers, it concluded: "This struggle, then, brought face to face the Old World and the New – Old England and Young America . . . The Englishman, looking at the American as he recoiled from his blows, could not but think with pride – 'It is I who have done this thing,' and yet he was also proud of the blows he received from the giant of the New World, for therein he could not fail to recognize the vigour of his race . . . The Englishman in this struggle appears as the faithful type of his nation. What are the attributes of the English race? What but endurance, patience and energy, often latent, but always fierce, and one that never knows defeat – an obstinacy that will never be conquered, and a secret oath to die rather than yield? Even in the story of the fight we find all these attributes. Even at the risk of offending the delicate taste of our readers, we will say that in the sternly obstinate and in-flexible resolution with which the Englishman, apparently unconscious of the pain in his right arm, supported, with his left arm only, the shock of the terrific avalanche which fell upon him, is, in our eyes, a triumph of moral force and a miraculous exhibition of will.

"Five and twenty times he was flung upon the sward, and five and twenty times he rose again, the living image of England in the field of battle. History tells us that Englishmen are always beaten in the first campaign. Like all men of strong character, they gather force from misfortune. It seems like Antaeus they must kiss the earth before they know their strength, for after a series of defeats we find them masters of the field of battle. If they are not thoroughly beaten at first, then their destruction will be a work of time."

The *Constitutionel* conformed to similar views as the *Debats* but other French publications saw it as a rude and disgusting exhibition. The tirade from the *Siècle* alluded to it as "barbarous and disgusting" and "the play of animal instinct."

*Bell's Life* severely censured Heenan for his conduct which, it claimed, "was not only unbecoming and unmanly, but also contra-vened rule 28 of the prize ring." (This rule was later amended and enlarged in its scope to prevent a repetition of similar incidents.)

The American press portrayed the battle in an entirely different aspect to that seen by the British. In short, after reading George Wilkes' report in *Frank Leslie's United States Illustrated News*, the Americans felt they had been cheated when he concluded:

"Round 37. The cries of "Police" now became perfectly deafening from Sayers' side; but Heenan still looked neither right nor left, but only at his man. He hit once on his back as he was running to his corner and, as Sayers struck back and missed, he seized him with his arms around his neck and held him for a minute in the air. Sayers, however, got up his hand and seized Heenan by the cheek, and pulled at his labby folds most painfully. This forced Heenan to lose his hold, and Sayers slipped down.

"Round 38. It was now plain from the noise around Sayers' corner, that it was the determination of his party to bring the fight to such a close as would save Sayers the belt; but still Heenan kept to his work and Macdonald kept steering him with judicious steadfastness. He was determined to fight and to do nothing else so long as he could get

Sayers to fight with him and, though the ring was on the point of being broken in, he went up to his man and fought as manfully and desperately as at first. He hit Sayers as he pleased and finally, seizing him by the neck, he bent his head under his arm and held him there against the ropes, completely at his mercy. Left to himself, Sayers must have sunk helpless to the earth, incapable to respond again to time, whereupon, finding a desperate crisis had arrived, the adherents of the champion actually took hold of Heenan's arms and, while they kicked and struck him, dragged the beaten champion from his hold.

"Round 39. The confusion was now so great that no appeals could possibly be heard, and the ring being broken in by friends of Sayers at the same moment, the referee, very improperly, got up and retired. Heenan, however, apprehending some new artifice to prevent him obtaining the belt he had so fairly won, remained in the ring, and when time was called went after Sayers again, through the centre of the crowd that now swarmed within the inner ropes of the arena. Sayers was pushed up towards him, but he easily hit him down or pursued him to the corner among his seconds, as a man would drive a boy.

"In the 40th and 41st rounds, this dishonourable treatment was repeated. Sayers neither time being brought up until Heenan presented himself before him and demanded he should come out and fight. Finally, when he came up the last time for round 42, finding that Sayers could not, or would not rise from his seat in the corner and his seconds refused to award him the victory that belonged to him by throwing up the sponge, he advanced upon him in the midst of his seconds and struck him where he sat. Being struck in return by someone else in that corner, he turned upon that other party and, in his just indignation at the outrageous manner in which the object of his ambition had been dishonourably wrested from him, he opened a free fight against them all. His friends, however, interfered, and carried him back to his corner, from whence, after declaring himself to be the winner of the fight and the true owner of the belt and title of Champion of England, he left the ring. Fair-minded and honourable Englishmen will decide whether these rights, so dearly and bravely won, shall not be given to him because he is a stranger to their soil."

After reading George Wilkes' preposterous and misleading report, about a dozen distinguished English gentlemen said they were prepared to swear on oath that Heenan had struck Sayers twice when he was down on two knees; he had struck and kicked Jemmy Welsh after he had knocked Sayers off his knee, and he had also struck Harry Brunton. The combination of all these acts would have constituted a foul and the referee, had he been present to have witnessed them, would have awarded the fight to Tom Sayers. In relation to these and other cogent reasons, it had all the hallmarks of being a lively meeting the following Monday.

It had also been reported in the press that "Tom Sayers would be presented with a purse containing the sum of 100 guineas on Saturday April 21, as a mark of approbation by members of the Stock Exchange, in tribute to the great courage he had displayed in his battle with John Heenan.

Throughout that Saturday morning, the main streets and through-fares leading to London's Stock Exchange presented a scene of bustling activity as crowds of eager people, from all walks of life, gathered to give him a rousing reception.

Although he made his appearance two hours ahead of schedule, the house was unusually crowded for the occasion and large numbers were already present awaiting his arrival. Accompanied by his old friend "Farmer" Bennett, Tom was first introduced to Sir Robert Carden and the principle members of commerce. Immediately the little party entered the general trading area, all business was suspended. The brokers left their desks and congregated around their celebrated visitor, all anxious to obtain a close glimpse of the man who, for the past four days, had been the subject of conversation in every corner of the land. Evidently taken aback by the warm and friendly reception, he was conducted around the room and introduced to the senior members of trade and commerce.

After completing his tour of inspection, he climbed up on a table in the French Market area and gracefully acknowledged the repeated cheers of the members. He seemed particularly moved by the extra-ordinary scene before him, and in a few homely words sincerely thanked all those present for the special kindness they had extended towards him and to Mr Bennett.

Except for his arm, which was still in a sling, he showed remarkably few signs of his tremendous castigation earlier in the week. One member expressed his surprise that he looked so well after his twenty knockdown blows.

A broad smile illuminated Tom's face when he replied, 'It's a bit of a wonder to me too. I'm only sorry I didn't have another ten minutes with The Boy.'

To renewed cheering from the great crowd gathered outside the building, he was escorted to a waiting cab by the member who had been instrumental in raising the subscription. Shaking Tom warmly by the hand, he presented him with a velvet bag containing 100 guineas.

Two days later, on Monday April 23, the executive managers and principle backers of both Heenan and Sayers met at the offices of *Bell's Life* to institute an amicable conclusion to the contest. Tom was an early arrival, but Heenan was not present, and no reason was given for his absence.

The meeting opened with a stormy outburst from Heenan's representatives who instantly laid claim to the silver belt of England which, they fervently believed, was lost by Sayers before the fight was stopped. The basis for their claim lay in George Wilkes' largely fictitious report that the English champion would have been defeated should the fight have been allowed to run its full course. Frank Dowling interjected by saying he had closed the conflict in compliance with the wishes of Heenan's friends. He explained that at the moment the ring was broken, he had been forced away and had remained on the outskirts of the crowd while the last three or four rounds were fought. It had actually been the friends of the American who insisted he should return to the ring and stop the fight and who, in accordance with the rules of the ring, maintained that when the enclosure was broken into, the combat should cease. It was these same people who made a passage through the crowd requesting him to return to the men and stop them, which he accordingly did, in spite of the wishes of the Sayers supporters, who were confident the English champion would win if given a few more minutes.

There was evidently a large element of truth in this statement, for after his impassioned speech tempers cooled and the strained relations gradually improved. The friends of both men now turned their attentions towards reaching a satisfactory settlement and, after debating the issue calmly and sensibly, proposed that Frank Dowling should have the deciding vote.

After some deliberation, he declared: Item 1. The contest would not be renewed due to the possibility of everyone going to jail.

2. That Heenan was in no condition to resume hostilities.

3. That in the present condition of Sayers' right arm, he was entitled by ring precedents (the fight having been interrupted) to a reasonable period of convalescence to restore his arm to its full use, and 4, that public opinion was radically opposed to these two extraordinary brave men who had contested so heroically and who, through no fault of their own, had been prevented from renewing their struggle after so much punishment, which was contrary to all dictates of humanity and fairness and which was the prized attribute of British boxing. Therefore, as the men had already proved their unflinching endurance to everyone's satisfaction, they need not be obliged to fight again and the contest be declared a drawn battle.

Everyone applauded Frank Dowling's wise and fair decision, but because several other measures needed to be taken into consideration, including the settlement of the battle money, the trophy, railway expenditure and profit, another meeting to finalize these issues would be held on May 18.

A letter appeared in *The Times* of May 7, purportedly written by Tom, but showing the unmistakably eloquent hand of John Gideon. It read:

"The period has arrived when it becomes my duty to thank the great British public for the patronage they have bestowed upon me. I did my best for the land of my birth and dearest affections. I had opposed to me one worthy of me and whose activity, rapidity and pluck, it was no small task to encounter. Sprung from our own race, the Americans inherit our best qualities and, as our conflicts with them in the progress of time ended in peace, so may every bitterness engendered by the late struggle for the championship pass away forever.

"To live to receive the kindly notice of the journal (The Times) which makes and unmakes reputations, which cheers the humble dwellings of the poor and makes tyrants tremble on their gilded thrones, is to have lived for a great and distinguished honour. Upon my own part and that of my children, I humbly offer my most grateful thanks, and I trust, to whatever period Providence will extend my life, will be unworthy of one who has received the notice of *The Times* newspaper.

I remain, Sir, your obedient servant,

Tom Sayers.
Champion of England."

But perhaps the *Cornhill Magazine* best summed up the public's feelings with its amusing anecdote: ". . . Well, if I were absolute king, I would send Tom Sayers to the treadmill for a month, and make him Sir Thomas on coming out of Clerkenwell. You are a naughty boy, Tom! But then, you know, we ought to love our brethren, though ever so naughty. We are moralists, and reprimand you and you are hereby reprimanded accordingly. But in case England should ever have the need for a few thousand champions, who laugh at danger; who cope with giants; who, stricken to the ground, jump up and gaily rally, and fall and rise again, and strike, and die rather than yield – in case the country need such men and you should know them, be pleased to send lists of the misguided persons to the principle police stations, where means may someday be found to utilize their wretched powers and give their deplorable energies a right direction. Then Sir Thomas, resist him to the death . . . and heaven bless you . . ."

Such was his popularity, that wherever he went, he was always surrounded by enthusiastic well-wishers, all eager to slap him on the back, buy him a drink or invite him for a meal. To mark their appreciation of his gallantry, the music halls, theatres and race tracks placed him on their free lists and he became a familiar figure at all the major events of the social calendar, always smartly dressed, often accompanied by John Gideon and, on the odd occasion, by Heenan.

On Derby Day 1860 Princess Mary of Cambridge asked for Mr Sayers to be presented to her in the Royal Box. Tom felt more than a little apprehensive about meeting Royalty, but she soon put him at ease and, shaking his hand warmly, presented him with an elegant mono-grammed lace handkerchief as a present for his daughter Sarah. The significance of this gift to a prize fighter, symbolized the first recognition of the prize ring by any member of the Royal Family since the days of the Prince Regent.

Later that afternoon, Tom was the victim of a pickpocket who stole the treasured handkerchief. However, thanks to the intercession of certain members of London's underworld, the handkerchief was later retrieved and returned to young Sarah.

At the final meeting to decide what should be done about the trophy, Sayers, Gideon and Jack Macdonald (representing Heenan) met with Frank Dowling in his office. In the three weeks since they last convened all sorts of ridiculous suggestions had been put forward. One idea had been for the belt to be cut in half and a subscription was actually raised to purchase the two halves.

With frequent objections and arguments from either side, it was ultimately proposed that the most sensible and logical solution was to place an order with Mr Hancock, the silversmith who designed the original belt, to manufacture two new belts, worked in frosted silver, and identical in every detail.

This decision was carried unanimously, and Mr Hancock promised to have both trophies ready within six days, in time for their presentation at Cremorne Gardens. However, two days later, on May 20, when Tom officially retired from the ring, it was announced that the venue had been changed and the ceremony would now take place in the circus ring of the Alhambra Theatre in Leicester Square, at nine o'clock on the evening of May 30, 1860.

At precisely to the minute on the appointed evening, the two men, linked arm in arm with the Master of Ceremonies, walked into the sawdust arena, waving gaily to the cheering audience. The M.C. read the address, and then presented each man with a cheque for his share of the battle money and a vellum containing the illuminated address. To more cheering from the spectators, the two belts, in red Morocco cases, were carried ceremoniously into the arena.

Heenan's belt was presented to him by John Gideon, who made a short speech, closing with the following remarks: '. . . Meanwhile, take this token, – cherish it as a well-earned, and well-deserved memento to the people of this country – and rest assured, that while pugilism remains a sport of Great Britain, so long will the name of John C. Heenan be remembered as one of the bravest men who ever entered a four-and-twenty foot roped ring.'

George Wilkes then made his presentation to Tom and, in a somewhat long-winded speech, called attention to the qualities of the Englishman, saying: '. . . Buckle it about your loins and treasure it; be proud of it; for it is a sure expression of the admiration of two nations, such as a man of your humble standing never had the proud fortune to receive before.'

Tom removed his coat and buckled the belt around his waist, a task he found none too easy, for since the fight he had put on quite a few pounds around the middle. Neither Heenan nor Sayers were orators but each mumbled a few words of thanks and, to the renewed cheers of the onlookers, linked arms and paraded around the arena until the ceremony ended. Sadly, however, the whole evening had a hollow ring about it, for neither belt had been fairly won in a fight and their true value was meaningless.

Within a few weeks of the great fight, the market place was flooded with souvenirs and memorabilia of every description. Portraits of the two boxers, priced at three pence each, sold in their thousands, while Toby jugs and clay pipes, inscribed on the bowl with Sayers and Heenan, were commonplace in the taverns of London. (Litho prints of the Farnborough battle and Staffordshire pottery figures, depicting Heenan and Sayers in fighting pose, are collectable items today and command high prices.) So great was the euphoria, that one man in Brighton had the words Tom Sayers tattooed across his chest. There was even talk of changing the ordnance survey maps to include crossed swords on the Farnborough meadow to mark the spot where England did battle with America.

The British tradition of admiration for courage and integrity now expressed itself in the form of a public subscription for Tom. The collection was started in the House of Commons where Lord Palmerston and leading members of both houses clubbed together their gold pieces and five pound notes. Tom's friends at the Stock Exchange, Lloyds and Mark Lane (the busy trading centre for City merchants) all contributed charitably to ensure the champion passed the remainder of his days in peace and free from the sorrows of poverty. The colossal sum of £3,000 was subscribed by his generous friends, but only with the un-compromising stipulation that he must never fight again in the prize ring. But, knowing well Tom's wayward nature, John Gideon's paramount concern was that he would not be coerced into entering the ring again with any false promises, thereby losing his £3,000 indenture and ending his days as a pauper. His lawyers drew up a deed and invested the £3,000 in the names of trustees, at 4½% interest in Great North Railway stocks, which guaranteed a modest income for the remainder of his life. Upon his death the money was to be divided equally between his two illegitimate children Sarah and Thomas, when they became of age.

A couple of months after the presentation of the belts, John Heenan announced his intention of returning to America. Immediately there came a great outcry from the British public when they learned of his decision and they tried every conceivable argument to make him change his mind. But he was restless and discontented. Adah Menken was seeking a divorce and nothing would induce him to stay. So in August 1860 he packed his bags, bid farewell to everyone in England and set sail for home.

On his return to New York, he received a rapturous welcome from the thousands of fight fans who packed into Jones' Wood open-air stadium to pay tribute to their hero. To add to their delight, he stage-managed, with the help of a local pugilist, how he had hammered Sayers in England.

After only a short stay in New York, he moved on to Chicago where he continued his notoriety with more exhibitions and the proceeds from public subscriptions. Later, while undertaking a tour of America, he was frequently seen in the company of a young lady named Harriet Martin who was subsequently cited in Adah Menken's divorce petition.

A few days after Heenan had sailed for America, John Gideon, who for the past few years had protected Tom's financial interests, departed for Paris on business. Left to his own devices, Tom decided it was time to enjoy the proceeds of his years of dedication to the prize ring. Now a moderately wealthy man, he had accumulated substantial riches from his guest appearances with Heenan and his benefits throughout the country, a large collection of silver plate donated by his admirers and a generous share of the railway excursion profits.

He moved from his humble little home in Bayham Street and went to live at 10 Belle View Cottages, a modest terraced house in Camden Street, Camden Town. Life now became very pleasant. He bought himself a gig and was often seen driving his dun cob through the streets of London, with his huge mastiff "Lion" seated on the tailboard.

The dog had been a present from Lord Derby who had told him, 'Tom, you are the best man in England and therefore you should have the best dog.'

During the school holidays that summer, young Sarah and Thomas came to stay with their father and the little family spent much of their time at play, romping with Lion, or going on picnics in the Highgate meadows. Although his wife Sarah still maintained regular contact with him and the children, visiting them at Belle View Cottage, he could not possibly have foreseen at this time how it would lead to such disastrous consequences in later years when she contested his will and inheritance. She probably regretted her actions in leaving her husband, and the riches of his position, for while she was currently employed operating a mangle in a laundry, James Aldridge was still driving his Hansom cab around London.

On the lamp above the George and Dragon, Harry Brunton proudly proclaimed himself Tom Sayers' favourite second.

# 22

## HOWES & CUSHING'S CIRCUS

In the summer of 1861, Tom chanced to meet up with and old acquaintance, a travelling showman named Jem Myers who was managing the American-owned Howes and Cushing's Circus. Under the auspices of its owner Joe Cushing, Tom had given numerous exhibitions bouts in the circus ring during the time Heenan had been in England. Despite a year having passed since the Farnborough battle, the name of Tom Sayers still held a big fascination to the British public, and when Myers invited him to make a few guest appearances on the present tour, Tom readily accepted.

The attraction of the animals and the free and easy life of the circus excited him tremendously and, during his travels around the country, he struck up a lasting friendship with the other performers of the troupe, who knew he was not afraid of getting his hands dirty undertaking all the onerous chores associated with a travelling circus.

But sadly, without the guiding hand of John Gideon, poor gullible Tom was no match for the slick, fast-talking American showmen, particularly when they offered him a major share in the business and the later option of buying outright the entire enterprise. The idea of owning his own circus appealed to him immensely and he listened attentively to their persuasive arguments that business could not possibly fail with the name of Tom Sayers heading the bill. Carried along on a wave of burning enthusiasm, he foolishly decided to invest his entire life's savings into the venture. The deeds were signed and he became the major shareholder. His first task was to reinstate his old friend Jem Myers as general manager and appoint Joe Cushing as his financial advisor.

He enjoyed to the full the thrills and excitement of his new vocation. With the brass band playing a rousing march, he would lead the circus into town, resplendent in a glittering clown's costume, or riding in a richly ornamented chariot drawn by his two performing mules, Barney and Pete. Often during the performances he appeared in the arena made up as a melancholy looking clown, throwing himself whole-heartedly into the act. The children loved him, and for a while every-thing went well.

He bought up the remaining shares, confident his future looked secure. But he was completely out of his depth. Other highly competi-tive circus owners were slowly squeezing him out of business and he began to incur ever-increasing debts. Uneducated, and with no qualifi-cations or business acumen, money problems worried him immensely. He discovered that his financial troubles appeared less tiresome after a few glasses of brandy and he started drinking heavily. By slow degrees, his former carefree life degenerated into one of excess and debility. His features developed a drawn and haggard expression and he began to show the first symptoms of a worsening illness. Several doctors were called in to treat him, but none could accurately diagnose his ailment.

One day, when he was feeling particularly indisposed, Joe Cushing prescribed a stiff dose of castor oil. He brought him a cup of brandy with the castor oil floating on top.

'Drink it, Tom' he said in a persuasive voice, 'It'll put you right in no time.'

Taking the cup in his hand, Tom stared at it for some time, making awful grimaces as he did so.

'Drink it I tell you', Cushing reiterated.

Tom raised the cup to his lips, and with a shudder exclaimed, 'Damn it, I can't.' Making a second attempt, he slammed it down on the table.

'I'll be damned if I can take it – there now – and one word is as good as a hundred.' For a while he sat staring at the cup, a look of abject distaste upon his face.

'Look here,' he cried. 'If I could only get my beak through the beastly stuff at the top and swig the brandy underneath, there'd be some sense in it; but no, I can't.'

'No oil, no brandy' said Cushing, 'Drink it Tom, be a man.'

Leaping to his feet, he growled with bitterness, 'Be a man indeed, I would rather fight fifty Heenans than be drenched with that infernal stuff. No, I can't take it and I won't take it.'

Joe Cushing often related this story, claiming that Tom Sayers met his match that day; the man who had been brave enough to stand and be punched, bruised and suffer untold agony had finally been beaten by a dose of castor oil.

When John Gideon returned to England at the end of 1862, he was horrified to learn that Tom's life savings were almost exhausted and he was on the brink of bankruptcy. Furious at the manner in which Tom had been deceived, he closed down the circus and sold off all the animals, tents, carriages and effects to settle the outstanding debts.

Poor Tom, the victim of an uncultured mind, was unable to cope with all the misfortunes. Disillusioned and heartbroken, he plunged into the depths of depression, shedding all restraints, and degenerating into a life of self-indulgence and dissipation. Losing weight drastically, he presented a gaunt, pathetic figure. With his dog Lion, now his constant companion, he spent most of his time in the infamous Britannia Tavern, or the equally iniquitous Mother Red Cap. Wearing a pair of riding boots adorned with tassels, and the words "TOM SAYERS – CHAMPION" embroidered across the knees, he would sit in his favourite corner next to the bar, a glass of brandy in one hand and a cigar in the other, drinking and carousing with the petty criminals, prostitutes and general riffraff of London, who made him their idol.

But nature's laws were not to be broken with impunity, and his indulgent life style soon began to have its inevitable effect. His conventional discipline of regular exercise and regulated diet, which had kept him in a constant pitch of physical perfection for more than ten years, now gave way to corpulence and debilitation. The symptoms of the

Tom Sayers seated beside his father in his famous trap, drawn by his dun cob. Tom's dog Lion is seated in his favourite position in the back seat.

illness he had contracted in his circus days returned and he developed a constant thirst which he was only able to quench with gallons of beer laced with brandy. He also observed significant deposits of a sticky substance adhering to his riding boots; the residue of sugar-impregnated urine.

When John Gideon saw him again he was astonished at the dramatic changes which had taken place over the course of a few months. Deeply concerned over his failing health, he suggested he should consult a doctor immediately.

Tom shrugged off his advice and for several weeks refused to listen to his repeated pleas. But inevitably, finding himself becoming progressively worse, he changed his mind and sensibly sought medical advice from his physician and friend, Doctor Adams. He gave him an exhaustive examination and after a series of stringent medical tests, informed him he was suffering from the rampant scourge of diabetes. He warned him that medical science was powerless to combat the illness, and unless he totally abstained from alcohol and adhered to a strict diet, it could soon prove fatal.

The news came as a bombshell. Shocked and alarmed at his doctor's diagnosis, he left his cottage in Belle View Terrace and went to live with his sister Eliza and Robert King in Claremont Square, Pentonville. Eliza would stand no nonsense from her younger brother. She ensured he conformed to his rigid diet and steadily reduced his fluid intake to an acceptable level. After a few weeks of diligent care and attention, he began showing encouraging signs of recovery, despite having lost a considerable amount of weight by sticking to his uncompromising diet. When his strength and inclination allowed, he loved to ride out in his gig, accompanied by his beloved mastiff Lion.

# 23

## HEENAN RETURNS

During the time Tom was convalescing at his sister's, the civil war in America was at its height. General Robert E. Lee had set his confederate army in motion for an invasion of the Northern States, and by the end of June 1863, his band of "Starving Ragamuffins" had marched through Maryland and was far into Pennsylvania.

On June 30, one of his brigades clashed with General George G. Mead's Union cavalry at the little farming community of Gettysberg. In the bloody battle which ensued, Tom's old adversary Aaron Jones, fighting with the Union forces, lay critically wounded on the battlefield. Initially listed as killed in action, he lay for many long hours among the dead and dying of both sides. Taken to the field hospital more dead than alive, the doctors were sceptical about his chances of survival, but his strength and iron-will prevailed and he survived his injuries and multiple wounds.

With the civil war nearing New York and most of the youth of America under arms, John Heenan's future looked very bleak indeed. Like most American mob heroes his popularity had waned and, with no one to challenge him in his own country, he was about to set sail again for England.

His return to the United States in 1860 had been particularly provoking for Sam Hurst, better known in fighting circles as the Stalybridge Infant. He had challenged Heenan before his fight with Tom Sayers to meet him in the ring, regardless of the outcome of their battle at Farnborough. Hurst had deposited his £50, with an equal amount from Heenan, but because the articles lacked a clause on any forfeiture, when Heenan decided to leave England, he had picked up his £50 and departed.

On Tom's retirement from the ring, the title of champion had been bandied about between Ben Caunt, Bendigo, Harry Orme, The Tipton

Slasher, Con Parker and Harry Broome. The Fancy, however, believed that as all of these were well advanced in years, the position would obviously have to be filled by someone prepared to defend it for the next three years, so when the Stalybridge Infant issued a challenge to fight any man in the world for £400, the sporting fraternity waited anxiously for a response. But to everyone's disappointment, the year of 1860 had slowly ebbed away and there had been no response to Hurst's challenge. At the eleventh hour, Tom Paddock came forward, but he stood no chance against the younger 6 feet 2½ inch, 13 stone challenger. Paddock was easily beaten and Hurst became the undeclared champion of England.

Unhappily for Hurst, his reign was short lived. He had broken his leg and had not fully recovered from the injury when he was beaten by Jem Mace on June 18, 1861.

One of Heenan's reasons for returning to England was to see his old advocate Jem Mace, after his two tremendous contests against Tom King. In their first battle, on January 28, 1862, Mace thrashed King in 43 rounds, but in the 18th round of their second engagement, King delivered one of the most crushing blows ever seen in the prize ring. The punch landed full on Mace's cheek, and seemed to cave in the whole side of his face. Mace crumpled under the impact and fell helpless to the ground. On coming up for the next round, still dazed, his left eye completely closed and bleeding from the eye, nose and mouth, King instantly felled him with his left. Mace struggled to the scratch once more, but King refused to hit him and simply pushed him down as his seconds threw up the sponge. Tom King now inherited the title, but he declined another meeting with Jem Mace, and by the time Heenan returned to England he had resigned the championship in favour of Mace.

Much to Heenan's surprise he found he was still a popular figure in Great Britain, and when it was whispered that The Benicia Boy was prepared to do battle for a sum not less than a thousand pounds, King's backers urged him to pick up the gauntlet. The articles were then endorsed for their contest to take place on December 8, 1863, with stakes of £1,000 a side.

With all the preliminary details settled, Heenan went to Camden Town to seek the whereabouts of Tom Sayers and to ask him to act as principle second in his match with Tom King. Tom was delighted to see him again and they spent several pleasant hours in Robert King's drawing room, reminiscing over old times and the events which had occurred since the Farnborough battle. Tom explained the complications associated with his recent illness, and said he felt confident that with several weeks remaining before the contest, he would be fit and well enough to perform his duties in Heenan's corner.

The battle between Tom King (left) and Jem Mace on November 26, 1862. In the eighteenth round, King delivered a crushing blow which seemed to cave in the whole side of Mace's cheek

The fight promised to be a natural sequel to the Farnborough conflict. Although Heenan was heavily fancied, Tom King had beaten many good men in his career and he was not an adversary to be taken lightly.

The battle took place on the outskirts of Wadhurst in Kent before a sizeable audience, but smaller than the one seen at Farnborough. Heenan's party evidently believed that the presence of Tom Sayers in The Boy's corner would cause gloom and dismay among the ranks of King's followers, but from the moment Sayers stepped into the ring, dressed in a fur cap, yellow flannel jacket, riding boots and a blue and white shawl twisted about his neck, it was plain for all to see that he was there for nothing more than effect. As he commenced attending to Heenan's preparations, he evoked a stir of comments, not only for his flamboyant style of dress, but also for his sickly and unhealthy complexion. At times he stood transfixed, gazing intently at Heenan, an expression of wonderment on his face as though marvelling at his own audacity in meeting this giant a few years earlier. But Heenan too, had changed. Heavy and cumbersome, his limbs now lacked the thews and sinews which had once been the envy of everyone.

Although King was in superb condition, his white skin glistening like polished ivory in the crisp morning sunlight, he remained silent and sullen during the preliminaries, scarcely exchanging any remarks with his seconds or the spectators.

A stony silence prevailed as they shook hands and moved imperceptibly closer. Suddenly the sounds of "Whack! Whack!" told of a couple of tremendous punches. Again the sounds of blows re-echoed across the fields, and as King recoiled from the slashing fists, Heenan bulldozed him back against the ropes. Instinctively the American's arm snaked around King's neck in a stranglehold. Remembering the similar situation at Farnborough, when Sayers' head had been held over the ropes by the same adversary, King lurched forward with all his might and pushed Heenan into the centre of the ring.

Yells came from the crowd, 'Get down Tom; he'll choke you if you don't!'

But King seemed oblivious to their advice and peppered away at Heenan's ribs until he relinquished his hold then, grappling with each other, they rolled over on the grass with King underneath. Frank Dowling, the referee, entered the ring and cautioned Heenan on his hugging tactics, pointing out that if he persisted in holding his opponent in this dangerous position, it could lead to his disqualification.

Throughout the fight, King's seconds, Jerry Noon and Bos Tyler took inordinate care with their man, which was more than could be said for Tom Sayers and his treatment of Heenan. He dithered and floundered, often just standing and staring with a look of strange be-wilderment on his face whenever Heenan urgently needed his assis-tance. At one stage during the conflict, he grabbed Heenan by the hair and pulled him off his opponent. The spectators were disgusted with his contemptuous performance, and his bizarre appearance.

Henry Miles, the editor of *Pugilistica*, reported: "How are the mighty fallen. Poor Tom was no more equal to his task than a child."

Heenan produced little of his old form, and King's general air of clumsiness did little to instil confidence. Admittedly the exchanges were heavy and severe, but many blows were aimed completely at random.

In round 18 Heenan seized King about the waist and, lifting him bodily into the air, he threw him with tremendous force head first into the ground and fell heavily across his body. When Heenan was lifted off, King was found to be unconscious, and it required the combined skills of his seconds to bring him round for the call of time.

In a mixture of anger and excitement, King's followers invaded the ring and it took several minutes for Frank Dowling and the ring-keepers to eject the impetuous demonstrators from the arena. The long intermission had given King ample time to recover and he tore into The Benicia Boy, inflicting some fearful punishment. Suddenly, Heenan was seized with a fit of vomiting which left him weak and vulnerable and entirely at King's mercy. As Heenan became weaker and wilder, so King's supremacy improved. He punished the American without com-passion until he was semi-conscious and nearly blind. At this point Heenan's backers took charge of the situation. It was obvious that any further action would only expose him to more unnecessary punish-ment, so they insisted he surrender and throw up the sponge. It had been a farcical and totally unscientific battle of 24 rounds, lasting 35 minutes.

John Gideon, businessman and entrepreneur, became Tom Sayers' principle backer and personal friend. It was through his ingenuity and guidance that Tom rose to stardom in the prize ring.

# 24

## LAST DAYS OF TOM SAYERS

After the fiasco at Wadhurst, the new wave of despondency which swept the Fancy plunged the prize ring into even greater depths of depression. King and several of his backers appeared at Maidstone Quarter Sessions, charged with a breach of the peace, but fortunately it ended in an acquittal and King retired from the ring. Heenan also declared he was finished with prize fighting, and nothing would ever induce him to enter the ring again. Although his performance at Wadhurst had not extinguished the affection of the British sportsmen, it ended his reign as a champion. He remained in England, living on his wits and his bookmaker's business until he returned to America at the end of the civil war.

As for poor Tom, he was painfully aware of his shortcomings and of the embarrassment he had caused. He knew he had been a bitter disappointment to everyone, particularly to those who still held him in high esteem and remembered him when he was the lion of his day.

Following the harsh criticism he received from the sporting press, he quietly faded from the discerning eyes of the Fancy. His main preoccupation now consisted of driving his dun cob through the streets of London, his faithful mastiff Lion by his side, stopping occasionally to chat or call out a cheery greeting to a friend or neighbour. He still had scant respect for red tape and petty bureaucracy, certainly no time for magistrates, or in the existence of someone he considered 'a stiff cove.'

This total disregard for the authoritative section of society was often the cause of friction between himself and his friends, who found his stubborn and defiant attitude difficult to control. He scorned the idea of "sponging" on anyone, and cared even less for being feted. One evening, when he was made the hero of a supper party, he simply lay down on a sofa when he had finished his meal and went to sleep. On another occasion, when attending a dinner party given by some young and irresponsible members of the aristocracy, he had the uneasy feeling he was being made the butt of some kind of sport for their warped sense of humour.

After listening patiently to their sarcasm and innuendos, he rose to his feet and growled, 'I'll presently walk all round this table, and punch all your heads.'

But his greatest love was racing and he seldom missed a major classic. On one occasion, when he was at Doncaster Races with some sporting friends, he received one of his greatest accolades. His features expressed his profound pleasure when Sir Tatton Sykes sought him out in the enclosure. He shook Tom's hand warmly and extended his congratulations on his past triumphs. The old Baronet then walked round Sam Hurst, hardly showing any signs of recognition and went over to where Nat Langham stood leaning on the rails. He removed his beaverskin glove, and grasped Nat's hand tightly. Nat reminded him that when he was in his prime, he was the only man to have beaten Tom Sayers.

Still holding his hand, he said in his quiet and gentle way, 'Well then, sir, I can now honestly say that I've shaken hands with two very brave men.'

Tom held a special place of affection in the hearts of London's citizens. They always remembered the day they were lining the streets to welcome the Prince of Wales' bride, The Princess Alexandra, when Tom, with an imperturbable expression of quiescence on his face, had driven down the whole route of the procession as if it were the hereditary right of the champion of England to perform this honour. To the cheers of the onlookers, not a single policeman along the entire route moved or did anything to impede his progress.

Sadly this was about the last time the great British public saw their "Little Wonder" for Mother Nature was soon to take her revenge.

As the year of 1864 had drawn to a close, his diabetes had progressed from bad to worse and he had wasted to a mere shadow of his former self. His strength had deteriorated from the torment of his hyperglycaemia and he had developed a hollow cough, betraying the symptoms of tuberculosis. On February 20, 1865 his sister Eliza sent for Doctor Adams, the family physician, who gave him a thorough examination. He carefully explained the implications of his illness and stressed that with care and attention, life could continue more or less as normal, providing he had a plentiful supply of fresh air and took his medicines as prescribed, but as consumption of the lungs was inoperable, and Victorian medical science lacked permanent preventive treatment, there was little prospect of a lasting cure.

Tom accepted his fate philosophically and thanked him for his prognosis, but it came as no great surprise for secretly he had feared the worst for several months. He sat for a while, deep in thought, staring silently out of the window. Then, shrugging his shoulders, he smiled benignly at Doctor Adams and thanked him for his honest opinion.

A few weeks later, one frosty morning in March, he was driving with his father near St Pancras Church when someone on the pavement, who presumably bore him some sort of grudge, insulted him with an obscene gesture. Tom pulled up instantly and handing the reigns to his father, jumped down from his gig to confront the man for his insolence. In his hurry, he slipped on the icy cobble-stones and landed heavily on his back. For a time he lay sprawled in the gutter, unable to move. His father jumped down and helped him back to his seat, but throughout the journey home he complained of a searing pain in his shoulder blades. When he returned to his sister's and removed his shirt, he was startled to find his back covered in one gigantic bruise. Doctor Adams was again called in, but he could only advise plenty of rest, and wait for the bruising to fade.

His health had improved slightly by the middle of April, and he went down to Brighton where he believed breathing his native sea air would be beneficial. For a while he felt much better, but at the Brighton race meeting he was caught without a coat in a heavy thunderstorm and was soon drenched to the skin. A couple of days later he was confined to bed at his father's house, suffering from an acute bout of influenza and a worsening cough.

Nevertheless, he would not miss the Derby, and at the Epsom meeting he met all his old pals of the racing fraternity. They were clearly shocked at his present condition and appearance; the familiar mahogany-tinted face of his fighting days now replaced by the deep flush of disease.

He felt much better in June, but during the long warm summer of July, he noticeably drooped day by day. He expressed a longing to see his beloved Tonbridge just once more before he died. It had been his favourite place in his days of health; the games of skittles he had enjoyed at the Castle Tavern, and when he had lived at the Brown Jug and trained on the Hadlow road. He drove down in his gig and took lodgings at The Bull.

A few days later he made the effort to drive down to Hastings, but he was so exhausted at the end of the journey he had to spend the next couple of days recuperating. His appetite became so feeble he could barely eat a new laid egg or swallow a few mouthfuls of a succulent partridge. By day, he would lie on a sofa in the smoking-room, and at eight o'clock in the evening, he retired to his bed only to face another long and restless night.

Each day his friends watched him grow weaker, and when at last he was only able to crawl out into the sunshine, he sold his gig and on September 16, he returned to London. Hailing a cab at the station, he went directly to his sister's house in Pentonville. The moment Eliza opened the front door, she was struck with horror at his poor emaciated face, the skin stretched like parchment across the bones. Valiantly fighting back the sparkling tears in her eyes, she could plainly see the end was near. She sent an urgent message to Dr Adams, telling him of Tom's condition, and requesting him to call at the earliest opportunity. He in turn called in Dr Brown, an independent specialist in chest complaints, but when he had completed his examination, he drew Dr Adams to one side and declared there was nothing to be done. Complete and absolute disease of the lungs had set in, and he could not possibly survive more than a few weeks. To corroborate his diagnosis, Dr Adams called in another eminent consultant, Dr Gull,[2] but he too shook his head and confirmed everyone's worst fears.

Tom knew perfectly well the end was near, and in October he expressed his desire to visit his old friend John Mensley, the man who had always manufactured his fighting boots. He stayed with him for about a fortnight, and during that time there was a progressive improvement in his health, giving renewed hopes he would survive the crisis. But it was only a temporary recovery, and when he returned to his sisters', he suffered a relapse.

Reluctant to be a burden to Eliza any longer, he returned to John Mensley's shoe factory in Camden Town's High street and asked for all his personal belongings to be sent to him there, in order that he might feel more at home. In the solitude of his sparsely furnished room above the factory, he often spent the long, painful hours of the night gazing compassionately at his favourite picture "Farnborough Morning" and at all the familiar faces of the friends who had attended that epic battle.

During his illness, scores of enquiries were made regarding his health. He received frequent visits from his family and close friends and from many who had been in contention against him in the ring. It was indeed a touching sight to see these big, burly prize fighters,

---

[2] According to a television series broadcast in 1988, Dr Gull was suspected of being Jack the Ripper, the man responsible for the Whitechapel murders in 1888. However, the £4m film made for Thames Television in conjunction with the American company Lorimar, was a complete hoax. Millions had been spent to perpetuate the folly of the involvement between John Netley (the coachman) and Sir William Gull. Later, its author Joseph Sickert admitted that there was no truth in branding Dr Gull, an honourable man and an outstanding physician, as the sadistic killer.

choking back their tears as he bid each and every one of them a fond and peaceful farewell.

Over the last two weeks of his life, he suffered intense and terrible pain, often waking up in the middle of the night screaming in agony as his hideous cough racked his frail body. His old friend the Reverend Litten, the assistant chaplain of the St Pancras workhouse, visited him regularly over his last few days on earth and during one of his coherent intervals of consciousness, requested him to administer the consolations of his religion.

For the last twenty-four hours, he lapsed into a state of semi-consciousness and could only recognize those about his bedside when they spoke to him or roused him from his slumbers.

At last, surrounded by everyone he loved, the end came with comparative peace. As his father gazed sadly down on his enfeebled body, and his two children sat on either side of the bed, each gently holding a hand, he passed away at 6 o'clock, on the evening of Wednesday, November 8, 1865.

Aaron Jones, who fought two tremendous battles with Tom Sayers, emigrated to America. On June 30th 1863, he was severely wounded and left for dead at the battle of Gettysberg.

# 25

## THE FUNERAL

The family mourners and personal friends of Tom had been notified that the funeral would take place at about four o'clock, on Wednesday November 15 and they were to assemble at John Mensley's shoe factory, 257 High Street, Camden Town.

Throughout that Wednesday morning, crowded gigs, wagonettes and small knots of people wandered slowly through the streets leading to Kentish Town and Camden Town.

Toward noon, the streets along the route the procession would take began filling with curious spectators, all waiting to pay their last respects to the man who had been the most distinguished in his profession and a general favourite with everyone. As a token of mourning to their hero, the drivers of London's omnibuses and Hansom cabs had wrapped their whips in black crepe, exactly as they did earlier that year for the funeral of Lord Palmerston.

The passing of Tom Sayers marked a milestone in the social history of the age, for he was the last representative of his class to hold the long-established and exalted rank of "Exponent of the Noble Art of Self-defence," and the last of the old guard of illiterate heroes who fought by instinct, and to the death if necessary. Such was his popularity, that everyone had quite expected to see some sort of demonstration, but none could have envisaged, or even vaguely anticipated the dramatic and moving scenes which were about to unfold.

In London's largest gathering of spectators for a funeral since that of the Duke of Wellington, nothing showed more conclusively the deep pride and respect they held for their champion when, long before the appointed hour, Camden Town High Street was partially blocked by the thousands of spectators who only left a narrow lane through which the traffic might pass. The small detachment of the local constabulary, who had never anticipated controlling such an enormous crowd, were almost overwhelmed until a large contingent of reinforcements arrived from Scotland Yard. Although there was a great deal of shouting, noise and a certain amount of levity from all classes, the crowd remained remarkably orderly and only one case of robbery was reported.

Except for his home town of Brighton, Camden Town had always held a singular place in Tom's affections. It was here he met his wife Sarah Henderson, his two children were born here, and where he opened his first business speculation – his beer shop. It was here he pitched his first circus tent, and it was here he returned to die among the friends he loved. His neighbours and the local tradesmen were determined to pay him that extra special homage reserved for only the most esteemed citizens. All the shops were wholly or partially closed, blinds were drawn, the windows, balconies and even the rooftops, were thronged by all those eager to be involved in the last ceremony connected with the name and fame of Tom Sayers.

Towering head and shoulders above most of the crowd congregated outside John Mensley's shoe factory stood Tom King, the last conqueror of Heenan. He looked particularly affected with emotion and, on being recognized, hurriedly hired a Hansom cab to drive him further along the road to where the crowd was less dense. It had been expected that John Heenan would join the family for the last journey to the graveside, and although eager faces searched the crowd, they were destined to be disappointed, for that day, the Benicia Boy was pursuing his bookmaker's business at Salisbury Races.

By three-fifteen, all the mourners had assembled in John Mensley's drawing room. The scene inside the apartment was sadly interesting: Tom's father sat motionless in his chair; his hands tightly clenched upon his knees, his silvery head bowed upon his chest, gazing steadfastly at the floor.

He raised his head only once to say in a trembling voice, 'I hoped never to have seen this day,' before lapsing once more into silence.

Tom's daughter Sarah tried desperately to put on a brave face, and fought valiantly to hold back the tears, but when her young brother entered the room, she broke down completely and the little brother and sister cried bitterly in each other's arms. When Eliza saw their unhappy faces, she too became terribly distressed and was forced to retire into another room for a time to regain her composure. Tom's two brothers, Charles and Richard Sayers, Nat Langham, Harry Brunton and Jemmy Welsh, were all silent in their grief, glancing at each other with sorrowful faces. When they were asked to take their seats in the carriage, poor Harry Brunton was so overcome with emotion, he broke down and wept openly.

At half past three the hearse arrived, drawn by a pair of black horses decked in lofty plumes and black cloths draped over their backs. Following behind came Tom's miniature mail phaeton, drawn by his dun cob. This caused a great sensation, for stretched out on the back seat, in the place he always occupied behind his master, lay Tom's mastiff Lion, his great head resting between his paws in a study of canine dignity. Had the dog been instructed to play the role he assumed, he could not have performed it better. This touching scene had such an awesome effect on the two children peeping timidly through the venetian blind, that once again they were overcome with grief. After this outburst, poor little Thomas never fully recovered his self-control.

The pony became very restive amidst all the noise and commotion, and the large body of policemen struggled in desperation to cordon off a path for the relatives and friends to take their respective places in the carriages. There were, however, quite a few raised eyebrows when the chief mourner was seen to be the dog Lion, followed by Tom's two children Sarah and Thomas. Behind them came Tom's father, his brothers Charles and Richard, Robert King, John Mensley, Mr Crofts, Henry Bennett, Henry Feist, Mr W.P. Warner of Hendon, Jemmy Welsh, Harry Brunton, Nat Langham, Mr Hunt, George and Master Mensley, Mr Ansell and Joe Phelps.

Many of Tom's friends had hired vehicles at their own expense and the cortege soon took on a very imposing appearance. The large numbers of traps and brougham's, many with family crests painted on their sides, clearly indicated that the aristocracy and gentry would not be excluded from the proceedings.

The rear was brought up by thousands of pedestrians and horsemen, which swelled to even greater numbers as the procession passed along the route to the cemetery.

As the crowd pressed relentlessly forward in their eagerness to see everything, the metropolitan police divisions, under the direction of Inspector Cox, linked arms to hold back the boisterous onlookers and clear a way for the hearse and the bearer of the sable plumes.

At a quarter to four, preceded by an excited multitude of men and boys, the procession moved off, led by a band playing "The Dead March in Saul."

For several days before the funeral, John Mensley had tried in vain to engage a military band for the occasion. He had applied to the various regiments stationed in London, requesting permission for a company of brass bandsmen to lead the procession but, for some un-accountable reason, all his petitions had been rejected by the senior officers.

At the very last moment, and by using his connections in London, he had recruited a band of musicians from the London music halls, but never having heard them play, he felt extremely apprehensive about their combined musical talents. However, he had no reason to have worried for all were experienced musicians and well accustomed to playing impromptu melodies.

Thousands of people lined the route through Camden and Kentish Towns, and almost every window and balcony was occupied by some sad-faced onlooker. The touching sight of Tom's vacant phaeton, with the pony and the faithful dog, provoked such a heart-rending response from the female population that many immediately burst into tears.

The atmosphere was electric as the band played the grand and impressive strains of the "Dead March in Saul," interspersed with Martin Luther's hymn "The Heavens are Telling." Flags floated at half-mast, and numerous banners were suspended across the road. In front of Mr Cookin's tavern, The Bull and Last in Kentish Town, a large black banner proclaimed "Peace to England's Champion," whilst another, near the Mother Red Cap, bore the inscription "Farewell Tom of the Lion Heart."

Never before had such a scene been witnessed as the crowd, estimated to be in the region of 30,000 assembled in the vicinity of Highgate Cemetery. On the arrival of the cortege, the spectators swarmed over the surrounding railings and the high embankments overlooking the chapel.

Only those dressed in deep black were admitted to the little chapel, where the plain black coffin lay upon the bier, surmounted with the black pall and a group of black plumes. The mourners were ranged on benches to the right and left of the coffin, but when young Thomas saw the bier he gave way again to his childlike grief and great heaving sobs shook his small body. He gazed from face to face with a sense of loneliness, even among the friends who surrounded him, for without his father the poor little lad felt desolate and alone in the world.

In a beautiful service, conducted in an unusually impressive manner, the Reverend Litten dwelt with special emphasis on the theme "Evil communications corrupt good manners," as though warning all those present of the errors which terminated the brief but brilliant career of Tom Sayers.

At the conclusion of the service the procession made its way on foot through the winding paths to the grave, situated in a very pleasant spot near a large weeping willow bending gracefully over the place where Tom was to lay. Among the hosts of celebrities who followed the coffin were titled men and women, famous actors, eminent literary men and hundreds of other public figures too numerous to mention. Many were

Tom's old adversaries and colleagues. John Gideon was there, so too were Dan Collins, Nat Langham, George Sims, Jack Grant, Bob Travers, Tom King, Jemmy and Billy Shaw, Bos Tyler, Jem Ward, Bob Fuller, Harry Cooper (the man who never missed a match), Jack Garrett (Tom's favourite clown) and many other circus friends who had travelled long distances to attend the funeral.

The scene at the graveside had a harrowing effect on many. Bob Travers was particularly conspicuous. His face bore an intensity of sorrow no one had seen before, and from the moment the coffin was lowered into the ground his eyes never left it for a moment, gently letting grains of gravel fall on the lid as the Minister pronounced 'Ashes to ashes, dust to dust.'

During the short service the onlookers were visibly moved and for quite some time after its conclusion, Tom's relatives and friends gazed down sorrowfully on the brass plate, simply inscribed "Thomas Sayers, born May 15th 1826, – died November 8th, 1865."

A party of photographers tried to record the proceedings but, hampered by the dusk of the November evening and the large congregation, they found their task an impossibility.

As the purple tints of the fine autumn evening fell over the leafless trees and deepened into cold, black shadows, the grave closed over poor Tom Sayers. Evening had set in and it was time to depart. The procession reformed and, with the band playing appropriate music, the immense crowd began the return journey, gradually dispersing to their homes as they retraced their steps through the main thoroughfares of the metropolis.

George  Wilkes, editor of Wilkes' Spirit of the Times, co-ordinated the arrangements
between England and America for the first World International Boxing Contest.

# 26

## END OF AN EPOCH

Later that same evening, in a room above the Duke of St Alban's Tavern in Swaines Lane, Henry Bennett, Colonel Napier Sturt, and Mr C.T. Perry, the trustees of Tom's £3,000 indenture, met with his solicitor Joseph Dale and members of the family for the reading of the will. A few nondescript pictures graced the walls of the high, sparsely furnished room, dominated at one end by a large gilt-framed mirror overlooking a warm fire blazing in the grate. In the centre of the room, ranged around a long table covered with a white table cloth, were twelve high-backed dining chairs.

When the company were comfortably seated, Joseph Dale arose from his chair in front of the fireplace and in a quiet voice, typifying the solemnity of the occasion, commenced to read the will, a long and tedious document, appointing Henry Bennett as sole executor to hold in trust the £3,000 indenture of 1861, stocks, funds and securities for his two illegitimate children Sarah and Thomas until reaching the age of twenty-one years. It also directed that should Sarah marry before reaching that age, then the money was to be equally shared to start in a trade or business, or whatever Henry Bennett thought befitting.

In accordance with Tom's wishes, Henry Bennett placed an advertisement in the press stating that at two o'clock on the afternoon of Friday December 1, 1865, Tom Sayers' entire collection of valuable silver cups, medals and belts, his mastiff Lion, the performing mule Barney, his fast-trotting dun cob, valuable jewellery, household furniture, clothing and a heterogeneous collection of sporting pictures in oils, water-colours, line-drawings and photographs, were to be auctioned on the express instructions of the executors of his will.

The sale of the effects aroused enormous interest, and for two days prior to the auction, the collection was open for viewing at Mr Shakell's Auction Rooms in Park Street, Camden Town. Admission was by the purchase of a shilling catalogue available from *Bell's Life*, *The Sporting Life*, John Mensley's, Mr Shakell the auctioneer, and at all the principle sporting houses of London.

A large and fairly respectable company assembled for the sale and a large measure of joking and good-humoured banter arose as the auctioneer's assistant exhibited the different lots. Bidding was brisk, although in many cases somewhat extravagant. The majority of the articles were bought by Tom's greatest friends; John Gideon paid £35 for Tom Cribb's celebrated silver cup. A richly chased silver cup (presently in the custody of Chichester City Museum) went under the hammer for 9 guineas. The elegant silver cup presented by Captain Webster, realized £31.10s.0d. A magnificent silver cup weighing 34 ounces, fell to the bid of Mr Bennett for £27.6s.0d. and the Championship Belt (gross weight 86 oz) presented by George Wilkes, was bought by Mr Michael of 42 Westbourne Park Road, Bayswater, for £38.12s.0d.

The sale of the trophies achieved £335.19s.0d; the pictures amounted to £26.2s.0d. and the furniture £37.16s.0d. The last lots to be disposed of were the animals, carriages and assorted effects. Lot 103 was the English mastiff 'Lion.' After a keen fire from the first bid of 20 guineas, the hammer fell in a few seconds to the nod of Mr Warner, the landlord of the Welsh Harp in Hendon. He paid the incredible sum of £40.19s.0d. for the animal which became the focus of attraction to his customers. The performing mule Barney yielded £13, and the last lot, the dun cob mare, was sold to John Mensley for £24.3s.0d; bringing the grand total to £524.6s.0d.

To ensure that Tom's father would not end his days in poverty and the workhouse, the executors decided he should receive the entire proceeds of the sale, but Tom had already shown sufficient foresight some years before to buy him a small cottage of his own in Brighton.

As the year of 1865 drew to its inevitable end, so too did the fortunes of the prize ring. After dominating the scene for 150 years, the grim old game had finally become too grim. Since that fateful day in 1860, when the ropes were lowered at Farnborough, the popularity of pugilism in England had swiftly declined. Too many influential people, many of whom had never witnessed a prize fight, had been sickened and disgusted at the appalling spectacle of sheer brutality and mob violence. Pressures from a rapidly changing society were seeking radical new changes.

No longer was it the fashion for wealthy patrons to encourage two men to thrash each other unmercifully for their gratification, or to settle a wager. A new era was dawning with a new code of rules drafted by the Marquis of Queensberry designed to eliminate three-quarters of all unnecessary brutality and to give men with science an equal opportunity to develop their own individual skills.

The great majority of sportsmen were pleased to see an end to the epoch and welcomed the change but, for the die-hards of pugilism, the nostalgia lived on for many years. They always remembered with pride the fistic celebrities whose exotic names conjured up romantic visions of old England; The Pet of the Fancy, The Black Diamond Merchant, The Game Chicken, The Sprig of Myrtle, The Nonpariel, The Yokel Jew, The Chimpanzee, The Pride of Westminster, The Gay Bristol Boy, Cicero of the Ring, The Coachman, The Phenomenon, The Cheshire Hero, Tricks, The Tinman, The Ball of Wax, Troopers Dakin and Shaw, the two pugilists killed at the battle of Waterloo, and of course Bendigo, whose greatest tribute was to have a town named after him in Australia. Some had been dubbed more savagely; Tom Tough, Death, The Old Ruffian, The Tipton Slasher, The Bulldog, The Jaw-breaker, Iron Arm Cabbage, and the Horrible Scroggins. Some had died from their terrible injuries; many more died in poverty and near starvation. Deaf Burke, who in his time had thrilled the crowds of two continents, died a lonely death in the street. Others ended their days in the workhouses and a great many more perished in the gutters, un-recognized, despised, or just simply forgotten.

Only a few survived and prospered and many of these in later years shunned their associations with the prize ring. John Gully, as member of Parliament for Pontefract, would frown and turn away with embar-rassment when he was reminded he once held the proud title of Champion of England. John Heenan's disgust became so abhorrent, he could scarcely be persuaded to talk of his days in the prize ring and his intimate friends were forbidden to mention the subject in his presence. A few lived to reach a ripe old age, but the majority were carried off in their prime.

Tom Hyer the American champion was aged forty-five when he died of cardiac dropsy on June 26, 1864. John Morrissey, who had been elected to Congress as a Senator in 1875, was forty-seven when he died at Saratoga on May 1, 1878. After his defeat at the hands of John Morrissey, Yankee Sullivan went to work in the Californian gold mines where, after committing some misdemeanor, he was killed by vigi-lantes. His contemporary O'Rourke also met a violent death while working in a Canadian lumber camp; having lost all his money in gambling debts, he was believed to have been involved in a smuggling operation when his murdered body was found by a fellow lumberjack.

John Heenan returned to New York, and in the next five years won and lost as many fortunes. The dispatch announcing his death on Saturday October 25, 1873 at Green River City, Wyoming territory, was confirmed a few days later by a telegram from Jim Cusick who had been nursing the thirty-eight-year old pugilist. Although Heenan's health was known to be deteriorating, his death still came as a shock to his friends in New York. The first dangerous symptoms had developed about three months before, when doctors Canochan and Parker were called to his bedside. After sounding his lungs, they formed the opinion that as there was no considerable development of a consumptive tendency, his lung haemorrhages were the sequel to an attack of pneumonia. Encouraged to hope for a life, which he believed he had few hopes of prolonging, he sought the dry, pure air of Colorado, but while en route for Southern California, a severe haemorrhage put an end to his sufferings.

Tom Paddock never fully recovered from his attack of rheumatic fever and died in 1863 aged thirty-nine. Bob Brettle's untimely death came at thirty-eight; Nat Langham was fifty when he died in London on September 1, 1871. Ben Caunt's demise came at the age of forty-six. The Tipton Slasher was in his sixty-second year when he succumbed at his home in Wolverhampton. Tom Spring, who passed away in Hertfordshire on August 20, 1851, was aged fifty-six. Bendigo was in his sixty-ninth year when his knee gave way from the old injury sustained turning somersaults. He fell headlong down the stairs and fractured his ribs. A bone splinter punctured a lung and three weeks later he died. Harry Brunton was sixty when he departed this world on June 9, 1886. John Gideon, the man responsible for most of Tom Sayers' greatest achievements, died in Paris in 1901, aged eighty-one. Harry Paulson, despite all his fierce encounters, lived to the ripe old age of seventy-two. On his death in 1890, all the Nottingham athletes, as well as other notable sportsmen, joined the family at the graveside.

His death closed a chapter in sporting history, for with him went the last link with the English prize ring. Although Jem Mace began his career in the prize ring and acquired the title of champion of England, he owes his place in history as the pioneer who established the form of boxing which came with the introduction of gloves and the Marquis of Queensberry rules.

In April 1868, Sarah Sayers contested Tom's will over the appointment of the £3,000 indenture settled in favour of his two illegitimate children Sarah and Thomas. She now claimed that three more children were the legitimate issue of Tom and herself. These three children, named respectively James Aldridge Sayers, Alfred Aldridge Sayers, and Charles Aldridge Sayers, were granted full legal rights to prove their entitlement to the fund, to the exclusion of the two children named by Tom in his will.

The claim of the Aldridge Sayers was opposed on the grounds that they were not Tom Sayers' children at all, either legitimate, or illegitimate, but the children of a man named Aldridge, with whom Mrs Sayers was alleged to have been unduly familiar after her separation from her husband. The evidence was directed to be tried before the Master of the Rolls on whether there was, or were, any child or children living at the date of the indentures of 1861, or born afterwards. This naturally posed the question of just how complete was the separation during the dates these children were conceived.

From the evidence adduced, the press reported, ". . . principally, it was too low and nasty to set forth in detail."

Despite corroboration that Tom Sayers was not registered as their father on their birth certificates, his Lordship ruled there was insufficient evidence to satisfy the court that the separation between Tom Sayers and his wife Sarah, had been so incomplete as to preclude his being the father of the three Aldridge-Sayers – James, Alfred, and Charles. These three children were the issue of one mother within her marriage to Tom Sayers, and must therefore be entitled to take the fund in question, to the preclusion of the two illegitimate children named under the trust and provisions of the deed of 1861.

So, vindictive to the very end, Sarah had, at last, taken her revenge.

Happily, Tom's two children did not remain impoverished. Young Sarah married George Mensley (a brother of John Mensley) at St Saviour's church, South Hampstead, on November 4, 1866. Sarah had ten children; two boys and eight girls. In the mid 1870's, the family moved to Newcastle Upon Tyne, where George became the owner of the Rosedale Hotel. Sarah died in March 1891, at the age of forty and was buried in Jesmond New Cemetery.

After his father's funeral, Tom junior returned to his boarding school at Harlow to finish his education. In his early twenties he travelled the music halls, entertaining the audiences with his fine singing voice. Then in 1874, in a partnership formed as Messrs Sayers and Elliot, he became proprietor of the New Tyne Concert Hall in New Bridge Street, Newcastle.

Two years later, in a move once contemplated by his father, he emigrated to Sydney, Australia. In a variety of occupations, he became successful as a vocalist, theatrical agent, and a bookmaker. On July 8, 1885, he married one Annie O'Brien from Maitland, N.S.W. Tom and Annie had three children; two girls and a boy. In July 1895, the three children contracted scarlet fever and all died within eight days.

Devastated at their loss, they returned to England. Tom Sayers died on January 25, 1936, and Annie passed away eleven months later. In accordance with their wishes, their ashes were taken to Australia and interred in the grave of their three children.

A lithograph by Richard Childs of Tom Sayers standing beside his championship belt, Tom Cribb's magnificent cup and lion-skin belt, and the silver cup presented by Captain Webster of the 79th Highlanders.

Following a long and complicated legal wrangle, the deeds of Tom Sayers' grave in Highgate cemetery were transferred in 1891 to his son Tom, then living in Australia.

Today, the "Friends of Highgate" operate guided tours of the cemetery where, amid the quiet lanes and pathways, the visitor suddenly comes upon the imposing monument to Tom Sayers, nestling under a canopy of shady trees. At the foot of the edifice, with its bas-relief of Tom's profile, lies the carved stone figure of his mastiff, Lion, recumbent, with its great head resting upon its paws.

Close behind the memorial lies the grave of Harry Brunton. In 1865, shortly after the death of Tom Sayers, Harry purchased a plot of ground where, upon his death, he could be near his dearest and devoted friend. So it is here, in the peaceful tranquillity of this unique piece of London's heritage, that the last great champion of the prize ring and his faithful second, sleep their last sleep side by side.

# THE DEATH OF TOM SAYERS

Give ear you gallant heroes,
 Of high and low degree,
Tom Sayers is gone to his last home,
 No more we shall him see;
His time is come, his glass is run,
 He's gone to that silent bourne,
Where he must lay till the judgment day
 No more he can return.

Poor Tom is gone to his long home,
 Where he in peace may rest,
With the champions belt of England,
 And the gloves upon his breast.

Tom was a gallant hero,
 No one could him defeat,
He could boldly stand and face his man
 Brave Tom was never beat.
The loss of Tom did cause his friends
 In sorrow to deplore,
As his funeral passed, they said, alas!
 Poor Tom is now no more.

He in the ring with Heenan stood,
 Long ere the fight did end,
Tho' Sayers Jack beat, and him defeat,
 They both proved valiant men;
There was never one could speak of Tom
 With envy or disdain,
But now he's gone, alas poor Tom,
 Will never fight again.

Tom Sayers was born at Brighton,
 Where passed his youthful days,
In eighteen hundred and twenty-six,
 The seventeenth of May;

Tom was twelve years a pugilist,
 No one did him defeat,
He fought sixteen hard battles,
 And only once was beat.

Tom fought with Couch and Collins,
 Grant and Martin, too, we see,
With Sims and Harry Paulson,
 And gained glorious victories;
He fought Aaron Jones and Paddock,
 And Benjamin, with joy,
And the last Tom beat and did defeat,
 Was the bold Benicia Boy.

At his residence in Camden Town,
 Alas! Tom Sayers died;
On the eighth day of November,
 Eighteen hundred and sixty-five.
Tom is by all lamented,
 Since his equal none can find,
Tom expired in the prime of life,
 At the age of thirty-nine.

Some silent tears was shed for Sayers,
 As his funeral pass'd along,
And did mournful say, as on the way,
 Alas! poor gallant Tom,
We'll never see thy face again;
 Thy loss we've deeply felt,
And as thou rest, upon thy breast
 We'll lay the champion's belt.

Alas! poor Tom, we cannot fail,
 Thee to regret with pain,
For thou art in thy silent tomb,
 Thou will never fight again.

# THE COMBAT OF SAYERIUS AND HEENANUS

Close round my chair, my children,
And gather at my knee,
The while your mother poureth
The Old Tom in my tea;
The while your father quaffeth
His rot-gut Bordeaux wine –
Twas not on such potations
Were reared those thews of mine.
Such drinks came in the very year –
Methinks I mind it well –
That the great fight of HEENANUS
With SAYERIUS befell.

These knuckles then were iron,
This biceps like a cord,
This fist shot from the shoulder
A bullock would have floored.
CRAWLEIUS his Novice,
They used to call me then
In the Domus Savilana*
Among the sporting men.
There, on benefit occasions,
The gloves I oft put on,
Walking round to show my muscle
When the set-to was done;
While ringing in the arena
The showered denarii fell,
That told of Crawleius' Novice
Had used his mauleys well.

Tis but some sixty years since
The times of which I speak,
And yet the words I'm using
Will sound to you like Greek.
What know ye, race of milksops,
Untaught of the P.R.,**
What stopping, lunging, countering,
Fibbing or rallying are?
What boots to use the lingo,
When you have lost the thing?
How paint to you the glories
Of BELCHER, CRIBB or SPRING –

To you, whose sire turns up his eyes
At mention of the Ring?

Yet, in spite of all the jaw
And gammon of this time,
That brands the art of self-defence –
Old England's art – as crime,
From off mine ancient memories
The rust of time I'll shake,
Your youthful bloods to quicken
And your British pluck to wake;
I know it only slumbers,
Let cant do what it will,
The British bull-dog will be
The British bull-dog still.
Then gather to your grandsire's knee,
The while his tale is told
How SAYERIUS and HEENANUS
Milled in those days of old.

The Beaks and Blues were watching
Agog to stop the mill,
As we gathered to the station
In April morning chill;
By twos and threes, by fours and tens,
To London Bridge we drew;
For we had had 'the office'
That were good men and true;
And saving such, the place of fight
Was ne'er a man that knew.
From East, from West, from North and
    South,
The London Fancy poured,
Down to the sporting cabman,
Up to the sporting lord;
From the Horseshoe in Titchbourne Street
Sharp OWEN SWIFT was there;
JEM BURN had left the Rising Sun,
All in the Street of Air;
LANGHAM had cut the Cambrian
With tough old ALEC REID,
And towered high above the crowd

* Savile House, in Leicester Square, renowned for its associations with sparring exhibitions.
** Prize ring.

Shone BEN CAUNT's fragrant weed;
Not only fighting covies,
But sporting swells besides –
Dukes, Lords, M.P.s and Guardsmen,
With county Beaks for guides;
And tongues that sway our Senators,
And hands the pen that wield,
Were cheering on the Champions
Upon that morning's field.
And Hark! the bell is ringing,
The engine puffs amain,
And through the dark towards Brighton
On shrieks the tearing train;
But turning off where Reigate
Unites the clustering lines,
By poultry-haunted Dorking
A devious course it twines,
By Wootton, Shier and Guildford,
Across the winding Wey,
Till by heath-girded Farnborough
Our doubling course we stay,
Where Aldershot lay snoring
All in the morning grey,
Nor dreamed the Camp what combat
Should be fought here today.

The stakes are pitched, the ropes are rove,
The men have ta'en their stand;
HEENANUS wins the toss for place
And takes the eastward hand;
CUSSICCIUS and MACDONALDUS
Upon the BOY attend;
SAYERIUS owns BRUNTONIUS
With JEM WELSHIUS for friend.
And each upon the other now
A curious eye may throw,
And from the seconds' final rub
In buff at length they show,
And from their corners to the scratch
Move stalwartly and slow.

Then each his hand stretched forth to grasp
His foeman's fives in friendly clasp;
Each felt his balance trim and true –
Each up to square his mauley's threw –
Each tried his best to draw his man –
The feint, the dodge, the opening plan,
Till right and left SAYERIUS tried –
HEENANUS' grin proclaimed him wide;
Then shook his nut – a lead essayed,
Nor reached SAYERIUS' watchful head.

At length each left is sudden flung,
We hear the ponderous thud,
And from each tongue the news was rung,
    SAYERIUS hath first blood!
Adown HEENANUS' Roman nose
Freely the tell-tale claret flows,
While stern SAYERIUS' forehead shows
That in the interchange of blows
HEENANUS' aim was good!
Again each iron Mauley swung,
And loud the counter-hitting rung,
Till breathless both, and wild with blows,
Fiercely they grappled for a close;
One moment in close hug they swing,
Hither and thither around the ring,
Then from HEENANUS' clinch of brass,
SAYERIUS, smiling, slips to grass!

I trow mine ancient breath would fail
To follow through the fight,
Each gallant round's still changing tale,
Each feat of left and right.
How through two well-fought hours and
    more,
Through bruise, and blow, and blood,
Like sturdy bull-dogs as they were,
Those well-matched heroes stood.
How nine times in that desperate mill
HEENANUS, in his strength,
Knocked stout SAYERIUS off his pins,
And laid him all at length;
But how in each succeeding round
SAYERIUS smiling came,
With head as cool, and wind as sound,
As his first moment on the ground,
Still confident and game.
How from HEENANUS' sledge-like fist,
Striving a smasher to resist,
SAYERIUS' stout right arm gave way,
Yet the maimed hero still made play,
And when in-fighting threatened ill,
Was nimble in out-fighting still –
Did still his own maintain –
In mourning put HEENANUS' glims,
Till blinded eyes and helpless limbs
The chances squared again.
How blind HEENANUS, in despite
Of bleeding face and waning sight,
So gallantly kept up the fight,
That not a man could say
Which of the two twere wise to back,

Or on which side some random crack
Might not decide the day;
And leave us – whoso won the prize –
Victor and vanquished, in all eyes,
And equal need to pay.

Two hours and more the fight had sped,
Near unto ten it drew,
But still opposed – one-armed to blind –
They stood, those dauntless two.
Ah, me! that I have lived to hear
Such men as ruffians scorned,
Such deeds of valor 'brutal' called,
Canted, preached-down and mourned!
Ah! that these old eyes ne'er again
A gallant mill shall see!
No more behold the ropes and stakes,
With colours flying free!
But I forget the combat–
How shall I tell the close?
That left the Champion's belt in doubt
Between those well-matched foes?
Fain would I shroud the tale in night –
The meddling Blues that thrust in sight –
The ring-keepers o'erthrown;
The broken ropes – th' encumbered fight –
HEENANUS' sudden blinded flight –
SAYERIUS pausing, as he might,
Just when ten minutes, used aright,
Had made the day his own.

Alas! e'en those brighter days
We still had Beaks and Blues –
Still canting rogues, their mud to fling,
On self-defence, and on the Ring,
And fistic art abuse!
And twas such varmint had the power
The Champions' fight to stay,
And leave unsettled to this hour
The honours of the day!
But had those honours rested –
Divided as was due,
SAYERIUS and HEENANUS
Had cut the belt in two.

And now my fists are feeble,
And my blood is thin and cold,
But tis better than Old Tom to me
To recall those days of old.
And may you, my great-grandchildren,
That gather round my knee,
Ne'er see worse men, nor iller times
Than I and mine might be,
Though England then had prize-fighters –
Even reprobates like me.